# Realizing
# Investment
# Value

# Realizing Investment Value

Edited by
WILLIAM D. BYGRAVE, MICHAEL HAY
and JOS B. PEETERS

FINANCIAL TIMES
PITMAN PUBLISHING

PITMAN PUBLISHING
128 Long Acre, London WC2E 9AN

A Division of Longman Group UK Limited

© Longman Group UK Limited 1994

First published in Great Britain 1994

**British Library Cataloguing in Publication Data**
A CIP catalogue record for this book can be obtained from the British Library.

ISBN 0 273 60336 1

Typeset by PanTek Arts, Maidstone.
Printed and bound in Great Britain by
Biddles Ltd, Guildford and King's Lynn.

# CONTENTS

# FOREWORD

I find this book a fascinating mixture of the illuminating and the alarming. It illuminates because it is one of the best researched sets of statements ever to have been published about the practical results of venture capital investing. It is alarming because, particularly to Europeans, it highlights the difficulties of making new innovative businesses the building blocks for growth of an enlarged economy. As a venture capital manager, I welcome *Realizing Investment Value* for its insights on both counts.

Firstly, so much generalized, anecdotal and downright inaccurate commentary has been written about venture capital in the last 15 years, particularly in Europe, that it is time for the record to be put straight. Venture capital management was originally formalized in the United States when investment bankers decided to trace their stream of initial public offering material back to its source. There they discovered individuals and families who have traditionally financed entrepreneurs investing at peppercorn share prices in high-technology start-ups. By organizing funds that helped with this process, the investment bankers gave themselves opportunities to fish in the stream. As some of the early funds in the late 1970s and early 1980s had spectacular success, two things happened. On the one hand, governments in other countries exhorted bankers to emulate the American experience. On the other, swarms of TV and tabloid journalists, consultants, accountants, lawyers and politicians gravitated towards the banks of this new river. Millions of column inches of articles, white and green papers, pamphlets, speeches and even whole books became available, produced, almost without exception, by people who had never bought, managed or sold an investment in their lives. As a result of this extraordinary level of interest in a relatively minor aspect of the investment business, expectations became diffused and unrealistic. A well-researched series of papers written and edited by practitioners either in the field or involved through their academic experience is, therefore, particularly welcome and timely.

Secondly, the book paints a particularly alarming picture of the prospects for the new, integrated, European economy if current trends continue. By highlighting the difficulties that European venture capital groups have in selling their investments, thus helping their investors to recycle their capital, the writers and editors of this book have uncovered an insidious threat to the growth potential of the European economy as it competes for world markets against the Americans and the Asians.

Venture capitalists, in the main, depend upon selling their portfolio companies to large multinational corporations, or to public markets, to realize their investments. At the present time, American and Asian corporations are the most visible and active buyers and Nasdaq the most aggressive seeker of new issues in Europe. In other words, despite all the grants, tax incentives, fine exhortations and the apparent assistance from those crowding the banks of the river, others see more potential in European business innovations than the Europeans see for themselves.

Where corporations are concerned, US-based multinationals in particular are much more experienced at tapping into the venture capital community for new ideas, technologies, products and markets, and see no reason why they should confine their playfulness to the United States. Acquiring a small, innovative European company can enable them to make a disproportionate strategic advance in Europe with a relatively low risk. The irony is that the major risk has already been taken by the European shareholders at start-up, but the business is now lost to Europe in management and exploitation terms. The centre of gravity normally moves to corporate headquarters in America. While the original European shareholders have presumably received fair return for their risk, the European taxpayer does rather worse. A business that had been subsidized through grants and tax losses on the understanding that it would become a building block for renewal of the European economy – managed by Europeans for Europeans – has slipped out of the net.

Allowing Nasdaq to dominate the initial public offering market for small innovative businesses in Europe, as they may well do, only aggravates the situation. European financial institutions on their own account and through encouragement of their clients must demonstrate a greater commitment to, and confidence in, a renewal of the European economy. They could do this, of course, by becoming significant investors in European-based, Nasdaq-quoted stocks. If they do not, historians will be forced to record that in the second half of the twentieth century Europeans continued to provide vast subsidies to agriculture, which employed a diminishing 4–5 per cent of the working population, while the new technology-based manufacturing and service businesses with the potential to galvanize Europe's industrial competitiveness were sold, albeit inadvertently, to investors in competing economies for a fraction of their true net present values.

In summary, therefore, for me this is the first book that documents adequately the urgent problems facing the European venture capital industry. It is a fitting tribute to Bert Twaalfhoven, the founder and continuing inspiration behind the European Foundation for Entrepreneurial Research (EFER), who, together with a number of sponsors, instigated the research papers leading to this book. He is also to be congratulated on convening an editorial team who are pre-eminent in their fields and complementary to the task. May their underlying messages be heeded.

*Richard Onians*
*Managing Partner*
*Baring Venture Partners*

European venture capital is an asset class which from inception has been shrouded in mystery, with little if any information on industry performance. Since European venture capital is a subset of the investment business where, ultimately, only performance counts, this situation is both intolerable and unhealthy especially when compared with its American counterpart about which much performance data is available. This book represents a professional well-researched effort to address this issue and as such is valuable reading for all those involved in or affected by European venture capital.

*Bryan R. Wood*
*September 1993*

# CONTRIBUTORS

**Mark E. Bleackley** is a doctoral candidate in Strategic and International Management at the London Business School. He holds an M.B.A. from London Business School and a B.A. in Economics and Statistics from the University of Sheffield. His interests include the effects of competitive collaboration, skill-based economic development and strategic change. His current research is examining the nature of competition among coalitions of firms in emerging high-tech markets.

He was previously a senior consultant with SRI International, where he led and participated in consulting assignments for multinational corporations and government bodies in Europe, Latin America, North America and the Middle East. Prior to that he was a research analyst in corporate banking with the International Division of National Westminster Bank.

**Johan Bruining** is Associate Professor of Business Organization at Erasmus University and Director of the Dutch Management Buy-out Research Unit. He undertook the first major study of management buy-outs in Holland, is the author of papers in *Entrepreneurship: Theory and Practice* and *Acquisitions Monthly* and is a contributor to the *Economist Guide to Management Buy-outs*. He is the author of two books on management buy-outs in Holland.

**William D. Bygrave** M.A., D. Phil. (Oxford), M.B.A., D.B.A., is the Frederic C. Hamilton Professor for Free Enterprise, Director of the Center for Entrepreneurial Studies at Babson College and Visiting Professor at INSEAD (The European Institute for Business Administration).

As an academic, he teaches and researches entrepreneurial finance. He and Jeffry Timmons are the authors of *Venture Capital at the Crossroads*, which examines the venture capital industry and its role in the economy. He has written more than 50 papers on topics that include nuclear physics, hospital pharmaceuticals, philosophy of science, venture capital and entrepreneurship. He wrote an award-winning dissertation on the US venture capital industry. He serves on the review boards of two entrepreneurial journals. He was the academic coordinator for the 1992 conference of the European Foundation for Entrepreneurship Research on *Realizing Enterprise Value: IPOs, Trade Sales, Buy-backs, MBOs*, which was held at the London Business School.

As a practitioner, he founded a venture-capital-backed high-tech company, managed a division of a high-tech company listed on the New York Stock Exchange, co-founded a pharmaceutical data base company, and was a member of the investment committee of a venture capital firm. His company won an IR100 award for introducing one of the 100 most significant new technical products in the USA in 1977.

His hobbies include pottering with computers, history and philosophy of science, container gardening by the ocean, and English village pubs. He and his wife Jane are the parents of four children.

**Yves Fassin** has an M.Sc. in Engineering and holds an M.B.A. degree from the Vlerick School of Management. He was Director of the Industrial Liaison Office of the University of Ghent from 1981 to 1988 and Secretary General of the European Venture Capital Association from 1988 to 1991. He is part-time professor of Technological Innovation at the FUCAM, University of Mons, Belgium, and partner of the Vlerick School of Management at the University of Ghent. His research interests include innovation, technology transfer, entrepreneurship, venture capital and IPOs, and issues of business ethics in these fields. He is a member of the Economic Circle of the Fondation Roi Baudouin.

**Michael Hay** is Dean of Executive Education and a member of the Faculty of Strategic and International Management at London Business School. He is author of *The Strategy Handbook*, with Peter Williamson; *Social Policies in Eastern Europe: The Transition to a Market Economy*, with Professor Sir Alan Peacock; and, with Steven Abbott, of a forthcoming study of venture capital funding of technology-based businesses, *Investing in the Future*. His current research interests include an examination of the barriers to small firm growth and management buy-out investment decision criteria.

**Arthur Herst** is Professor of Financial Economics at the University of Limburg. His research interests include management buy-outs and corporate finance. He has published papers in *Entrepreneurship: Theory and Practice* and *Acquisitions Monthly* and is a contributor to the *Economist Guide to Management Buy-outs*. He is author of a book on management buy-outs in Holland.

**Robert Joachimsson** is Senior Lecturer in Business Studies at the University of Uppsala. He is a contributor to the *Economist Guide to Management Buy-outs*.

**Benoît Leleux** is a doctorial candidate at INSEAD specializing in Corporate Finance and Venture Capital. His experience includes four years of consulting work in South East Asia, where he was primarily involved in the financial problems of development businesses and large-scale start-ups in the agribusiness sector and the development of an agribusiness management curriculum for a leading Jakarta business school. His current interests span various strategic issues surrounding the pricing and timing of initial public offerings on American and European markets and the efficiency implications of trading suspensions in corporate control transactions in France. Other interests include the latest developments in corporate finance and venture capital and their influence on entrepreneurial activities. He holds a M.Sc. (equiv.) in Agricultural Engineering and an M.A. (equiv.) in Education from the Université Catholique de Louvain (Belgium), and an M.B.A. from the Virginia Polytechnic Institute and State

University (USA). Benoît Leleux received a Sasakawa Young Leaders Fellowship Award for his research at INSEAD and is currently a Fellow of the College for Advanced Studies in Management (CIM) in Brussels.

**Churchill Lewis** is a former principal in the investment banking firm Alex Brown & Sons Incorporated where he was responsible for financial services for the retail industry. In this capacity, he was the lead banker in more than 20 public equity offerings and numerous private financing and merger and acquisition transactions. His work entailed extensive contact with the venture capital industry in the United States, which supported many of the companies brought public by Alex Brown.

Since 1991, Churchill Lewis has been Programme Manager, Private Sector, for the United Nations Development Programme's Division for Eastern Europe and the Commonwealth of Independent States. In this capacity, he was responsible for UNDP's programme of support for privatization and the strengthening of the market economy in the region. He established an office in Vienna for this work in 1991, shortly after arranging the meeting organizing an association of privatization officials responsible for implementing market economy reform in Poland, Czechoslovakia, Hungary, Romania, Bulgaria and several republics of the former Yugoslavia. These officals meet in informal workshops to share experiences relating to concrete implementation issues and develop regional action plans for addressing common problems identified in these workshops. Topics have included Public Offerings as a Technique of Privatization, Joint Ventures and Direct Sales as a Technique of Privatization and Preparing Enterprises for Privatization: Business Appraisal. Officials of the Baltic states and other republics of the former Soviet Union are becoming increasingly involved in the activities of this association.

**Sophie Manigart** is Professor at the Department of Applied Economics at the University of Ghent in the field of Corporate Finance. She gained a doctoral degree in Management in 1993. From September 1990 and July 1991, she was a visiting scholar at the Snider Entrepreneurial Center at the Wharton School, University of Pennsylvania, with Professor I.C. MacMillan. She obtained an M.B.A. in 1986 from the Vlerick School of Management and a degree in Electronic Engineering in 1985, both from the University of Ghent. From September 1989 until May 1990 she served as a researcher on the Valuation Committee of EVCA. Her main research interests are the financing of start-ups and growing enterprises. She has published in the *Journal of Business Venturing* and the *Journal of Managerial Finance,* among others.

**Asko Miettinen** is Professor of Management at the Lappeenranta University of Technology, Finland. He is currently spending the 1993–4 academic year at the Vienna University of Economics (Wirtschaftuniversität Wien) as a Visiting Professor. He received his M.A. and Ph.D. from the University of Helsinki and his M.Sc. (Econ.) from the Helsinki School of Economics and Business Administration. Prior to teaching at the LUT he was at the Finnish Institute of Management and worked in Finnish industry.

Dr Miettinen earned his ITP Certificate at the London Business School and has been a visitor at Harvard Business School and MIT. He has also worked as a full-time faculty member at the European Institute of Advanced Studies in Management (EIASM) in Brussels. Miettinen's current research interests are small business management and innovations.

**Daniel F. Muzyka** is an Associate Professor of Entrepreneurship at INSEAD, where he holds the IAF Professorship of Entrepreneurship and is Director of Entrepreneurship. Dr Muzyka conducts research and seminars in several dimensions of entrepreneurship as related to new ventures, and is actively involved in developing models of entrepreneurship and transformation for larger organizations. He holds a doctorate from the Harvard Business School, an M.B.A from the Wharton School and an M.A. (Astrophysics) from Williams College.

**Jos B. Peeters** is Managing Director of Capricorn Venture Partners n.v., a venture capital operation in collaboration with Baring Venture Partners, oriented at financing technology-based growth companies in the heart of Europe. In the past seven years he has been managing director of BeneVent Management, a Belgium-based venture capital operation associated with the Kredietbank-Almanij group.

Jos Peeters holds a Ph.D. in Physics from the University of Louvain and has been involved for more than 10 years with the application of new technologies for industrial and commercial purposes. He worked at Bell Telephone Manufacturing Company (now part of Alcatel) and thereafter was with the international, technology-based consulting group, PA Technology. He is co-founder and first chairman of the Belgium Venturing Association and is a past chairman of the European Venture Capital Association (EVCA). He is an adviser of the European Foundation for Entrepreneurship Research (EFER) and chaired the Programme Committee of their 1992 conference in London on Realizing Enterprise Value.

**Kaj-Erik Relander** is an investment manager at the venture capital unit of the Finnish National Fund for Research and Development (SITRA). He began his career in management consulting, then started a computer company, sold it successfully and moved into venture captial. He has personally made over 20 venture capital investments in high-technology companies included syndications with such companies as Repola and United Technologies Corporation. Relander has directed an extensive venture capital research project funded by SITRA and written a book and published articles on venture captial and technology acquisition. He presently serves as a director of venture-funded companies in emerging industries in Finland and in the US. He has an M.Sc. in Economics and an M.B.A. in Finance from the Helsinki School of Economics, where he teaches a course in venture capital. Relander has been a visiting scholar at the Wharton School of the University of Pennsylvania.

**Ken Robbie** is Research Fellow at the Centre for Mangement Buy-out Research at the University of Nottingham. He has extensive industrial and financial experience in negotiating management buy-outs. He has contributed papers to a range of academic and professional journals including *Strategic Management Journal; Journal of Business Venturing; Entrepreneurship: Theory and Practice; Omega; Financial Accountability and Management; International Journal of Bank Marketing.* His books include *Touche Ross' Management Buy-outs* (with M. Wright and J. Normand) and *Buy-ins and Buy-outs: New Strategies in Corporate Management* (with M. Wright, S. Thompson and B. Chiplin). He has recently completed the first major study of management buy-ins.

**Antti-Pekka Syrjänen** M.Sc. (Eng.) was born in Finland in 1966 and is a graduate of Helsinki University of Technology, where he majored in industrial management and international business. Before joining SITRA, the Finnish National Fund for Research and Development, he designed management information systems for a Scandinavian chemical industry corporation. In SITRA he prepared investment analyses and conducted research on venture captial in cooperation with Kaj-Erik Relander. After SITRA, Antti-Pakka Syrjänen joined the corporate planning team of Nokia Mobile Phones, Europe's largest and the world's second largest manufacturer of cellular phones. He has published papers at Helsinki University of Technology and in cooperation with Kaj-Erik Relander arising from international management conferences.

**Steve Thompson** is Senior Lecturer in Business Economics at UMIST and from the beginning of 1994 has been appointed as Professor of Managerial Economics at the University of Nottingham. In addition to management buy-outs, his research has also focused on internal organization and corporate governance and executive remuneration in financial services. He has published papers in the *Strategic Management Journal; Journal of Business Venturing; Entrepreneurship: Theory and Practice; Journal of Industrial Economics; Accounting and Business Research; International Journal of Industrial Organisation*; and *Journal of Economic Behaviour and Organisation*. He is the UK editor of *Managerial and Decision Economics.*

**Yves Romanet** is Professor of Finance in the Department of Accounting and Finance at the École Supérieure de Commerce, Lyons. His research interests include management buy-outs, venture capital and the financial problems of small and medium-sized firms. He is author of *Financie d'Entreprises* and has extensive experience in consulting for small and medium-sized businesses.

**Mike Wright** is Professor of Financial Studies and Director of the Centre for Management Buy-out Research at the University of Nottingham. He has published numerous papers in academic and professional journals such as *Strategic Management Journal; Journal of Business Venturing; Entrepreneurship: Theory and Practice; Accounting and Business Research; Journal of Business Ethics; Soviet Studies; Omega; Journal of Management Studies; Journal of Marketing Management*. His research interests include management buy-outs, mergers and divestment, privatization, venture capital and entrepreneurship, marketing financial services and corporate governance. His recent books include *Marketing Financial Services* and *Cases in Marketing Financial Services* (both with C. Ennew and T. Watkins); *Buy-outs and Buy-ins: New Strategies in Corporate Management* (with S. Thompson, K. Robbie and B. Chiplin); and *Readings in Management Buy-outs*. He is currently completing a Technical Note on Privatization by Buy-out in Central and Eastern Europe for the European Bank.

# ACKNOWLEDGEMENTS

We are indebted to every one of the researchers and practitioners who made presentations at the conference on *Realizing Enterprise Value: IPOs, Trade Sales, Buybacks, MBOs, and Harvests* held at London Business School in December 1992. That conference was organized by the European Foundation for Entrepreneurship Research (EFER). It is a privilege to thank EFER, its indefatigable chairman Bert Twaalfhoven and his dedicated staff, especially Nada Spendal and Karen Levolger-Schweigler, for organizing and supporting this conference. In designing that conference, we appreciated the encouragement of the European Venture Capital Association's (EVCA) members. Matts Andersson, EVCA's 1992–1993 chairman, and William Stevens, EVCA's secretary-general, were steadfast supporters, as was George Bain, the Principal of London Business School. Caroline Hodgkinson played an invaluable role in organizing the conference in London.

In addition to the EFER leadership and administration, this particular conference also involved a wide array of individuals who constituted a Programme Committee. This committee was responsible for setting the direction and establishing the content of the conference. The individuals who were a part of this programme committee and their organizations are listed below:

| | |
|---|---|
| Mr. Matts Andersson | SITRA (Finland) |
| Professor William Bygrave | Babson College (US) and INSEAD (France) |
| Mr. Marco Cecchi de Rossi | SOFIPA (Italy) |
| Mr. Yves Fassin | De Vlerick School (Belgium) |
| Mr. Hennie Gieskes | Spaarne Compagnie (Netherlands) |
| Dr. Michael Hay | London Business School (England) |
| Mr. François Lacoste | Private Investor (France) |
| Professor Daniel Muzyka | INSEAD (France) |
| Professor Hubert Ooghe | De Vlerick School (Belgium) |
| Mr. Richard Onians | Baring Venture Partners (England) |
| Dr. Jos Peeters | Capricorn Venture Partners (Belgium) |
| Professor Sergio Pivato | Instituto Lorenzetti (Italy) |
| Professor Yves Romanet | ESC Lyon (France) |
| Mr. William Stevens | EVCA (Belgium) |
| Mr. Dennys Watson | Eurotechnology (Belgium) |
| Mr. Neil Williamson | 3*i* (England) |

We wish to add special thanks to the financial sponsors of the conference. These included: Atlas, Netherlands; Electra Innvotec, United Kingdom; Ernst & Young, United Kingdom; EVCA, Belgium; Gilde Investments Funds, Netherlands;

SOFIPA, Italy. We would like to recognize the special contribution made by Diederik Heyning and Leendert Van Driel of Gilde Investments Funds with their funding of the 'Best Paper' prize.

William Bygrave thanks Babson College for granting the sabbatical leave that enabled him to spend the 1992–1993 academic year at INSEAD, where he undertook much of his work on this book. He is very grateful to INSEAD for appointing him to a visiting professorship. INSEAD's faculty and staff were wonderful hosts. Special thanks are offered to Daniel Muzyka, Dean Claude Rameau, Dean Ludo Van der Heyden, Céline Polisset, Hennie Escoffier, Gerda Rossell, and Benoît Leleux for their generous help. Numerous colleagues have helped Bill Bygrave with the research that is the basis for Chapter 1. In particular, Jeff Timmons, Michael Stein and the staff at Venture Economics merit special acknowledgement.

Chapter 3 draws extensively on the results of research conducted in Europe by Umberto Cherubini, Marco Ratti, Björn Hansson, Alexander Ljungqvist, Daniel Muzyka, Rémy Pailard, Bernard Belletante, Ahmad Rahnema, Pablo Fernandez, Eduardo Martinez-Abascal and Bart Rogiers. May they all be recognized here for their contributions. The numerous comments received from the editors also proved immensely valuable. Benoît Leleux also gratefully acknowledges the financial support from INSEAD's Research and Development Department and the *Collège Interuniversitaire pour les études Doctorales en Sciences du Management* (CIM) in Brussels.

The authors of Chapter 4 would like to thank Christine Ennew, Tom Lamb, Chris Ward, Angela Haygarth, Bill Bygrave, Michael Hay and participants at the EFER conference. Financial support for the Centre for Management Buy-out Research at the University of Nottingham (CMBOR) from Touche Ross Corporate Finance and Barclays Development Capital Limited is gratefully acknowledged. The research assistance of Marcel Bonnet and Kunle Ajayi is also acknowledged.

The authors of Chapter 5 would like to acknowledge the support of Murray Johnstone who sponsored the research on which this chapter is based. We would particularly like to thank Iain Tulloch for his insightful and constructive comments. We should also like to record the assistance of CMBOR and Securities Data Corporation for granting access to their comprehensive data sources.

With regard to the Pan-European Study discussed in Chapter 7, we would first like to thank INSEAD for its financial support of this research project. INSEAD was responsible for collecting and collating information from a consortium of schools. Gerda Rossell and Benoît Leleux were instrumental in the collection and analysis of the information. We would also like to thank the consortium member institutions and participants: Belgium: Vlerick School (Hubert Ooghe, Yves Fassin, Sophie Manigart and Bart Rogiers); France: ESC Lyon (Remy Palliard and Yves Romanet); Germany; Dortmund University (Kai Thierhoff, Bjorn Manstedeten, Heinz Klandt); Italy: Bocconi University (Sergio Pivato, Anna Gervasoni); Spain: IESE (Ahmad Rahnema); Sweden: IMIT (Clas Wahlbin, Christer Olofsson); United Kingdom: London Business School (Michael Hay and Mark Bleackley). Without the commitment and effort exhibited by these institutions, the study would not have been possible. The institutions and participants provided access to the venture capital-backed entrepreneurial community across Europe.

Finally, Jos Peeters acknowledges the immense contributions made by Boudewijn Baron van Ittersum, John Wallinger, Brian Winterflood, Françoise Vappereau, John Wall, Richard Onians, Evert Elbertse and Ronald Cohen to our understanding of the issues with which this book is centrally concerned. He thanks William Stevens from EVCA, Maurice Anslow from Venture Economics and Simon Thornton from Initiave Europe for providing valuable background information.

# INTRODUCTION

*William D. Bygrave, Michael Hay and Jos B. Peeters*

## BACKGROUND

One of Britain's leading venture capitalists recently stated that liquidity of funds is the biggest issue facing the European venture capital industry in 1993 (Onians, 1993). To be precise, it is illiquidity that has become a major concern as opportunities for successful exits of venture capital investments have become less abundant in Europe. Nowhere is that more apparent than for flotations. With the major European secondary stock markets in the doldrums, initial public offerings (IPOs) of stock by venture-capital-backed companies – indeed, by small and medium-size enterprises in general – are relatively infrequent. Hence, perhaps the most important issue facing not only venture capitalists but all investors in private businesses is how can they realize the value in their investments?

The organized venture capital industry in Europe is not much more than 10 years old; in contrast the US industry is just three years short of its fiftieth birthday. True, there were a few players in Europe before 1980, most notably the UK firm now named 3*i*, and at least one American-style venture capital firm – which was not a success – that was set up in the 1960s. But it was during the entrepreneurial era of the 1980s that European venture capital grew explosively. From 1984 through 1992, the venture capital funds under management in Europe grew from ECU 3.6 billion to ECU 38.5 billion (EVCA, 1991; 1992; 1993; 1 billion = 1000m throughout this book). Today, the total capital under management in Europe rivals the figure for the USA.

However, unlike the USA, where divestments and investments have been roughly in balance, the amount of money being invested in portfolio companies by European venture capital funds far exceeds the amount being divested. For instance, over the five years 1988 through 1992, ECU 21.2 billion was invested in portfolio companies but only ECU 9.4 billion was divested. Consider these numbers: divestments actually declined slightly from ECU 2.06 billion in 1990 to ECU 2.0 billion in 1991, then increased to ECU 2.3 billion in 1992, whereas investments increased from ECU 4.13 billion in 1990 to ECU 4.63 billion in 1991, and increased again to ECU 4.7

billion in 1992. Of course, some of that imbalance is because the total pool of venture capital continues to grow. But that is only a partial explanation because the amount of new funds raised has been declining since it peaked in 1989. If the 1990 to 1992 trend continues, a log jam of unrealized investments is building up.

By the end of 1992, the European venture capital industry reluctantly acknowledged that much of that investment–divestment imbalance was due to the relative scarcity of successful realizations. European venture capitalists will have to improve their realizations if they are to earn a respectable return on the ECU 20.4 billion in their portfolios at the end of 1992.

Nowhere is the lack of successful realizations more apparent than in the UK. Of the venture capital invested in portfolio companies in the UK from 1983 through 1990, 57 per cent financed management buy-outs (MBOs) and management buy-ins (MBIs) (Bannock, 1991, p. 24). But, to date, an insufficient number of those investments has been harvested. For instance, according to a study by the Centre for Management Buy-out Research, of 158 MBOs completed in the period 1983 to 1985 only 45 had been harvested by June 1992 (Wright et al., 1992). Looked at another way, it means that more than 70 per cent of those MBOs had not been harvested successfully. That lack of successful exits is particularly acute with smaller MBOs/MBIs, which abound in venture capital portfolios. Of MBOs/MBIs consummated during the 10 years 1981 to 1990, 92 per cent had an initial value of less than $18 million. By the end of June 1992, only 27 per cent of the 1981–2 generation of MBOs/MBIs in that category had been exited by an IPO, trade sale or secondary MBO/MBI (Wright et al., 1992). So almost three-quarters of those 10-year-old investments had not been exited successfully.

It is a formidable task to earn an adequate return on an investment held for five years, let alone 10, because time exacts a fierce penalty on the rate of return. Typically, a successful venture capital investment returns at least 40 per cent compounding annually over a holding period of four to five years. A yield of 40 per cent compounding annually for five years requires that 5.4 times the original investment be returned; but the same yield over 10 years requires 28.9 times the original investment. Delays in the realizations depress returns on investments. To be blunt, a venture capital investment that is unrealized after 10 years is long past its 'sell-by' date in all but a few rare instances.

At the start of the 1990s, European venture capitalists, especially in the UK and The Netherlands, were frustrated with their exit opportunities. Their frustration gave rise to a number of new initiatives designed to facilitate exits. Among them were proposals for a pan-European private secondary market for venture capital investments (Onians, 1993) and for a local participation market for Dutch venture capital investments (Elbertse, 1993).

## EXITS OVERALL

It was not until 1991 that EVCA – the European Venture Capital Association – began to gather statistics on the overall divestments of venture capital, so it is impossible to look at trends in exits. The 1991 snapshot revealed that trade sales accounted for 41 per cent of the total amount divested, IPOs and subsequent sales of shares for 10 per cent, and divestment by other means (such as management buy-backs and redemption of preference shares) 18 per cent. The remaining 31 per cent was attributable to write-offs.

The following are excerpts from EVCA's 1992 yearbook on the exiting of venture capital investments in different countries.

### Austria

'No secondary market for sales of unlisted securities exists in Austria. The most common method of exiting venture capital investments is by means of corporate acquisition.'

### Belgium

'The secondary market was created in 1985, but it has not been successful in terms of the number of listings ... Investments are often repurchased by the other shareholders, this being an especially common factor in the large number of investments in small and medium-sized, traditionally family-owned, businesses. Exits from larger investments are most often achieved by trade sale to (usually foreign) corporate investors.'

### Denmark

'Venture investments in Denmark are mainly exited through mergers and acquisitions. The Danish secondary market is not highly active, and provides little opportunity for exiting venture capital investments in small and medium-sized companies. According to industry specialists, a common stock exchange quotation system for Denmark, Sweden and Norway (the planned "Nordic Ring") would improve the liquidity of the Danish secondary market.'

## Finland

'As in many European countries, most exits are achieved by corporate acquisitions. The Helsinki OTC [over-the-counter] market, established in 1984, provides the only public route on which venture-backed companies would become quoted. At present, prospects of achieving an exit through the Helsinki OTC market are poor.'

## France

'Since 1987 the number of venture-backed flotations has decreased dramatically, but a booming M&A [merger and acquisition] market has more than compensated for the absence of a liquid secondary market during recent years.'

## Germany

'The prospects of achieving an exit through the flotation of a portfolio company on the German stock market continue to be poor. Trade sales to previous associates, other companies and institutional investors therefore remain the primary exit option for many German investments.'

## Ireland

'The number of companies floated in the Stock Exchange has decreased since 1989. Most venture capital investments are realised through trade sales, and this trend is likely to increase in the future.'

## Italy

'Neither the principal stock exchange nor the secondary market present significant opportunities for exiting venture capital investment in Italy ... Exit by private or trade sale continues to present the only option for venture capitalists.'

## The Netherlands

'The main stock exchange presents financing options for larger companies. A secondary market ("Parallelmarkt") also exists and can serve as an exit for venture capital companies ... Merger and acquisition activity is also an important source of exits for Dutch venture capitalsits. Plans are underway to create an auction mechanism for trading shares between venture capital companies and institutional investors in more mature companies.'

## Norway

'No unlisted securities market for secondary sales on shares in small companies existed in Norway in 1991. In conjunction with the fiscal reform, however, a new stock exchange for these shares has been created and will be operational by mid-1992 ... Despite the new exchange, exits will be adversely affected by the on-going recession. Investors often find engagements continuing longer than originally anticipated. The exits from venture capital investments that are completed are most commonly carried out through trade sales and mergers and acquisitions.'

## Portugal

'There now exists an unlisted securities market which will play an important role in exiting, which at present is mainly taken through corporate acquisitions.'

## Spain

'Trade sales are expected to represent the shortest exit route for most venture investments ... Although a secondary market was launched in 1986, it has not been very active ... Initial public offerings of venture-backed companies are rare, due to the small number of portfolio companies in the Spanish venture field.'

## Sweden

'Although the Swedish OTC market, established in 1982, is one of the most active secondary markets in the region, the majority of exits from venture capital investments are made through corporate acquisitions.'

## United Kingdom

'The formation of the Unlisted Securites Market (USM) in November 1980 and the level of mergers and acquisitions in the 1980s were major triggers for the development of the UK venture capital industry. Both the USM and the main market have played a major role in providing exit routes for venture capital investors and entrepreneurs alike. More recently, however, the levels on new listings obtained by venture backed companies in the UK have been relatively low, due to the lingering recessionary climate. Despite the comparatively large number of exits achieved through stock market flotation in the UK historically, acquisition or trade sale remains numerically the more important exit route for UK venture capital firms, even when stock market conditions are buoyant... Trade sales are expected to continue to provide the majority of venture capital exit opportunities.'

## IPOs

The correlation between the IPO market and the health of the venture capital industry is well documented in the USA (Bygrave, 1989; Bygrave and Timmons, 1992). As yet, the relationship has only been glimpsed in Europe. During the 1980s, a number of European nations set up second- and third-tier stock markets in order to facilitate public flotations by small companies that could not meet the requirements of the main market. Three of the most successful were the Unlisted Securities Market in the UK, the Second Marché in France, and the Parallel Market in the Netherlands. A surge in venture capital in the UK, France and The Netherlands coincided with a boom in these countries' secondary markets.

But alas, the success of the second markets was short-lived, and now they show little or no sign of reviving. According to some observers, the formation of the USM in November 1980 was a major trigger for the development of the UK venture capital industry. But after peaking in the mid-1980s, the USM has steadily declined in popularity, so that by 1992 it was all but dead. No question, in their heyday, the USM, Third and OTC markets in the UK provided an excellent mechanism for harvesting investments in private companies via stock flotations. From 1981 through 1987, 142 MBOs floated stock on one of those three stock markets, averaging 20 per year. But in 1989 the figure fell to only seven, followed by just one in each of 1989, 1990, and 1991 (Wright et al., 1992). Similarly, the number of venture-capital-backed flotations on the French Second Marché has decreased dramatically since 1987. And likewise, the number of flotations on the Dutch Parallel Market in recent years has been insignificant.

The extent of the problem with European secondary markets is strikingly illustrated by the figure, which shows that while the annual trading volume on the USM and the Second Marché was dwindling away in the 1990s, the Nasdaq (National Association of Securities Dealers Automated Quotations) small-capitalization market was flourishing as never before.

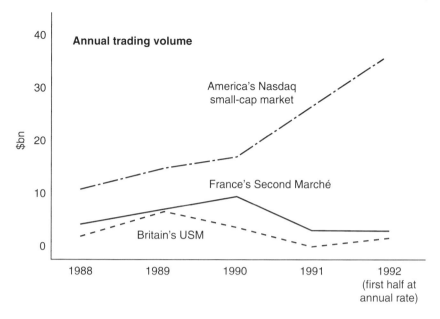

*Figure A  The differing trends of America's Nasdaq small-capitalization market and secondary markets in France and Britain*

(*Source: The Economist,* 18 July 1992)

## TRADE SALES

Trade sales of venture-capital-backed companies are still a viable exit route, although the number is decreasing due to the severe economic recession that is blanketing Europe in 1993. In the UK, which is experiencing its longest recession since the Great Depression of the 1930s, the number of trade sales of MBOs averaged 39 per year from 1981 through 1988, but fell to 15 in 1989, 8 in 1990, and 3 in 1991. Fortunately, trade sales in other European nations have not been as severely affected.

## EXITING CRISIS

As is clear from even this brief review, the European venture industry, along with the entrepreneurs in whose companies the industry has invested, faces something of a crisis. The essence of this crisis can be simply stated: it is at root a crisis of liquidity. The strands of this crisis can be defined in terms of certain core issues. First, there is an accumulating log jam of unrealized investments. The number of investments being carried by venture capital companies in their portfolios and the rate at which this number is being added to with new investments far exceed both the number and rate of investment realizations or harvests. It is as if more and more liquidity is being put into one end of a pipe but less and less is being realized at the other end.

Second, this system problem of lack of liquidity is not simply a problem for the venture capital community. It profoundly affects entrepreneurs themselves; they, like their venture capital investors, require access to funds whether to fund the further growth of their business or to realize the value of the investment they have built up. On this issue the interests of both venture capitalists and entrepreneurs coincide. Although the problem is more acute in some markets – notably the UK – than in others, none the less the problem is of genuinely European dimensions.

Third, the mechanisms that have been developed to resolve the problem and ease the log jam, most notably the proliferation of second and in some countries third stock markets, have singularly failed to meet the challenge. After an initial surge of activity these markets have, in the main, petered out.

The ramifications of this crisis are profound. A flourishing venture capital industry requires an equally healthy market or other set of mechanisms through which the value of matured investments can be realized. Similarly, a flourishing community of entrepreneurs committed to building real value in their businesses requires some route both to further finance and, at the appropriate time, to an exit from the business. The situation currently prevailing in Europe is marked by a clear imbalance between what one might call 'entry' (investment and business start-up) and 'exit' (realizing or harvesting investments). It is with this imbalance that this book is centrally concerned. Our purpose in assembling this international group of authors is to provide an authoritative assessment of the situation and, more positively, to outline a set of practical solutions or ways of tackling it.

We start by placing the problem in the broader context of the rates of return from venture capital. Our opening chapter therefore draws directly on the pioneering work undertaken by William Bygrave, who was involved in creating the Venture Economics returns data base on which all subsequent work in this area has relied. (Venture Economics is a research company specializing in venture capital.) Having outlined the experience of US venture funds and identified the key factors influencing actual rates of return, William Bygrave proceeds to sketch out the situation prevailing in Europe. Here little more than a sketch is possible, since little or no information is available. None the less, such information as does exist, including what can be derived from sources such as the annual report of 3*i*, has been pieced together to provide some European counterpoint to the wealth of returns data available from the US.

A key determinant of the health of the venture capital industry is the vitality of the market for initial public offerings. Not only does an IPO provide an efficient exit route for both investors and entrepreneurs alike, it is clear from the evidence that it is the route which generally provides the best opportunity of maximizing the rate of return itself. In our second chapter we focus therefore on IPO markets in both Europe and the US. Yves Fassin and Churchill Lewis provide an overview of activity on both the Nasdaq market in the US and a wide range of secondary markets operating in a number of European countries. The way the IPO process actually works in practice is described along with a set of 'IPO games' or mechanisms used to manage the price and performance of a company's shares after its flotation.

Post-IPO price performance has been the subject of exhaustive research, particularly in the US. In Europe rather less is known, at least on a systematic basis, about what happens to the share prices during the period following the IPO. This raises a series of fundamental questions relating to the initial pricing of a share, the impact that the timing of an offer has on the price realized and, most importantly, the actual performance of the share price in the longer run. In addressing these issues in chapter 3, Benoît Leleux and Sophie Manigart draw on a range of empirical work recently undertaken in six European countries – France, the UK, Belgium, Spain, Germany and Italy.

In keeping with this pan-European focus we move in chapter 4 to an examination of the life cycle of the typical management buy-out in four countries – Sweden, Holland, France and the UK. The harvesting of an MBO potentially exposes basic conflicts of interest between the managers involved in the MBO and their investors. How these conflicts manifest themselves and are resolved is an issue addressed by Mike Wright and his fellow-authors, who set this particular issue in the broader context of the factors influencing both the timing and the form of the harvest of an MBO, the average length of time for which an MBO investment is held in different countries and the fate which befalls the management once the investor has exited from the MBO.

Quite what determines the incidence of MBOs over time is the subject of chapter 5 where Mark Bleackley and Michael Hay attempt to answer a set of questions including: Where do MBOs come from? What is the relationship between the economic cycle and MBOs? What impact does M&A activity have on the MBO market? What effect does the availability of debt have on the size and level of buy-out deals? Given the scope of these questions they are answered here in the context of one country, the UK.

If it is clear that the vitality of the IPO market is decisive in determining the level of returns on venture capital investments, it is equally clear that this is not the route through which most investment realizations are made. This role is played by another form of exit, the trade sale, the importance of which is almost certain to increase during the next few years. Hitherto very little work has been done on the trade sale phenomenon. In chapter 6 Kaj-Erik Relander, Antti-Pekka Syrjänen and Asko Miettinen go a long way towards filling this gap in our knowledge. In doing so they consider the impact that trade sales have on entrepreneurs, particularly those whose companies are acquired by a much larger corporation for whom the acquisition of small, technology-based companies may provide an ideal means of gaining access to a new technology. But what is really original in this analysis is the question the authors pose in terms of the extent to which venture capitalists plan their mode of exit at the time of making the original investment. Drawing a distinction between those investors for whom the manner and timing of an exit is primarily opportunistic and those who endeavour to plan the process at the outset, Relander, his colleagues and Asko Miettinen present a series of highly suggestive cases which explore the impact that planning – or the lack of it – has on the value of the price realized through the trade sale.

Exit is a critical issue for venture capital companies. It is of equal importance for entrepreneurs. But we know remarkably little about how entrepreneurs actually view different forms of exit, where they go for advice and how they assess the various options open to them. This realization prompted us to set up a major pan-European study expressly designed to replace current anecdotal evidence with something more solid and substantial. Thus eight leading business schools, working under the auspices of the European Foundation for Entrepreneurship Research, joined forces to mount a major survey of entrepreneur attitudes in Europe. The results of this unique exercise are presented in chapter 7 in which William Bygrave and Daniel Muzyka, who coordinated the project, discuss the implications for both entrepreneurs and venture capital practitioners alike.

Finally, chapter 8 adopts an explicit policy orientation and, specifically, outlines a set of practical recommendations and proposals for redressing the imbalance between entry and exit that gives the book its central impetus. Having examined various dimensions of the crisis facing the European venture capital industry, particularly in comparison with the situation prevailing in the US, Jos Peeters, a former chairman of the European Venture Capital Association, advances the case for creating a pan-European market geared specifically to the needs of smaller, rapidly growing companies on which the economies of Europe will increasingly depend. In putting forward this radical proposal, our intention is to initiate a wide-ranging and fundamental debate well grounded in the empirical evidence that this book provides.

# References

Bannock, G. (1991). *Venture Capital and the Equity Gap*. London: Graham Bannock and Partners.

Bygrave, W.D. (1989). Venture capital investing: a resource exchange perspective. Doctoral dissertation, Boston University.

Bygrave, W.D., and Timmons, J. (1992). *Venture Capital at the Crossroads.*, Boston: Harvard Business School Press.

Elbertse, E. (1993). Developing exit mechanisms in your market. Presentation at EVCA business seminar on Exiting in Europe, Venice, 11–12 Feb.

EVCA (1991). *Venture Capital in Europe: 1991 EVCA Yearbook*, Zaventem, Belgium: EVCA.

EVCA (1992). *Venture Capital in Europe: 1992 EVCA Yearbook*, Zaventem, Belgium: EVCA.

EVCA (1993). *Venture Capital in Europe: 1993 EVCA Yearbook*, Zaventem, Belgium: EVCA.

Onians, R. (1993). A European secondary market. Presentation at EVCA business seminar on Exiting in Europe, Venice, 11–12 Feb.

Wright, M., Robbie, K., Romanet, Y., Thompson, S., Joachimsson, R., Bruining, J. and Herst, A. (1992). Realizations, longevity and the life-cycle of management buy-outs and buy-ins: a four-country study. Presented at the EFER 92 Forum, London Business School, 12–14 Dec. (See also Chapter 4 below.)

# 1

# RATES OF RETURN FROM VENTURE CAPITAL[*]

*William D. Bygrave*

## LESSONS FROM AMERICA

In 1982, an economist at the National Science Foundation characterized venture capital as an industry 'shrouded in empirical secrecy and an aura of beliefs' (Boylan, 1981–2). Nowhere was that more true than when it came to rates of return, which, according to industry folklore, ranged from 30 per cent to 50 per cent and even higher. A 1983 US Congressional survey found that venture capital firms expected annual returns of 31 per cent at a minimum (US Congress, 1984). In the mid-1980s, it was reported that limited partners were expecting returns of 40 per cent – 60 per cent, and some were hoping for 75 per cent (Stevenson et al., 1986) – high enough to arouse even the sleepiest pension fund manager. However, there was an astonishing paucity of reliable information supporting such high expectations. As one pension fund manager said in 1985: 'Depending on whose [rates of return] we believe, we should have anywhere from as little as 5 per cent to as much as 50 per cent of our portfolio in venture capital.'

In 1985–6, in response to the need for valid and reliable data on the actual returns from venture capital funds, I assisted Venture Economics in starting its returns data base. By 1989, Venture Economics data base contained 42 per cent of all the funds formed from 1970 through 1987 and 65 per cent of the capital under management. That sample of 197 funds represented the universe remarkably well, with 3 per cent seed stage, 16 per cent early stage, 74 per cent balanced, and 7 per cent late stage investments. In its 1991 annual edition of *Investment Benchmarks Report: Venture Capital*, Venture Economics reported returns based on 403 funds formed since 1969.

The first publication by Venture Economics of the actual returns on those funds caused quite a commotion. The results – to put it mildly – were

\* Parts of this chapter are excerpted from *Venture Capital at the Crossroads* published by Harvard Business School Press.

disappointing. After 1980, overall returns briefly peaked at around 30 per cent in 1982–3, at the time of the initial public offering (IPO) frenzy, and then slid relentlessly to single digits by 1988. The headline of the *Wall Street Journal* of 8 November 1988 said it all, 'Recent Venture Funds Perform Poorly As Unrealistic Expectations Wear Off.'

In this chapter, we will first look at historical US rates of return to see if there was ever any support for those folklore returns of 30 – 50 per cent. Then we will examine the actual returns. We will explain why those returns were so poor – perhaps an all-time low – at the end of the 1980s and why they are recovering in the 1990s. We will end with a discussion of what little information we have about returns in Europe.

## HISTORICAL RETURNS IN THE US

The industry abounds with anecdotes and hearsay. For example, everyone knows about American Research and Development's investment in Digital Equipment Corporation. It is part of the folklore of the industry. Even if the amount invested varies from $60 000 to $70 000 and the amount returned in about 12 years varies from $500 million to $600 million depending on who recounts the tale, the annualized rate of return of 130 per cent or thereabouts is the stuff that legends are made of (Bygrave and Timmons, 1992). But what is the reality? Table 1.1 lists the rates of return for venture capital (VC) published in the scholarly literature. Even with as spectacular an investment as Digital Equipment Corporation in its portfolio, American Research and Development's annualized rate of return for the 20 years 1946 to 1966 was only 14 per cent (Rotch, 1968). In 1966, of course, the value of its investment in DEC was still growing. By the late 1970s, when DEC had been harvested and ARD had become part of Textron, ARD's annualized rate of return fell into the single digits (Gervirtz, 1985).

Two of the best-known private venture capital firms are Bessemer Securities and Hambrecht & Quist. According to Poindexter, Bessemer reported a 17 per cent compound rate of return for the period 1967–74, and Hambrecht & Quist a 15 per cent compound rate of return over several years through 1972 (Poindexter, 1976).

Most tests on venture capital profitability have used small samples of publicly held Small Business Investment Companies (SBICs). A study of 14 public venture capital firms found the rate of return to be 11 per cent on average (Faucett, 1971). Hoban (1976) constructed a portfolio composed of 110 actual venture capital investments made by four different venture capital firms in 50 different companies during the period 1960–8. The four venture capital firms were a publicly held SBIC, a private partnership, a private corporation owned by a wealthy family, and a subsidiary of a large bank holding company. He found the gross (before management fees and income taxes) annualized rate of return of the portfolio to be 22.9 per cent for the period through the end of 1975. Poindexter gathered data from 29 publicly held firms consisting of 26 SBICs and three companies investing in venture capital. The geometric mean of the annual rate of return for the 29 firms over the period 1961 to 1973 was 11.6 per cent. Over the same period, Poindexter found that the annualized rate of return of the Standard & Poor's (S&P) 500 was 7.1 per cent (Poindexter, 1976). It is worth noting that rates of return for the sample of venture capital firms depended strongly on the calendar period over which they were computed. For example, it was 10.7 per cent for the period 1961–6, 31 per cent for 1967–71, and 1.2 per cent for 1972–3.

**Table 1.1 Venture capital: compound annual rates of return**

| | | |
|---|---|---|
| 14% | **American Research and Development** (1946–1966) | *Rotch, 1968* |
| 14% | **92 Firms** | *Poindexter, 1976* |
| |   13% 59 VC firms managing a third of VC pool | |
| |       (rate of return from firm's birth through 1974) | |
| |   12% 29 Public VCs (mainly SBICs, 1961–1973) | |
| |   17% Bessemer Securities (1967–1974) | |
| |   15% Hambrecht & Quist (few years through 1972) | |
| 11% | **14 Public VCs** (primarily SBICs) | *Faucett, 1971* |
| 23% | **110 Actual Investments in Portfolio Companies** | *Hoban, 1976* |
| | (gross return before annual management fee) | |
| 27% | **Public VCs** (based on stock prices, 1974–1979) | *Martin and Petty, 1983* |
| | **267 Firms** (SBICs, Independent-Private and Corporate) | *US Congress, 1984* |
| |   19% SBICs (based on capital appreciation, 1982–1984) | |
| |   31% independent firms (based on capital appreciation, 1982–1984) | |
| |    4% corporate (based on capital appreciation, 1982–1984) | |
| 16% | **Public VCs** (based on stock prices, 1959–1985) | *Ibbotson and Brinson, 1987* |
| 24% | **Simulation of Hypothetical VC Investments** | *Wells, 1974* |
| 15% | **Simulation of 100 Funds** | *Stevenson, Muzyka and Timmons, 1986* |

Martin and Petty (1983) analysed the performance of 11 publicly traded venture capital firms, of which all but two were in Poindexter's sample. They computed the compound rate of return on the publicly traded stock of those 11 firms for each of the six years 1974–9. The average rate of return on the publicly traded stock of the 11 venture capital firms over that period was 27 per cent. Unfortunately, Martin and Petty's rate of return on publicly traded stock was not the actual rate of return on the firm's venture capital investments. The two should not be compared because there may be little or no relationship between their values at any one time. For example, Arthur D. Little, former chairman of Narragansett Capital Corporation, which was in both Poindexter's and Martin and Petty's samples, stated that in the mid-1970s Narragansett's share price fell to 80 per cent below the book value of the assets in its portfolio (Wayne, 1988).

A study by First Chicago Investment Advisors used a method similar to Martin and Petty's to study the rates of return of public venture capital companies from 1959 through 1985. The compound annual rate of return over the 26-year period was 16 per cent (Ibbotson and Brinson, 1987, pp. 99–100).

It is not easy to get the data needed to calculate the actual rates of return of venture capital investments – not even for publicly held funds such as Poindexter's sample of 29. Poindexter commented that it was an arduous task. To get the actual rate of return, it is necessary to dig into the financial statements in annual reports and Securities and Exchange Commission (SEC) filings, such as 10K reports, to get operating expenses, interest expenses, income dividends, capital gains dividends, operating expenses, interest expenses, net assets, long-term debt and net worth. Those numbers must be adjusted to allow for any additional public offerings and stock splits. The reliability of the net asset figure may be questionable because most of its value resides in a fund's portfolio. The value of that portfolio is an estimate of the current market value of the companies in the portfolio, and most of those companies are private.

Poindexter surveyed 270 venture capital firms that managed the bulk of the domestic venture capital pool. He estimated that the respondents who supplied rate-of-return data managed one-third of the domestic pool of venture capital. They were asked to estimate their firm's compound rate of return since inception. The mean of the estimated rates of return of the 59 firms was 13.3 per cent, with a range of 35 per cent and –40 per cent (Poindexter, 1976).

The 1983 study by the Congressional Joint Economic Committee found that independent private venture capital firms expected a minimum annualized rate of return on individual investments that ranged from 75 per cent for seed-stage financing to about 35 per cent per year for bridge financing. The same study found that independent private venture capital firms experienced a 31 per cent annual net capital appreciation rate over the period 1982–4. The report went on to conclude that 'the persistence of above average rates of return on venture capital investments suggests that capital markets may be under-allocating funds to risky, entrepreneurial investments.'

Unfortunately, the methods used to obtain the rates of return reported in the US Congressional study were methodologically flawed (Bygrave, 1989). Hence, it would be incorrect to conclude from the Joint Economic Committee's survey that the annualized rate of return of all venture capital managed by independent firms was 31 per cent for the period 1982–4.

There have been a number of models simulating the rates of return of venture capital firms. Wells (1974) studied the decision-making process of venture capitalists. He asked them to estimate the rates of return they expected from 17 investments. From that he constructed a hypothetical venture capital firm that drew its ventures from the distribution of estimated rates of return. He found his simulated portfolio for his hypothetical venture capital firm produced a compound rate of return of 24 per cent.

Stevenson, Muzyka and Timmons (1986) used a Monte Carlo simulation model that was developed with published data on venture capital fund performance and interviews with fund managers. Their simulation of the returns of 100 funds showed an average return of 15 per cent with a range from 10 per cent to 35 per cent, with one fund returning greater than 35 per cent. A potential flaw in their model was the assumption that there was zero correlation among investments for both the investment partnership and for the investment domain as a whole.

## Summary of the historical data

Our survey of returns is from scholarly research published in the academic literature as opposed to anecdotal accounts printed in the business press. It shows, in summary, that contrary to the folklore figure of 30 – 50 per cent, actual venture capital returns have most often been in the teens, with occasional periods in the 20 – 30 per cent range and rare spikes above 30 per cent.

## ACTUAL PERFORMANCE IN THE US

The inflow of US venture capital dried to a mere trickle by the mid-1970s. A common complaint by entrepreneurs at that time was that there was not enough venture capital available. It was an investor's (or seller's) market. Then, at the end of the 1970s, the floodgates opened and the United States was awash with venture capital. The situation of the mid-1970s was suddenly reversed. It had become an investee's market (or buyer's market). What effect did that have on the rates of return? That question will be answered as we look at the results of a study of the performance of the venture capital funds in the Venture Economics data base.

# Method

The US venture capital industry is dominated by venture capital partnerships composed of limited partners and general partners. The limited partners provide the money and the general partners provide the management. Venture capitalists in one venture capital firm may be general partners in several partnerships under the management umbrella of that firm. Some of the older venture capital firms manage half-a-dozen or so partnerships. In return, the general partners receive an annual management fee and a share of any profit that the partnership makes. The general partners' annual management fee is usually 2 – 3 per cent of the paid-in capital, and the general partners' share of the profit, known in the industry as the partners' carried interest, is usually 20 per cent; the other 80 per cent goes to the limited partners. Partnerships generally have a 10-year life, which can often be extended.

When a new partnership is formed, the money committed to the partnership is paid in several instalments (takedowns) over the first two or three years. The general partners send reports and financial statements to the limited partners, usually quarterly. From those financial statements, limited partners can calculate their share of the book value of the partnership (the residual value). The residual value consists of any uninvested capital and the estimated partnership's share of the value of portfolio companies in which the partnership has invested. When a company in the partnership's portfolio goes public, the limited partners may receive their share of the stock in that company, although the venture capital partnership often holds back stock for a period before distributing it. That is called a disbursement. It is usually valued at the offering price per share of the public offering. When a stock carries restrictions on its sale, its price is often discounted by 20 – 30 per cent. Besides stock, there may be other disbursements such as cash from trade sales and dividends.

Traditionally, venture capital partnerships do not disseminate information from which it is possible to determine their performance, specifically their rates of return. However, limited partners have information on takedowns, disbursements, and residuals from which internal rates of return can be computed.

## Computations of IRRs

There is no industry-wide standard method for computing the financial returns of venture capital funds. Increasingly, limited partners are computing their internal rate of return (IRR) based on their cash-on-cash returns plus their share of the residual value of the venture capital funds holdings of cash and investments in portfolio companies that have yet to be distributed to the limited partners.

The algorithm for computing the IRRs is fairly simple in principle. The residual, the disbursements, and the takedowns are each reduced to their present value on the date of the first takedown. A disbursement of D dollars has a present value of $D/(1 + IRR/100)^t$, where IRR is the annualized internal rate of return in per cent, and t is the time in years from the date of the first takedown to the date of the disbursement. The present values of a takedown of T dollars and a residual of R dollars can be computed the same way. Then, by iteration, the value of IRR is computed at the end of each calendar quarter by finding its value when the present value of the takedowns equals the present value of all the disbursements plus the present value of the residual.

## Limitations

In practice, it is not quite so simple. First, there are limitations in some of the data sets. Some pension funds record the actual dates of the transactions, others record them at the end of the month in which they occur. To put them all on the same basis, transactions are computed as if they occurred on the last day of the month.

Second, although it is easy to construct an algorithm that computes the limited partners' share of a residual, it is difficult to compute it reliably without knowing the intricate details of the partnership agreement, specifically when and how the general partner's share of the profit is recognized. In principle, the general partner does not get any share of the profit until the limited partners have received all the money that they paid into the fund. After that the profit is split, usually on a 20:80 basis. However, once the residual plus disbursements exceeds the sum of the takedowns, the fund is making a profit on paper. Most funds then recognize the unrealized profit that is in the residual. After that point is reached, the general partner holds back its anticipated share of future profits from subsequent disbursements to the limited partners.

The following simplifying method is used to compute the limited partner's residual value: (1) When the sum of the distributions is less than the sum of the takedowns (paid-in capital), the total value of the fund's residual is multiplied by the limited partner's percentage ownership of the fund; (2) When the sum of the distributions exceeds the sum of the takedowns, the total value of the fund's residual is multiplied by the limited partner's percentage ownership of the fund multiplied by the limited partner's percentage of the allocation of the profits.

A third limitation is the reliability of the valuation of the residuals. Most funds have a valuation committee that estimates the value of its portfolio of investments in companies that have no publicly traded stock. Thus, the value of the residual is a somewhat subjective judgement of each fund's valuation committee. This problem is mitigated to some extent because there are different funds, and there is no reason to believe that there is any overall bias either high or low by the valuation committees.

Before we present the actual rates of return, we should point out that the venture capital industry has been debating the issue of how portfolios should be valued. An ad hoc committee of the National Venture Capital Association charged with developing guidelines recommended a standard valuation method in 1990 (see *Venture Capital Journal*, June 1990, pp. 1–2). Among those guidelines is a recommendation that while data should be collected during the first few years of a fund's life, no rates of return should be compiled until the end of the fund's third year. Venture Economics, which compiled the returns presented in the next section, goes even further: in its annual *Investment Benchmarks Report*, it includes returns only for funds with at least four years of operating history.

## Annualized rates of return

The annualized rates of return for all the funds in the data base are presented in Figure 1.1. It shows the capital weighted average, median, and top quartile of the IRRs by calendar year for all funds formed from 1969 through 1985. The median IRR peaked in 1982 at 27 per cent. The capital weighted average also peaked in 1982 at 32 per cent. The top quartile (the point where 25 per cent of the returns of a group are higher and 75 per cent are lower) peaked one year later at 44 per cent. These overall returns are in line with what we learned from our historical survey of the scholarly literature: overall returns from venture capital are typically below 20 per cent with only brief spikes above 30 per cent. However, the top-quartile funds performed much better, with returns above 20 per cent in 9 out of 16 years, above 30 per cent for four of those years, and above 40 per cent for one year.

Venture Economics has developed a return measure that takes account of the long-term nature of venture capital investing. At the end of 1991, the 10-year return was 8.9 per cent on average and 15.7 per cent for the top quartile; the 15-year return was 17.7 per cent average and 23.0 per cent top quartile; and the 20-year return was 15.0 per cent average and 21.3 per cent top quartile (Reyes, 1992).

The information presented in Figure 1.1 must be viewed with caution

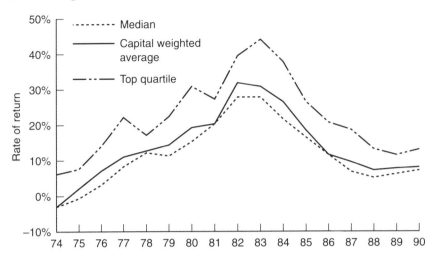

*Figure 1.1 Overall rates of return of venture capital funds*

(*Source of data*: Venture Economics)

because it agglomerates the IRRs of all funds at least five years old in a given year regardless of the age of the funds. To do so is potentially misleading because it is expected that as funds grow older, their portfolio companies move closer to being harvested (through initial public offerings, mergers, etc.) or have actually been harvested. Thus it is likely that the rate of return of a fund will increase with age, all other things being equal. Of course, all other things are not equal. One important factor is the calendar date, which can have a major effect on IRRs. For example, as Figure 1.1 shows, IRRs peaked in 1982–3. The year when a fund was started can also have a major effect. A new fund typically invests its money in portfolio companies during the first three to four years of its life. Hence, for example, funds started in 1978 had portfolio companies that went public in the hot 1983 IPO market.

## Consequence of timing

The funds were grouped in annual vintages according to the year in which they were started. (In the context of the venture capital industry, vintage has the same meaning as cohort, the term demographers use for people born in the same year who pass through life's cycles together.) The average IRRs of all funds and the top quartile IRRs for each vintage are presented in Figures 1.2 and 1.3 (Reyes, 1992). The 1976–9 vintage performed well, with an

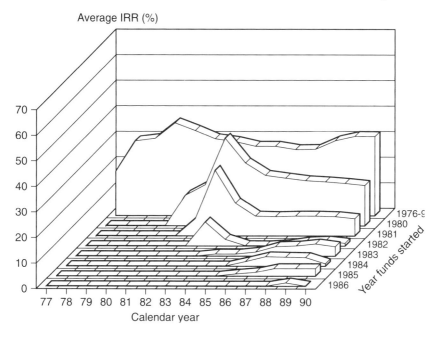

Average IRR (%)

*Figure 1.2 Average IRRs of venture capital funds for each vintage*

(*Source of data*: Venture Economics)

average rate of return in the range 26 per cent to 32 per cent. If the average fund performed well, then the top quartile performed spectacularly; they produced a return ranging from 46 per cent to 60 per cent. The 1976–9 vintage of top quartile funds truly fulfilled the expectations of their investors.

Funds formed after 1979 did not perform as well. After peaking in 1983 at 34 per cent, the average return of the 1980 vintage slid steadily down to 16 per cent by the end of 1990. The 1981 vintage fared worse, following an early spike of 26 per cent in 1983, the average return fell to 8 per cent two years later and ended 1990 at 7 per cent. The average returns of the 1982, 1983, 1984, 1985 and 1986 vintages had never risen out of the single digits by 1990; in a few years, average returns of some vintages were slightly negative.

The top quartile return in the 1980 vintage peaked at 36 per cent in 1983, dropped to 17.5 per cent by 1985 and climbed back to 21 per cent by the end of 1990. Subsequent vintages ended 1990 with the following top quartile returns: 1981, 21 per cent; 1982, 9 per cent; 1983, 15 per cent; 1984, 13 per cent; 1985, 13 per cent; 1986, 10 per cent.

Top-quartile IRR (%)

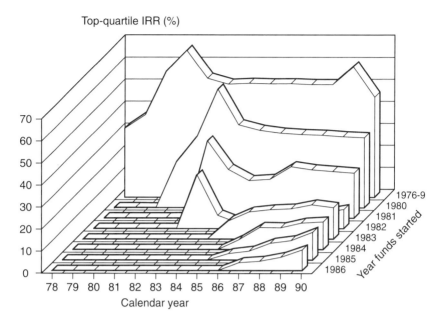

*Figure 1.3 Top-quartile IRRs of venture capital funds for each vintage*

(*Source of data*: Venture Economics)

## Type of fund

According to finance theory, early stage funds should outperform later stage and balanced funds because of their greater risk. Clearly, investments in high technology companies that have yet to develop products and markets are a lot chancier than investments in management buy-outs of a low technology company with mature products and developed markets. That appears to be true in practice: early stage funds yielded somewhat higher returns than later stage and balanced funds. Later stage funds had the lowest returns (Bygrave and Timmons, 1992). According to a study of 203 companies representing essentially all the start-up investments between 1978 and 1988 by three venture capital funds investing primarily in technology-oriented companies, the annualized rate of return for financings made at the start-up stage was 38 per cent compared with about 28 per cent for those made at the early expansion and follow-on stages (Keeley and Turki, 1992). That study concluded that seed and start-up financings had low failure rates, which is contrary to the perception held by many venture capitalists that the risk of loss is very high for seed stage and start-up stage investments (Ruhnka and Young, 1991).

Not all funds manifested returns consistent with Keeley and Turki's findings. For instance, a study of investments by TA Associates primarily in US high technology companies between 1977 and 1990 found that companies at the start-up stage when TA invested returned – 6.5 per cent and those at the development stage 14 per cent; whereas companies producing profits when TA invested yielded 32 per cent, and ones generating revenues but not profits 25 per cent (Landry, 1992). Hence TA's experience is more in line with the perceptions reported by Ruhnka and Young (1991).

## Ecstasy–agony cycle

The early 1980s were glorious days for venture capital. Returns climbed steeply to heights not seen since the late sixties, which was the previous glory era. But the euphoria was short-lived. After reaching their lofty peak in 1983, returns began a downward slide that continued through the end of the eighties. When compared to the performance of the stock markets in recent years, venture capital returns have been well below risk-adjusted expectations since 1983. An article from *Forbes* called 'Too much money, too few deals' summed it up this way:

> Even the top performers are hurting. Take Boston-based TA Associates, one of the most successful of the large firms, with over $400 million under management. The 41% average return it has enjoyed over the past 11 years masks the fact that money invested in 1983 has returned less than a passbook 5.5%.
>
> 'It used to be hard not to make money,' TA Associates general partner P. Andrews McLane says ruefully. 'It's definitely not as easy now.' (*Forbes*, 7 Mar. 1988, p. 144.)

Many factors contributed to the declining returns. If some observers said it was too much money chasing too few deals, others said it was too much money chasing too many good deals. No question, the United States in the early 1980s was rather suddenly awash with venture capital. There was a shortage of quality deals to invest it in. Complicating that problem was a shortage of experienced venture capitalists to seek out deals, evaluate them, invest in them and oversee the investments. Then, when it was time to start harvesting the quality deals that had grown into successful companies, investors had lost their appetites for IPOs. Stock flotations were impossible for most venture-capital-backed companies. Or if they were possible, valuations were down. Let's look at those factors underlying falling returns in more detail.

*Availability of capital and deals*

In the 1980s, institutions, especially pension funds, supplied more and more capital to venture capital funds. It was causing concern that the flood of money would lower returns. As a 1988 *Business Week* article reported:

> [Venture capitalists] spent years cajoling pension funds to invest part of their $3 trillion kitty in startups. Now the funds are complying – with a vengeance. They're 'preparing to unleash hundreds of millions of dollars on venture capitalists who already have too much money,' frets Don Valentine, a general partner of Sequoia Capital in Menlo Park, Calif. Many other veteran venture capitalists share his worry that the flood of venture capital will force prices of fledgling companies higher while lowering returns for most investors. (6 June 1988, p. 126.)

That sentiment was expressed earlier at the National Venture Capital Association annual meeting in May 1987, when William Hambrecht, another leader of the venture capital industry, commented that what was happening in the industry at that time was 'Economics 101'. There were too many dollars coming into the industry, and competition for deals was pushing returns down. (*Venture Capital Journal*, May 1987, pp.1–2.)

*Availability of venture capitalists*

In 1978, there was no shortage of applicants who wanted to enter the venture capital profession. What was in short supply, however, was venture capitalists with 10 or more years of experience in the industry. The number of professionals in the industry increased from 597 in 1977 to 1494 in 1983 – a 150 per cent increase. The capital under their management increased from $2.5 billion to $12 billion – a 379 per cent increase. And the average capital per professional increased from $4.2 million to $8.1 million – a 93 per cent increase. (*Venture Capital Journal*, July 1984, p. 4.)

The rapid growth of the venture capital industry depleted the availability of experienced venture capitalists (Kozmetsky et al., 1984). For the industry as a whole, venture capitalists were managing more money but were less experienced in 1983 than in 1977. In the 61 new partnerships formed in the period 1977–82 – new partnerships being new venture capital funds raised by new firms, rather than follow-on partnerships, where new venture capital funds are raised by existing firms – the level of the general partners' experience was only 5.2 years. (*Venture Capital Journal*, Oct. 1982, pp. 8–10.) The level of experience of general partners in new funds dropped further in 1983.

*All-important stock market*

The returns in the figures above demonstrate the dramatic effect of the frenzied IPO market of 1983 when 121 venture-capital-backed companies went public, more often than not with spectacular offerings. Valuations of venture capital portfolios skyrocketed. Price-to-earnings ratios of 40–60 for venture-capital-backed IPOs were common (Sahlman and Stevenson, 1986). Some were much higher. At the height of the feeding frenzy, for example, Stratus Computer went public with an offering price of almost 200 times its annualized earnings. Other companies had no trouble going public even though they had lost money every quarter since they were founded. It confirmed what others such as Poindexter had noted: hot IPO markets are by far the most important cause of peaks in venture capital returns.

Alas, after the collapse of the 1983 hot market, small-capitalized stocks went through eight lean years in which they markedly underperformed the big ones. That was almost certainly the biggest factor underlying the disappointing performance of venture capital from 1985 through 1990.

There can be little doubt that the market in initial public offerings is the most important determinant of the returns on US venture capital investments. When the IPO market is buoyant, it's comparatively easy to float new issues of venture-capital-backed companies at high valuations. That causes venture capital returns to rise. The correlation between returns on venture capital and the performance of small-cap stocks is demonstrated convincingly in Figure 1.4, which plots the top-quartile return on venture capital and the difference between the returns on small-cap stocks held for 10 years and the S&P 500 stocks held for the same period.

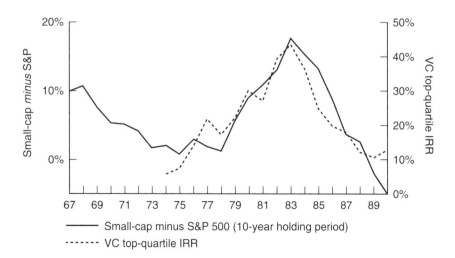

*Figure 1.4 The correlation between returns on venture captial and the performance of small-capitalization stocks, 1974–1990*

(*Sources of data*: Ibbotson Associates; Venture Economics)

## IPOs: the golden harvest

A healthy IPO market gives the venture capital industry its vitality. Without IPOs the venture capital investment process would not be viable. When venture-capital-backed companies go public, the returns on the original investment are sometimes spectacular. Returns of 50 times the first round of venture capital – or even more – have occasionally been realized. Examples of impressive returns of venture-capital-backed IPOs during the last decade include Apple, with a 235 times return, Lotus 63 times, and Compaq 38 times. It is heady stuff for investors.

### *IPOs and other types of realizations*

Many venture capitalists believe that an IPO produces a higher price than the outright sale. That belief appears to be supported by the fact that the average valuation of IPOs between 1988 and 1992 was $106.9 million versus $37.4 million for private sales (*Venture Capital Journal*, Feb. 1993, pp. 30–5). But when considering that fact and the evidence that will be presented next, it is very important to be mindful that companies floating IPOs are mostly stars or potential stars, whereas those that are sold include not only stars but also many mediocrities with no hope of going public.

The gains realized through IPOs were almost five times greater than the next most profitable methods, according to a study of how 26 venture capital funds exited 442 investments from 1970 to 1982 (Soja and Reyes, 1990, p. 191). That study found that 30 per cent of the exits were through IPOs, 23 per cent private sales, 6 per cent company buy-backs, 9 per cent secondary sales, 6 per cent liquidations and 26 per cent write-offs. Using a calculation of gain or loss of (amount returned minus amount invested)/amount invested, gains were produced by IPOs (1.95 times investment), private sales (0.40 times), company buy backs (0.37 times), and secondary sales (0.41 times). Losses were suffered in liquidations (–0.34 times investment) and write-offs (–0.37 times). Relatively few of the companies in the portfolios of those venture capital firms produced large gains whereas almost a third lost money and another third either broke even or produced only nominal gains.

Almost 50 per cent of the final total value of a portfolio came from only 6.8 per cent of all its investments, and 75 per cent of the final value came from only 17.7 per cent, according to an analysis of 383 investments that were harvested by 13 venture capital funds from 1969 to 1985 (Khoylian, 1988, p. 6). In contrast, money was lost on 34.5 per cent of the investments. The average holding period of those 383 investments was about four years, which varied little according to the exit route. When gains and losses are sorted by the stage of the company at the time of the investment, early-stage investing produced proportionately more big winners (≥5 times the investment) and total losers than either expansion or buy-outs. This is what finance theory predicts. It is interesting that the ratio of big winners (≥5 times) to other winners/mediocrities/partial losers to total losers was almost exactly 2:6:2, which happens to be a rule of thumb for a successful venture capital portfolio.

Sevin Rosen, one of the hottest venture capital funds throughout the 1980s, is a textbook example of the 2:6:2 rule. According to Ben Rosen, his firm invested in 36 companies. Eight went public, eight went bankrupt and 20 were still in incubation at the beginning of 1988 (*PC World*, Jan. 1988, pp. 110–14). Its two funds, both specializing in early stage computer and semi-conductor companies, earned several hundred million dollars on an investment of $85 million (*PC Week*, July 1987, pp. 125–32). Among its winners were Lotus Development, Compaq Computer, and Silicon Graphics, and among its losers were Osborne Computer, Synapse Computer, and Enmasse Computer.

Sevin Rosen's $2.5 million investment in Compaq was worth $40 million at the IPO, and its $2.1 million bet on Lotus was worth $70 million at the IPO. Its $400,000 invested in Osborne was a total loss. Since just two of its investments were worth $110 million at the time of the IPO (and much more subsequently), it shows that a fund needs a few spectacular winners if it is to make high returns on its entire portfolio.

## *Venture capital returns from high-technology IPOs*

A study of 77 high-tech companies backed by venture capital that had IPOs between 1979 and 1988 found that the times returns (times return = amount returned/amount invested) on the venture capital investment at the initial offering price was 22.5 times for the first round; 10.0 times for the second round; and 3.7 times for the third round (Bygrave and Stein, 1989, 1990). Four years after the IPO the times return was 62.7 times for the first round, 38.1 times for the second, and 13.5 times for the third.

The average compound annual rate of return for the first round of venture capital at the time of the IPO was 220 per cent; four years after the IPO (about seven years after the first round of venture capital), it had declined to 57 per cent. So although the times return increased from 22.5 times to 62.7 times, the rate of return declined because of the longer holding period. It shows why it is important to consider not only the rate of return but also the times return when evaluating the performance of venture capital investments.

To see what happened to the returns on the first three rounds of venture capital, a subset of 36 companies, each of which had at least three rounds of venture capital, were examined. The returns on rounds one, two and three for those companies are shown in Figure 1.5. At the time of the IPO, the return on the first round was 192 per cent, the second round 163 per cent, and the third round 208 per cent. Because those three rounds of venture capital were held for different lengths of time before the IPO, we found that four quarters after the IPO the returns were 107 per cent, 80 per cent, and 65 per cent; eight quarters, 82 per cent, 57 per cent, and 41 per cent; 12 quarters, 82 per cent, 62 per cent, and 43 per cent; and 17 quarters, 71 per cent, 55 per cent, and 30 per cent. Again, that is what would be expected because risk decreases with each successive round of venture capital.

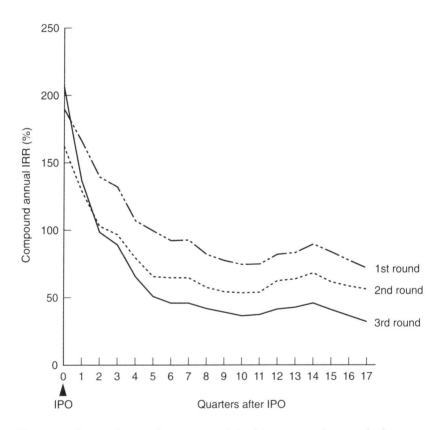

*Figure 1.5 Internal rate of return on original investment by round of venture capital*

(*Source of data*: Bygrave and Stein, 1989)

*IPO returns versus expectations for venture capitalists*

According to industry wisdom, venture capitalists financing seed and start-up high technology companies are looking for compound annual returns of 50 per cent or more; for second-stage financings they tend to look for 30 per cent to 40 per cent; while third-round investors may expect returns of 25 per cent to 30 per cent (Morris, 1985). A rule of thumb is a return in five years of seven times on the first venture capital (a compound rate of return of 48 per cent).

The overall returns of the venture-capital-backed IPOs in our sample appear to be in line with industry wisdom. The companies in our sample were in emerging technologies. The median time from their founding to receiving their first venture capital was 10 months. Thus early-stage, high-technology companies predominated in our sample. Those types of companies are among the riskiest of venture capital investments. Five years after the first venture capital was invested, the average rate of return on the first round was 73 per cent; on the second round, 54 per cent; and on the third round, 33 per cent. Seven years after the first round of venture capital was invested, its rate of return was 57 per cent. Thus the returns on our sample were at the high end of industry expectations.

If the venture capitalists sold their stock at the time of the IPO, or soon after, their rate of return was very much higher than if they held on to it and sold it 'long term'. The median rate of return on the first round of venture capital was 136 per cent at the IPO. But they did not sell much of their holdings at the IPO. Management and investors in the sample of 77 companies sold only 6.4 per cent of their holdings at the IPO. Although a 'rate-of-return maximizer' would have sold as much as possible of the stock at the IPO or soon after, in practice that was not feasible. Management and original investors still owned 72.2 per cent of the stock after the IPO. Thus they could only sell it 'slowly' due to SEC rules restricting the sale of unregistered stock and because they did not want to flood the market with stock and depress the price.

The median times return on the first round of venture capital at the IPO was 7.5, but the mean was 22.5. The mean was much higher than the median because the distribution was skewed. Some of the times return in our sample were greater than 100, and one (Apple) was greater than 200. Those numbers are in line with the findings of others (such as Davis and Stetson, 1985).

By any measure, the returns on venture capital invested in companies that went public over the period 1979 to 1988 more than met venture capitalists' expectations. Yet, as we saw earlier in this chapter, the overall returns of the funds started in the 1980s have fallen far short of expectations. The explanation lies in the IPO market. The public lost interest in speculative IPOs because – in sharp contrast to the returns of venture capital investors – the returns to the public fell far short of expectations.

*Returns to buyers of IPOs*

How well did ordinary investors fare if they bought stocks of all 77 venture-capital-backed IPOs in our data set? They did well for the first year or so, but if they held on to their stocks, they began to lose money after two years. The median compound annual rate of return 17 quarters after the IPO was –6 per cent; 58 per cent of the stocks had negative returns; 23 per cent had returns below –20 per cent; and only 19% had returns above 20%. They got the message: beware of venture-capital-backed IPOs. If they bought stock in all 77 IPOs in our data set of venture-capital-backed high technology companies, they made money if they sold it quickly. But if they held on to the stock, they started to lose money after about two years. Their losses continued for at least the next two years. They did better in IPOs of profitable companies that did not rush to go public than in losing companies that rushed to go public. Of course, the higher the quality of an IPO, the less likely that 'outsiders' can buy it. It is no wonder that the public lost its voracious appetite for high-tech IPOs after the feeding frenzy of 1983. In the years that followed, many of those IPOs turned out to be dismal investments. Some IPOs, such as Victor Technologies and Priam went bankrupt, and investors lost everything. Consequently, while holders of S&P 500 and Dow Jones stocks were enjoying record-breaking gains, public holders of venture-capital-backed high-tech stocks in our data set were, on average, enduring losses.

*IPO gap*

Because public investors lost their appetite for speculative IPOs from 1984 through 1990, many venture-capital-backed companies were unable to go public. Hence venture capital funds were unable to reap their expected harvest. Some companies postponed their IPOs, others – usually, but not always, the less promising ones – were acquired by other companies. Figure 1.6 says it all. The number of venture-capital-backed IPOs fell sharply after its 1983 peak and, apart from 1987–8, did not recover until 1991, while the number of private sales rose until 1987 then levelled out. As we saw earlier, returns on private sales are not nearly as lucrative as those on IPOs. Hence it is not surprising that the overall returns on venture capital declined.

Starting in 1991 and continuing through 1992 into 1993, there was a renewed interest in small-cap stocks. The National Association of Securities Automated Quotations index set new highs. As 1992 came to a close, the Nasdaq index, at a record high, was up 14 per cent for the year compared with a mere 5 per cent for the big-company S&P 500. The average price-to-earnings (P/E) ratio on Nasdaq stood at 35 compared to 24 for the S&P 500.

To no one's surprise, many private companies seized the opportunity to go public. Wall Street floated $20 billion of newly public companies in 1992, up 34 per cent over 1991 (Morgenson and Ramos, 1993). Of that $20 billion, $12 plus billion was raised by more than 400 IPOs listed on Nasdaq. The 1992 bumper crop of 151 venture-capital-backed IPOs surpassed the previous record of 121 first set in 1983 and equalled in 1991. The hot IPO market that began in 1991 heralded a significant improvement in venture capital returns.

In 1991, the number of venture-capital-backed IPOs exceeded the number of private sales for the first time since 1983. The ratio of IPOs to private sales was almost two to one in 1991, which was a stunning reversal of the previous year's ratio of one to two. In 1992, the ratio of IPOs to private sales increased further to 2.2 to one. With IPOs surging, venture capital returns started to improve; investors again paid attention to venture capital; new money again flowed into the industry. After shrinking by an average of

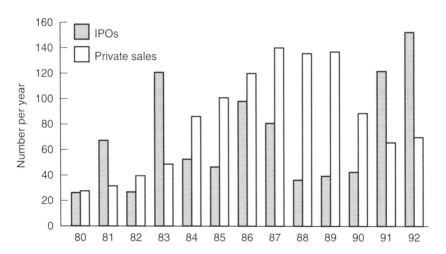

*Figure 1.6 Numbers of IPOs and private sales of venture-capital-backed companies, 1980-1992*

(*Source of data: Venture Capital Journal*)

25 per cent a year for four years, new money raised by venture capital firms in 1992 doubled over 1991.

One observer wrote that 1992 was 'the first "up" year in what appears to be the start of a new cycle in venture capital' (Vachon, 1993). A new cycle it may be, but will it match the boom of the early 1980s when the industry earned 30 per cent returns? It is unlikely – probably impossible – because stock markets cannot absorb enough new issues to produce returns above 30 per cent. Sahlman in 1989, for example, argued that venture capital funds would have owned 50 per cent of the total market value of all the Nasdaq stocks if their returns had been 25 per cent; 68 per cent of the total market value if their returns had been 35 per cent; and 110 per cent of the total market value if their returns had been 50 per cent. Clearly, that is unimaginable.

After 1983, the IPO market's ability to float new issues of venture-capital-backed companies did not keep pace with the rate of creation of such companies. Bygrave and Timmons (1992) estimated that the cumulative gap between the number of venture-capital-backed IPOs needed to produce industry-wide returns of 30 per cent and the actual number was about 500 for the period 1984 to 1989. Although the red-hot IPO market that began in 1991 has partially closed that gap, it will have to get white-hot and stay at that temperature through 1994 before industry-wide average returns again rise above 30 per cent. Leading venture capitalists seem to have realized its ramifications for the industry as a whole – if not for themselves – because according to a fall 1988 survey, they expected returns of about 15 per cent for all venture capital funds but 23 per cent for their own funds over the next 5 to 10 years (Bygrave and Timmons, 1992).

## Implications

We reiterate that a robust IPO market is crucial for the venture capital industry. However, as the evidence in this chapter makes clear, the IPO market is very uncertain. Perhaps it is too uncertain to be relied on as the main harvest route for venture capital investments. Traditionally, IPOs have yielded a harvest much more bountiful than mergers. But hark back to what was written earlier in this chapter: in general, only the cream of the crop goes public, whereas trade sales include everything from companies in distress to huge successes. Giant companies buying venture-capital-backed companies for strategic purposes often value them higher than the IPO market would. That has become very apparent in the biotech industry. It's nothing new. In 1969, Xerox bought Scientific Data Systems (SDS), an eight-year-old venture-capital-backed minicomputer company with $100 million annual sales and $10 million net income, for almost $1 billion. Xerox paid an astronomical sum, even when measured against the super-hot IPO market of 1969. But perhaps what is new in the 1990s is the recognition by venture capitalists and entrepreneurs alike that merging a company with a large strategic partner may be as viable a harvest objective as a public stock offering. That has important implications for how a start-up company is developed.

## EUROPEAN RETURNS

Unlike the USA, where published venture capital returns are comprehensive, European returns are cloaked in secrecy. What little information is available sometimes has questionable validity and reliability. Initiatives are now underway both by the British Venture Capital Association (BVCA) and Europe's Venture Capital Association (EVCA) to rectify this situation; but it will probably be several years before either association begins to publish extensive returns information. It is important to bear this in mind as you consider the information on European returns in this chapter. The returns that we discuss here have either been published in articles or presented at conferences.

### The Netherlands

Without doubt, of all the European venture capital associations, the one in the Netherlands, the Nederlandse Vereniging van Participatiemaatschappijen (NVP) has made the most concerted effort to produce information on the returns earned by venture capital firms headquartered in its nation. According the NVP study, Dutch venture capital earned an average annual return on investment of 13 per cent for the period 1986-90, which compares favourably with average returns of 4 per cent on stocks, 2 per cent on bonds, and 6 per cent on deposits over the same period (Versteeg, 1992).

The NVP returns were derived from data provided by about 50 Dutch venture capital funds that comprise the 'vast majority' of institutional venture capital with only one significant player not participating. The data were for investments made between 1981 and 1990 that were subsequently divested during the same period. The average holding period was 4.3 years. The cash-on-cash returns were computed for all realized investments including both successful harvests, such as flotations and trade sales, and unsuccessful ones, such as bankruptcies and write-offs.

Because the NVP returns did not include the value of portfolio companies that had not been harvested – that is the residual value of the portfolio – they have been criticized as being unrealistic. For that reason and because the returns make no allowance for management fees and managers' carried interest, the Dutch returns cannot be compared directly with the US returns, which are net of fees (1-3 per cent of the capital invested) and carried interest (usually 20 per cent of the capital gain). But if we set aside the problem caused by excluding the value of the residual, we can deduct 23 per cent from the NVP returns to compare them on the same basis with the US returns. Thus the NVP average annual return of 13 per cent was equivalent to 10 per cent for a US fund. Hence it appears that the Dutch average return was, very approximately, similar to the capital weighted average annual US return of slightly more than 8 per cent for the 1986-90 period.

Although the NVP did not examine the returns by fund it did report anecdotally that they ranged from below zero to more than 25 per cent. One large independent private Dutch fund, Atlas Venture, recorded a 15 per cent average annual net return to its investors over a 10-year period (de Haan, 1992).

When the overall return of 13 per cent was broken down by stages there was a substantial variation. The 38 per cent earned by bridge financing was the highest return, followed by 25 per cent for buy-out, 11 per cent for later stage, 8 per cent for turn around, and –3 per cent for early stage financing. Those returns, which are not congruent with the risks, will be discussed later in this chapter.

As we saw with the US returns, the year of the investment made a big difference to the returns. The NVP study found that the highest returns came from investments made in 1981–2, at the depth of the recession when prices were low, and exited in 1986–7 when stock prices were sky-high. Those investments produced an average return of 20 per cent. But as the economy improved and more and more venture capital was chasing companies in which to invest, prices rose and too many deals were done at prices that were too high. Consequently, returns fell to 17 per cent for the 1983–4 vintage of investments, 13 per cent for 1985, 13 per cent for 1986 and 11 per cent for 1987.

## United Kingdom and France

The most developed venture capital industries in Europe are in the United Kingdom, France and the Netherlands. At the end of 1991, the United Kingdom accounted for 49 per cent of the venture capital in Europe; France almost 20 per cent; and the Netherlands accounted for about 5 per cent. But whereas, relatively speaking, the Dutch industry has been forthcoming with information on returns, the UK and French industries have published virtually nothing.

The largest fund in Europe – indeed, in the world – is the British 3*i* Group, which made over 800 investments totalling £424 million in its financial year 1992 (*Venture Capital Journal*, Mar. 1993, p. 21). It publishes reports from which it is possible to estimate its annual return. In some respects it is not a typical fund inasmuch as it is evergreen rather than a set of partnerships with finite lives, most of the money that it invests is raised with bond issues and debt, and when it invests it uses an array of debt and equity instruments. Hence, to compare 3*i*'s returns with those of other venture capital, it is necessary to estimate 3*i*'s return on its equity investments, net of expenses. It has been estimated that 3*i*'s annual returns computed on that basis from published information were 18 per cent in 1986, 20 per cent in 1987, 15 per cent in 1988, 17 per cent in 1989, 4 per cent in 1990, and 2 per cent in 1991 (Brown, 1992).

Although the validity of the computation that produced these returns can be challenged, the trend in unmistakable. Between 1986 and 1989, 3*i* performed very well – better than the top quartile of US funds – but then returns fell precipitously with the onset of the worst UK recession in more than 50 years and the virtual collapse of the Unlisted Securities Market. In view of 3*i*'s dominant position in the UK, it seems reasonable to assume that its returns reflect what happened to the UK industry as a whole. The decline in returns almost certainly deterred investors, and the result was a 36 per cent decrease in the amount of new venture capital raised by UK funds in 1991 as against 1990 (EVCA, 1992).

Top Technology, the managers for the Hambro Advanced Technology Trust, a UK fund specializing in early-stage, high-technology deals, achieved a realized rate of return of some 33 per cent per year over the 1982–9 period. Six of HATT's exits were by successful flotations on the main stock exchange (Bannock, 1991).

The only available numbers for French venture capital are those from the CDC Participations study which covered 20 venture capital organizations with an average age of 6.5 years, representing about 9 per cent of the French venture capital. The 20 organizations produced an average return of 14.6 per cent on realized investments. CDC forecast a cash return after management fees of 18.7 per cent. Approximate annual returns were 11 per cent in 1979, 15 per cent in 1982, 17 per cent in 1986, and 12 per cent in 1987. It was estimated that returns from venture capital were a few percentage points higher than those for bonds regardless of the year when the investment was made. The generalizability of the study is questionable because of the limited number of funds participating (for some years, the return is for only one fund) and those that did participate were focused on late stage investing (Brown, 1992).

## INFERENCES

It is premature to draw firm conclusions from the skimpy information on European venture capital returns. Nevertheless, with the US returns as a guide, perhaps we can glimpse some tentative inferences.

European overall returns appear to be similar to US returns. Actual returns seem to be somewhere in the mid-teens rather than the mid-twenties or even higher that investors have been expecting from venture capital returns. Before arguing that a 15 per cent return or thereabouts is inadequate, it is necessary to look at the returns versus the riskiness of the investment. To date, the only information relating to risk came from the NVP study, which showed that the early stage investing actually lost money while bridge financing returned a whopping 38 per cent. That defied finance theory, which predicts that bridge financing, which is substantially less risky than early stage investing, should have a lower return.

That inversion in the returns, if it is generalizable, presumably explains why most European venture capital has moved away from classic venture capital, which invests in early stage companies, towards merchant capital, which invests in later stage financings and buy-outs (Bygrave and Timmons, 1992). Only 6.9 per cent of the European venture capital invested in 1991 went to early stage companies – a sharp decline from its peak of 12.3 per cent in 1988 (EVCA, 1992).

Nowhere is that trend more apparent than in the case of 3*i*. At the start of the 1980s, when early-stage, high-tech venture capital was red-hot in the USA, the 3*i* Group founded 3*i* Ventures to specialize in classic venture capital. It opened offices in Newport Beach and Boston to get closer to US high tech. It had some impressive successes, including the funding of LSI Logic, a California semiconductor manufacturer, and Rodime, a UK hard-disk pioneer – both exited with very rewarding public stock offerings. But as 3*i*'s returns fell in 1990-1, the company retrenched. Today, 3*i* Ventures no longer exists as a separate entity. Its team of high-tech venture capitalists was disbanded. Its Newport Beach office was closed. And it is winding down its US operations. Granted, Top Technology's excellent performance and 3*i* Venture's successes show that early-stage, high-tech investing can sometimes produce returns big enough to compensate for the relatively high risk involved. However, returns on these types of investments are very vulnerable to downturns in both the economy and the stock market for new flotations.

In its recent advertisements 3*i* is stressing that it is a private equity investor. It seems to have dropped the term venture capital from its publicity. If the trend away from classic venture capital continues, as it undoubtedly will unless returns from early stage investing improve, perhaps the European industry should follow 3*i*'s lead and call its activity private equity investing rather than venture capital.

What will it take to put the venturing back into venture capital? Or, put differently, how can confidence in classic venture capital be restored in Europe? Based on the experience of the US industry, a hot market for small-cap stocks will do it. But that is easier said than done. The USM appeared to be on its death-bed at the end of 1992, and other European second-tier stock markets, including those in the Netherlands and France, were ailing. More and more European venture-capital-backed companies are going public on US stock markets, primarily Nasdaq. So this is the challenge: how can Europe develop small-cap stock markets that are as viable as Nasdaq?

# References

Bannock, G. (1991).*Venture Capital and the Equity Gap*, London: Graham Bannock and Partners.

Boylan, M. (1981–2). What we know and don't know about venture capital. American Economic Association meetings, National Economist Club, 28 Dec.1981. 19 Jan. 1982.

Brown, D. (1992). Presentation at EVCA symposium on Venture Capital, Madrid, June.

Bygrave, W. D. (1989). Venture capital investing: a resource exchange perspective. Doctoral dissertation, Boston University.

Bygrave, W. D. and Stein, M. (1989). A time to buy and a time to sell: a study of venture capital investments in 77 companies that went public. In *Frontiers of Entrepreneurship Research 1989*. ed. N. C. Churchill, J. Katz, B. Kirchhoff, K. Vesper and W. Wetzel, Jr, pp. 288-303, Wellesley, Mass.: Babson College.

Bygrave, W. D. and Timmons, J. A. (1992). *Venture Capital at the Crossroads*, Boston: Harvard Business School Press.

Davis, T. J., Jr. and Stetson, C. P., Jr (1985). Creating successful venture-backed companies. In *Pratt's Guide to Venture Capital Sources*, 9th edn, ed. S. E. Pratt and J. K. Morris, Wellesley Hills, Mass.: Venture Economics.

de Haan, M. (1993). Presentation at EVCA symposium on Venture Capital, Venice, Feb.

EVCA (1992). *Venture Capital in Europe: 1992 EVCA Yearbook*, Zaventem, Belgium: EVCA.

Faucett, R. B. (1971). *The management of venture capital investment companies*. Masters thesis, MIT.

Gevirtz, D. (1985). *The New Entrepreneurs: Innovation in American Business*, New York: Penguin.

Hoban, J. P. (1976). *Characteristics of venture capital investing*. Ph.D. dissertation, University of Utah.

Ibbotson, R. G. and Brinson, G. P. (1987). *Investment Markets*, New York: McGraw-Hill.

Keeley, R. H. and Turki, L. A. (1992). New ventures: how risky are they? In *Frontiers of Entrepreneurship Research 1992*, ed. N.C. Churchill et al., Wellesley, Mass.: Babson College.

Khoylian, R. (1988). *Venture Capital Performance*, Needham, Mass.: Venture Economics.

Kozmetsky, G., Gill, M. D., Jr. and Smilor, R. W. (1984). *Financing and Managing Fast-Growth Companies: The Venture Capital Process*, Lexington, Mass.: Lexington Books.

Landry, K. (1992). Presentation at EVCA symposium on Venture Capital, Madrid, June.

Martin, J. D. and Petty, W. P. (1983). An analysis of the performance of publicly traded venture capital companies, *Journal of Financial and Quantitative Analysis*, 18(3), 401–10.

Morgenson, G. and Ramos, S. (1993). Danger zone, *Forbes*, 18 Jan., 66–9.

Morris, J. K. (1985).The pricing of a venture capital investment. In *Pratt's Guide to Venture Capital Sources*, 9th edn, ed. S. E. Pratt and J. K. Morris, Wellesley Hills, Mass.: Venture Economics.

Poindexter, J. B. (1976). *The efficiency of financial markets: the venture capital case*. Ph.D. dissertation, New York University.

Reyes, J. (1992). Presentation at EVCA symposium on Venture Capital, Madrid, June.

Rotch, W. (1968). The pattern of success in venture capital financing, *Financial Analysis Journal*, 24 (Sept.–Oct.),141–7.

Ruhnka, J. C. and Young, J. E. (1991). Some hypotheses about the risk in venture capital investing. *Journal of Business Venturing*, 6(2), 115–33.

Sahlman, W. A. (1989) The changing structure of the American venture capital industry. Paper presented at the National Venture Capital Association meeting, Washington D.C., 10–12 May.

Sahlman, W. A. and Stevenson, H. H. (1986). Capital market myopia, *Journal of Business Venturing*, 1(1), 7–30.

Soja, T. A. and Reyes, J. E. (1990). *Investment Benchmarks: Venture Capital*, Needham, Mass.: Venture Economics.

Stevenson, H. H., Muzyka, D. F. and Timmons, J. A. (1986). Venture capital in a new era: a simulation of the impact of the changes in investment patterns. In *Frontiers of Entrepreneurship Research 1986*, ed. R. Ronstadt et al., Wellesley, Mass.: Babson College.

US Congress (1984). *Venture Capital and Innovation*, Joint Economic Committee study by R. Premus, Dec.

Vachon, M. (1993). Venture capital reborn, *Venture Capital Journal*, Jan., 32–6.

Versteeg, N. (1992). Presentation at EVCA symposium on Venture Capital, Madrid, June.

Wayne, L. (1988). Management's tale, *New York Times Magazine*, 17 Jan., 42.

Wells, W. A. (1974). *Venture capital decision making*. Ph.D. dissertation, Carnegie-Mellon University.

# 2

# IPO MARKETS IN EUROPE AND THE UNITED STATES: PRINCIPLE AND PRACTICE

*Yves Fassin and Churchill Lewis*

## INTRODUCTION

In both Europe and the United States an IPO occurs when the privately owned equity in a company is offered for sale to the public, in accordance with the disclosure requirements of the relevant national securities laws. Following its IPO a company is thereafter subject to clearly defined periodic disclosure and reporting requirements applicable to all 'public' companies, irrespective of the percentage of their shares that are transferred to public ownership via the IPO.

In the United States the public financing of smaller companies through an IPO typically takes place on the Nasdaq market, the origins and performance of which are described below. Essentially what Nasdaq offers is a single, homogeneous market specifically set up to deal with the particular needs of smaller, growing companies. In Europe the situation is very different. The 1980s witnessed the birth – and in some instances the rebirth – of a whole series of separate national stock markets established with the express purpose of providing smaller companies with access to public capital. Since these markets typically grew up alongside well-established stock exchanges in a particular country they acquired the generic title of 'secondary markets'. Good examples of this phenomenon include the Unlisted Securities Market in London, the Second Marché in Lyon, the Marché Hors-Côté in Paris, Milan's Mercato Restritto, Amsterdam's Officiële Parallelmarkt and the German Geregelte Markt. In each case there are pronounced country-specific differences between the markets in terms of the regulations by which they are governed, the eligibility criteria that companies have to meet and the reporting requirements to which companies whose shares are publicly quoted on these markets become subject. Thus these diverse secondary markets differ significantly when it comes to the size, type and number of companies whose shares are traded.

   This introduces a particular point of difficulty for those studying the area. In the United States Nasdaq has been the subject of exhaustive research, in part made possible by the abundance of readily available data on which to draw. In Europe the researcher is afforded no such luxury. While country-specific studies do exist (for example those by Dawson and Reiner, 1988; Jenkinson, 1990), as do descriptive overviews of the initial public offering process in a particular market (see for example Gilardoni, 1989; and that by Paribas Belgique, 1985), there is little or nothing of a systematic, comparative nature. Such comparative work as has been done is typically restricted to descriptive statistics of activity and trading levels, supplemented by summaries of the regulatory regimes prevailing in different countries (Peyrard, 1992). In addition, organizations such as the International Federation of Stock Exchanges (Fédération Internationale des Bourses de Valeur, FIBV) in Paris and the Brussels-based Federation of Stock Exchanges in the European Community (Fédération des Bourses de la C.E.) publish yearly statistics.

   It is against this background that this chapter should be seen. Our purpose here is threefold. First, to provide a brief overview of what is actually happening on both the Nasdaq market and the different European secondary markets, particularly in terms of the relative scale of activity and contribution being made by these markets to the funding of smaller firms. Second, to give the reader some insight into how the initial public offering process works in practice. Third, to identify and briefly describe a series of what we have called 'IPO games'; that is, the range of techniques that have been developed to influence or manage the share price of a newly quoted company.

   In describing what is happening in Europe we shall draw directly on a study undertaken in 1991 by one of the authors which, in addition to an exhaustive search of publicly available data, comprised 30 direct interviews with secondary market representatives, bankers, accountants and other professionals in London, Paris, Milan and Brussels. Our outline of the IPO process itself will draw primarily on the United States for a simple reason. The diversity that exists within Europe makes it almost impossible to produce an overall description of the IPO process that also does justice to that diversity. At the same time, many of the key features characteristic of the process in the US apply, at least in principle, to European secondary markets. The implications of the proliferation of secondary markets in Europe, a number of which have performed disappointingly, will be considered in Chapter 8 below, where the case will be made for the creation of a pan-European secondary market designed to overcome many of the weaknesses we are about to describe. We start by reviewing the situation in Europe.

# IPO MARKETS IN EUROPE: AN OVERVIEW

At first glance European investors and entrepreneurs appear to be provided with a wide choice of secondary markets through which they can raise new capital or realize the value of an investment. As can be seen from Table 2.1 there are 12 operational secondary markets, supplemented in some countries by much smaller so-called 'third markets' such as the Freimarkt in Germany, the Terzo Mercato in Italy and the Paris Hors-Côté. But what also becomes clear from this table is that in the case of some markets the total number of

**Table 2.1 Secondary stock exchanges in Europe**

|  | Name | Date created/ relaunched | Number of companies listed | Minimum requirements | Other markets |
|---|---|---|---|---|---|
| UK | USM | 1980 | 550 | 10% | OTC |
| Germany | Geregelte Markt | 1987 | 145 | DM 500m | Freimarkt |
| France | Second Marché | 1983 | 189 | FF 10mm | Hors-Côté |
| Italy | Mercato Restritto | – | 37 | L 1mm 10% | Terzo Mercato |
| Netherlands | Parallelmarkt | 1982 | 65 | G 5mm | |
| Spain | Barcelona | 1982 | 4 | No minimum | |
| Belgium | Second Marché | 1985 | 3 | | |
| Denmark | | 1982 | – | | |
| Greece | | 1990 | 5 | Dr 100mm | |
| Luxemburg | | – | – | | Hors-Côté |
| Ireland | | 1980 | 25 | | OTC |
| Portugal | No official or parallel | – | 29 | | OTC |

*Sources:* Peyrard, 1992; yearbooks of FIBV, Fédération des Bourses de la C.E, EVCA.

companies listed is in fact very small, with markets such as those in Barcelona or Brussels being barely viable in terms of the number of companies trading on them. Table 2.1 also gives the minimum flotation requirements in terms of the percentage of a company's shares offered for sale and, in some instances, minimum value of an offering.

Table 2.2 shows the number of companies quoted on secondary markets (or similar) in different European countries, and the capitalization of the secondary markets in millions ECU. The ratio has been calculated between the capitalization of the secondary market to the capitalization of the first market. The ratio of the capitalization of the first market to the gross national product gives an idea of the importance of the stock exchange in a specific country.

**Table 2.2  Companies and capitalization of secondary markets in Europe, 1990**

| | Number of listed companies | Capitalization secondary market, ECU million | % 2nd market of 1st | % 1st market of GNP | Average capital per company, ECU million |
|---|---|---|---|---|---|
| England | 425 | 7 671 | 1.2 | 82 | 18.0 |
| France | 184 | 16 928 | 7.6 | 24 | 92.0 |
| Netherlands | 39 | 688 | 0.8 | 51 | 17.6 |
| Italy | 37 | 9 374 | 8.6 | 13 | 253.4 |
| Germany | 236 | 14 872 | 5.7 | 23 | 63.0 |
| Spain | 3 | 12 | 0.0 | 23 | 4.0 |
| Ireland | 25 | 698 | 9.2 | 29 | 27.9 |
| Portugal | 29 | 327 | 5.0 | 20 | 11.3 |
| Belgium | 5 | 436 | 0.9 | 40 | 87.2 |
| Greece | 5 | 77 | 0.7 | 27 | 15.4 |
| Europe | 988 | 51 083 | 3.3 | 38 | 51.5 |
| USA | 4 700 | | | | |
| Japan | 342 | | | | |

*Sources:* As Table 2.1.

A total of about 1 000 companies are quoted on the European secondary markets, compared to 4 700 on the Nasdaq in the US and 350 on the OTC Market in Tokyo. In absolute terms, nearly half of all companies listed on European secondary markets are in fact listed in London (425 out of 983). However in terms of absolute value of companies listed on secondary markets, the Second Marché in Lyon shows the highest market capitalization (ECU 16 928 million), closely followed by the Geregelte Markt in Germany (ECU 14 872 million), with the USM in London some way behind (ECU 7 671 million).

Bigger differences in type of companies appear after calculation of the average market capitalization per company : on average ECU 51.5 million for Europe as a whole but ECU 253.4 million for Italy, where a number of 'banca populare' are quoted. France also shows a high average, due to a few big companies quoted on the Second Marché. The average capitalization per company falls from ECU 51.5 million to 31.9 million per company if the Lyon and Milan markets are excluded. The capitalization of secondary markets is dwarfed by the first markets. For all European markets combined, the capitalization of second markets is 3.3 per cent of the main markets. The amount of the capitalization of the secondary markets related to the first market ranges from a high 9 per cent for both Italy and Ireland to less than 1 per cent for Belgium and The Netherlands. In contrast, the ratio of Nasdaq to the New York Stock Exchange (NYSE) was 51 per cent in 1992.

The disparity between the secondary markets and the first markets becomes even clearer when measured in terms of the total value of all the shares traded annually, as shown in Table 2.3. The ratio of secondary market ECU volume to first market ECU volume for Europe as a whole was only 0.89 per cent in 1990.

**Table 2.3 ECU volumes of first and secondary markets, 1990**

|  | Secondary market, ECU million | First market, ECU million | % 2nd market of 1st |
|---|---|---|---|
| UK | 2 047 | 430 561 | 0.48 |
| France | 5 605 | 93 336 | 6.01 |
| Netherlands | 421 | 32 129 | 1.31 |
| Italy | 782 | 33 318 | 2.35 |
| Germany | – | 405 477 | – |
| Spain | 8 | 28 428 | 0.28 |
| Europe | 9 315 | 1 045 813 | 0.89 |

As an indication of the relative importance of flotations as a means of realizing venture capital investments, Table 2.4 shows the number of divestments encompassing all realizations and write-offs of venture capital portfolio companies; the total number of IPOs on both main and secondary markets occurring in 1990; and the number of companies quoted on the secondary markets by country. Given that only a fraction of the total number of IPOs were backed by venture capital, it shows what a small part flotations played in providing an exit route for venture capital investments in 1990. To put the 1990 figures in context, Table 2.5 sets out in summary form the total number of IPOs occurring in seven European countries in 1989, 1990 and 1991.

**Table 2.4 Numbers of all venture capital divestments, IPOs on all markets and listed companies 1990**

|  | All VC divestments | All IPOs | Companies listed 2nd market |
|---|---|---|---|
| UK | 1 060 | 51 | 425 |
| France | 232 | 11 | 184 |
| Netherlands | 162 | 10 | 39 |
| Italy | 32 | 4 | 37 |
| Germany | 240 | 47 | 236 |
| Spain | 70 | 4 | 3 |
| Europe | 2 071 | 151 | 983 |

**Table 2.5 Numbers of IPOs, 1989–1991**

|  | 1989 | 1990 | 1991 |
|---|---|---|---|
| UK | 77 | 51 | 20 |
| France | 29 | 17 | 13 |
| Netherlands | 10 | 10 | 9 |
| Italy | 1 | 4 | 6 |
| Germany | 88 | 47 | 36 |
| Spain | 1 | 0 | 1 |
| Belgium | 3 | 3 | 2 |
| Europe | 267 | 151 | 94 |

## IPO Markets in Europe: summary

From this review of European IPO secondary markets, a number of features stand out:

- The capitalization of all secondary markets is only 3.3 per cent of the total capitalization of the first markets.
- The capitalization of secondary to first markets ranges from less than 1 per cent for Belgium and The Netherlands to 9 per cent for Italy and Ireland.
- The total value of all the shares traded in the secondary markets per year is less than 1 per cent of the turnover of the first market, with a range from 0.3 per cent (Spain) to 6 per cent (France).
- The European secondary markets play a marginal role in Europe for harvesting venture-capital-backed companies.

As we shall now show this picture is in marked contrast with the US where the Nasdaq market plays a vital role.

# NASDAQ: ORIGIN AND GROWTH

In the past 20 years in the United States, initial public offerings have grown dramatically in number and volume. One can only conclude that of the various items available in the securities market, the equity sold in initial public offerings (also referred to as 'new issues') is increasingly popular. Why? The proliferation of IPOs and the increasing volume of capital moving in these transactions have in and of themselves been important factors in the success of this market. The increasing number of new issue securities in public hands has increased the volume of subsequent trading, improving the ease of buying and selling such securities (liquidity) and enhancing their value. Securities firms making the underwriting, sales and trading of these equities their core business have prospered, and new institutions dedicated to buying and owning these new issue equities have multiplied. Consequently, this segment of the institutional investor market has been distinctly classified as 'small capitalization' or 'high growth' investing in reference to the equity capitalizations of investee companies of generally less than US$1 billion and the rapid growth rates (greater than 20 per cent) associated with these companies. All this has enhanced the demand side of the market.

Yet the underlying fundamentals of the product must have been and continue to be attractive for this market to have become so successful. The sophisticated buyer of financial instruments is interested in those with superior risk-reward characteristics. Buyers of IPO stocks must believe that they can make money by owning these instruments. Classification of this activity as 'high growth' investing reveals the anticipation of superior growth rates in revenue and profits of investee companies. The value of stock in these companies, assuming that stock price as a multiple of earnings does not change, should appreciate more quickly than the value of stock in larger but lower-growth companies. The expansion in the market for IPO securities shows that this expectation has, at least to some extent, been fulfilled.

The reasons for this customer satisfaction, however, lie as much in the environment in which the buying and selling of IPO securities takes place as in the underlying performance of the investee companies. The dominant feature of this environment, which can in fact be credited with the emergence of significant new brokerage firms and institutional investors dedicated to small-capitalization stocks, is the separate market which developed to foster sales and trading of these securities. The National Association of Securities Dealers (NASD) established this market in 1971. The impetus behind this initiative was the perception by smaller brokerage and underwriting firms (securities dealers) of an economic opportunity in the combination of the demand for capital by high-growth small and medium-size businesses and the public interest in owning stock in rapidly growing companies.

Existing floor-based securities markets such as the New York Stock Exchange and American Stock Exchange (Amex) did not lend themselves to transactions in equity securities of smaller companies because all trades pass through a floor specialist. Smaller companies imply fewer and smaller trades with lower aggregate transaction revenues for brokers and traders than trades in stock of bigger companies. Since the amount of time a transaction requires is generally the same regardless of size (and smaller transactions in a floor exchange may require more time since buyers and sellers are fewer and therefore harder to match), larger stock transactions for larger companies will be favoured. There is no incentive for the trading market in stock of smaller companies to improve in a floor-based system serving larger companies.

The NASD innovation was to give each securities firm the opportunity to make its own market in the stock of a given company, using computer technology to centralize trading reports and to make buy and sell quotations of market-makers in the same stock available to each other. Multiple market-makers improved throughput while competition between market-makers narrowed spreads (the separation between bid and ask quotations), both enhancing the ease of buying and selling (liquidity characteristics) for stockholders. Because of the automated quotation (AQ) aspect of this market, it has come to be known as the NASDAQ market.

The success of the Nasdaq market is evident from its growth in absolute terms and in market share. The market's annual share trading volume increased from 8.4 billion shares in 1982 to 48.5 billion shares in 1992. This

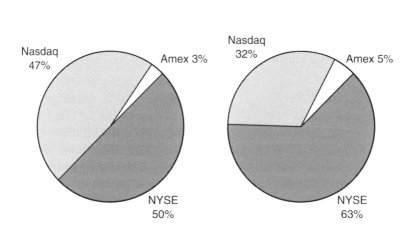

Figure 2.1 Proportions of shares traded on Nasdaq, NYSE and Amex, 1992 and 1982

trading volume represented 32.1 per cent of shares traded on the three leading exchanges in the United States in 1982 as contrasted with 46.8 per cent in 1992 (Figure 2.1). The dollar volume of the stocks traded on the Nasdaq market placed it second among all markets in the world in 1992 and represented 33.3 per cent of the total of the three leading US exchanges, which was more than double its 1982 percentage (Table 2.6). The Nasdaq composite index has increased 191 per cent in the 10 years 1982 to 1992.

**Table 2.6  Ten-year comparison of Nasdaq, NYSE and Amex**

|  | *Nasdaq* | *NYSE* | *Amex* |
|---|---|---|---|
| *Companies by year* | | | |
| 1992 | 4113 | 2089 | 814 |
| 1991 | 4094 | 1885 | 860 |
| 1990 | 4132 | 1769 | 859 |
| 1989 | 4293 | 1719 | 859 |
| 1988 | 4451 | 1681 | 896 |
| 1987 | 4706 | 1647 | 869 |
| 1986 | 4417 | 1573 | 796 |
| 1985 | 4136 | 1540 | 783 |
| 1984 | 4097 | 1543 | 792 |
| 1983 | 3901 | 1550 | 822 |
| *Issues by year* | | | |
| 1992 | 4764 | 2658 | 942 |
| 1991 | 4684 | 2426 | 1058 |
| 1990 | 4706 | 2284 | 1063 |
| 1989 | 4963 | 2241 | 1069 |
| 1988 | 5144 | 2234 | 1101 |
| 1987 | 5537 | 2244 | 1077 |
| 1986 | 5189 | 2257 | 957 |
| 1985 | 4784 | 2298 | 940 |
| 1984 | 4728 | 2319 | 930 |
| 1983 | 4467 | 2307 | 948 |
| *Share volume (millions) by year* | | | |
| 1992 | 48 455 | 51 376 | 3600 |
| 1991 | 41 311 | 45 266 | 3367 |
| 1990 | 33 380 | 39 665 | 3329 |
| 1989 | 33 530 | 41 699 | 3125 |
| 1988 | 31 070 | 40 850 | 2515 |
| 1987 | 37 890 | 47 801 | 3506 |
| 1986 | 28 737 | 35 680 | 2979 |
| 1985 | 20 699 | 27 511 | 2101 |
| 1984 | 15 159 | 23 071 | 1545 |
| 1983 | 15 909 | 21 590 | 2081 |

Initial public offerings on the New York Stock Exchange, the American Stock Exchange and other United States markets are also possible and even encouraged by those institutions, now that IPOs are a prevalent feature of the equity securities business in the United States. The Nasdaq market, however, is very strongly preferred by issuers and underwriters for IPO transactions. From January 1982 through early December 1992, there were 3328 IPOs on the Nasdaq market, 285 on the NYSE, and 151 on Amex. The trend between 1988 to 1992 is shown in Figure 2.2 and the relative importance of the Nasdaq market to the other major stock markets of the world are shown in Figure 2.3.

In its advertisements, the Nasdaq market claims to be the stock market for the next 100 years. And it may well be right to judge from its growing popularity. The key to its success is its market-makers and the electronic trading system. A typical stock has 12 market-makers, who compete with one another. Of the market-makers, 20 per cent do 80 per cent of the business. Some 60 per cent of the transactions are done online automatically, which guarantees the buyer the best price that is listed electronically at the time of the offer. The only way that a market-maker can get out of the way of a bid is by raising the price. However, Nasdaq does have its detractors. A critical article in *Forbes* asserted, 'No question that Nasdaq is a vital and lively market, but if you are an individual investor, those spreads and price manipulations will eat you alive. The odds are firmly stacked against you.' ('Fun and games on Nasdaq', 16 Aug. 1993, pp. 74–80).

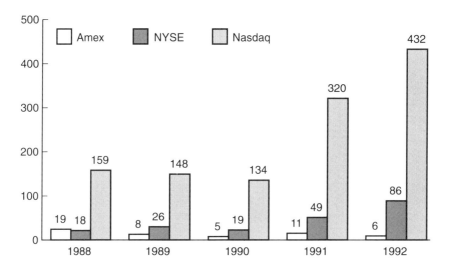

*Figure 2.2 Numbers of IPOs on the Amex, NYSE and Nasdaq markets, 1988–1992*

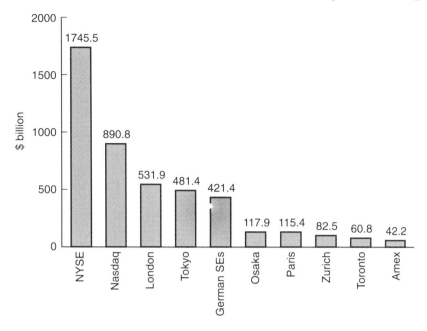

*Figure 2.3 Dollar volumes of equity markets, 1992*

Now that we have surveyed recent activity on European secondary markets and the Nasdaq market, we go on to look at how the IPO process works in practice in the USA.

## MARKETING THE IPO

The initial public offering process begins with the filing of a preliminary 'registration statement' with the Securities and Exchange Commission. This document contains information about the offering and the business whose stock is to be sold, including three years of audited financial statements. The key aspects of this document, including the financial statements, are printed for circulation as a preliminary prospectus or 'red herring', so called because of the text printed in red on the document warning that no discussion among sellers and prospective purchasers of the stock may take place independent of this document. In practice, nothing about the offering that would stimulate interest in the offering may be printed for distribution other than the preliminary prospectus for a period starting several months prior to the filing of the preliminary registration statement and ending several weeks after the stock has been sold. News articles for which an issuing company provides information and which might be construed as arousing interest in the company in the months prior to filing the preliminary registration statement can elicit an SEC order postponing the offering for a 'cooling off' period. Discussion of the offering or possible offering in the months before filing the preliminary registration statement must therefore be carefully circumscribed.

Once this document has been filed, the planned offering is public information and discussion of its terms is unavoidable. The SEC reviews the document and makes comments as to how the registration statement should be amended before the stock is sold. This review period from filing to comment is generally five weeks and gives the issuing company and its representative time to present the merits of the business and the terms of the offering to prospective buyers. Without directly approving the practice, the United States securities laws implicitly allow sales presentations of initial public offerings linked to the preliminary prospectus. This therefore makes the preliminary prospectus not only a legal disclosure document but also a marketing document that can highlight the strengths of a company.

Companies issuing stock in initial public offerings typically engage one or two investment banks to manage the initial public offering process so that the stock is effectively sold at an attractive price. The technical framework for this engagement is that the investment banks 'underwrite' the offering, that is purchase the stock in the offering at an agreed price and thereafter bear the risk of its resale. In practice this underwriting commitment is not made until the end of the five-week review period described above, by which time indications of interest have been obtained from prospective buyers and a price linked to the level of demand can be ascertained. The underwriters 'go effective' with the sale usually on the morning after the underwriting agreement has been signed, and indications of interest from prospective buyers become confirmed orders. The underwriters' period of exposure is therefore typically managed to last no more than 12 hours, and this exposure is syndicated to investment banks other than the managers to further reduce the risk.

The issuing company, if it is performing well, will generally have numerous potential managing underwriter(s) to choose from, all having established resources to bear the underwriting risk and to organize the syndication and sale of the stock. The selection criteria relate rather to the investment bank's reputation for representing successful companies; its ability to help the issuing company tell its story in such a way that it obtains an attractive price for its stock; and its sponsorship of the issuing company after the sale through research coverage and trader support, so that the stock continues to appreciate in value. Investment banks that achieve consistency with respect to these criteria acquire 'brand name' recognition with the investor community, which reinforces their ability to satisfy these criteria for the issuing company.

The issuing company selects the managing underwriter (lead investment bank) no later than two to three months before the registration statement is to be filed. As part of the competition to be selected for this business, the investment bank will have analysed financial information about the company and made a preliminary assessment of the value of the company's stock. The issuing company will typically be represented by a law firm (counsel) with at least some experience of securities law. This law firm and the company's auditors prepare a draft of the registration statement on behalf of the company, which is ultimately responsible for the accuracy of the document. The managing underwriter and a further law firm specializing in securities law selected by the underwriter then take an active role in shaping the document with the issuing company, its counsel and auditors. The managing underwriter focuses on positioning the company for an effective presentation of its business strategy and competitive advantages in the language of the document, while assuring itself of the completeness and accuracy of the financial and operating information presented.

The combined effort on the preliminary prospectus is the basis for the joint preparation by the issuing company and the managing underwriter of a presentation using slides for use at meetings where company management explains the offering to the institutional investor community. Known as the 'road show', these meetings take place towards the end of the five-week review period after the preliminary registration statement has been filed. The road show will be presented on sequential days in key institutional investor cities including New York, Boston, Baltimore, Chicago, Minneapolis, San Francisco and Los Angeles and one or two major cities in the region of the country where the company is based. The compression of the road show in a period of one to two weeks maintains national focus on the offering for a concentrated period of time. Company management may also present the offering in important Western European institutional investor markets if the offering size and company capitalization are larger than average for initial public offerings or if the technology or nature of the business is likely to be of international interest.

## SELLING THE IPO

The IPO marketing process is geared to institutional investors (mutual funds, pension fund managers, insurance companies, etc.) because of their importance in the equity capital markets in the United States. Sale of stock in the offering is usually divided so that one-third or more is placed in a so-called 'institutional pot' for sale by the managing underwriters to institutions sufficiently active in the initial public offering capital market so that their trading behaviour after the offering can be fairly readily predicted. This placement practice provides a core of stability for the stock which helps the lead underwriters manage trading so that buying of the stock exceeds selling and the stock price goes up, satisfying the interests of both investors and the issuing company. This is discussed more fully below. The remaining free stock in the offering is allocated among underwriting syndicate members (and a few brokers who may receive shares to sell although they are not in the syndicate, called the 'selling group'). A significant amount of this stock (perhaps half) is also sold to institutional buyers rather than individuals. While over half of an offering can therefore typically be expected to be sold to institutional investors, over time trading activity will cause stock to accumulate in institutional hands, settling at a level around 80 per cent of the stock publicly traded.

If the issuing company and lead underwriters have done a good job positioning the company and convincing the investment community that the suggested price range for the stock on the preliminary prospectus is consistent with that positioning and the company's underlying value, the order indications during the marketing period and prior to sale will generally be at least several times the stock available for sale in the offering. Offerings that elicit strong demand may have orders for five or more times the stock available for sale in the offering. In such cases, buyers' original orders are cut back to the extent necessary to match supply and demand. The lead underwriters are typically granted an option to sell additional shares equal to 15 per cent of the shares shown as available for sale in the offering (the 'green shoe'). While this option helps the underwriters to satisfy excess demand, its real purpose is to allow the lead underwriters to oversell the offering. They then have a choice of supplying the stock oversold from stock purchased in the market in the early hours of trading after the offering is effective or from the green shoe. This permits the lead underwriter to act as a buyer immediately following the offering with reduced financial exposure. This buying power helps support the stock price and push it in the desired upward direction following the offering.

If the order indications for the stock in the offering are five or more times the amount of stock offered, the managing underwriters will typically suggest a sale price for the stock at the upper end of the price range per share shown on the preliminary prospectus (the 'filing range'). More rarely, the stock will be sold at a price higher than the filing range but generally not more than 20 per cent above the filing range. More rarely still, the size of the offering will be increased but generally by not more than 15 per cent. To permit these adjustments, they are included in the amended registration statement which will be filed in any case two or three days before the offering in response to comments from the Securities and Exchange Commission. They may even be shown in a second amendment to the registration statement.

If demand for the offering is weak (order indications of less than twice the stock on offer), the price agreed with the issuing company may be below the filing range shown on the preliminary prospectus. How much the price is below the filing range is a function of what price level will generate sufficient demand for a stable offering. Prices more than 20 per cent below the suggested range may result in postponement or even cancellation of the offering.

The reason why changes in price and size of IPOs from what is represented on the cover of the preliminary prospectus are carefully circumscribed is that substantial changes in terms of the offering, as well as in information about the underlying operations of the business, may constitute a 'recirculation issue'. That is, the stock may not be sold until all buyers have seen a new document containing the new information. This recirculation entails considerable cost in printing and distribution of new documents but, more importantly, interferes with the momentum and psychology of the offering process. Recirculation will delay the offering by at least a week and, since it is unusual, will raise the presumption of a problem in the minds of the buyers. In practice, changes from the preliminary prospectus are rarely considered sufficiently material to require recirculation.

The final registration statement, however, will reflect all changes, including the offering price finally agreed on between the issuing company and the managing underwriters. Once this document is filed with the Securities and Exchange Commission (the morning following agreement on price), the offering is declared effective and, shortly thereafter, trading in the stock begins. A final prospectus based on this final registration statement is printed and sent to all buyers of the stock with their order confirmations. Importantly, this final prospectus is the legal document which will subsequently be consulted in any legal dispute concerning the adequacy of disclosure in the offering. Even though buyers do not see this document until after the offering and their purchases are accomplished facts, they have typically received something very close to it in the form of the preliminary prospectus many weeks prior to the offering.

## PAYING FOR THE IPO

The price paid by buyers of the stock is a gross price which includes compensation to the lead investment banks, other investment banks in the underwriting syndicate and other brokers in the selling group. This compensation is approximately 7 per cent of the gross price in initial public offerings in which stock with a value of more than $15 million is sold. Smaller or more speculative offerings (for companies with a limited or questionable operating history) may pay compensation of 8 per cent or more, while initial public offerings in which stock with a value of $70 million or more is sold will generally pay between 6 per cent and 7 per cent. Investment banks generally must substantiate this level of compensation based on recent IPOs of comparable size and quality. The investment banks particularly well known for quality work in managing IPOs may be able to command a slight premium above the average (a fraction of a percent) in the level of compensation which they are able to negotiate with the issuing company. This compensation is called the 'gross spread' because it represents the difference between the gross selling price and the amount of money which the underwriters have committed to pay to the issuing company for each share of stock. In addition, the issuing company must pay other expenses in connection with the offering, including fees to its lawyers, the costs of printing preliminary and final prospectuses (including working time in the printers' offices) and filing fees to the Securities and Exchange Commission, state commissions (if any) and the NASD or other market on which the stock will be listed. The 'gross spread' and these other expenses are disclosed in the final registration statement.

The 'gross spread' consists of three components. Approximately 20 per cent is the 'management fee', which is generally divided equally among the managing underwriters, if more than one, assuming they are of the same stature in the investment banking business (a matter of consensus among syndicate desks of investment banks, which are constantly working together in underwriting groups).

Another 60 per cent of the gross spread is the 'selling concession', which is paid to members of the syndicate and selling group on the basis of how much stock they were each allocated to sell. This percentage may be slightly higher or lower depending on the level of difficulty in placing the stock with buyers. The managing underwriters also receive a significant portion of this segment of the gross spread, both because they are almost always paid by institutional investors for stock sold from the previously mentioned institutional pot (since institutions recognize that the lead banks in the offering control the placement of this stock) and because they allocate to themselves outright large amounts of the stock to be sold. The institutional pot may be 'competitive' or 'non-competitive', which highlights the distinction between the lead managing underwriter and co-managing underwriters (if there is more than one). Once managers have been selected by the issuing company, cooperative and open communication among them is desirable even if they were fiercely competitive in seeking the business. None the less, practicality dictates that one of the managers control the syndication and selling process. The issuing company will designate one manager as lead manager (whose name appears by convention on the bottom left of the prospectus cover). The lead manager may press this 'first among equals' advantage by having the issuing company agree to a competitive pot. In this arrangement, the selling concession on stock sold from the institutional pot goes to the investment bank which the buying institution designates. This will almost always be one of the managing underwriters as an inducement for them to fill the order to the maximum extent possible, although the buyer may use the opportunity to pay a favour to some other bank. As among managing underwriters, the lead manager will receive most of the indications, particularly in offerings for which there is strong demand, since the buyer recognizes that the lead manager ultimately controls the stock's distribution. In a competitive pot, the lead manager therefore receives a greater portion of the gross spread than other managers who are otherwise equally situated. In a non-competitive pot, the managers split selling concessions directed to any of them equally.

The final 20 per cent of the gross spread is the 'cost to underwrite'. This money is used to pay the underwriters' expenses in the offering, including the cost of counsel to the investment banks, advertisement of the offering on its conclusion and the so-called 'closing dinner' to honour the issuing company and to strengthen the anticipated continuation of a client relationship with the lead investment banks. The money is also available to help stabilize the stock once the offering is effective, that is to serve as an additional pool of capital which the managing underwriters may use to create demand for the stock in the market if necessary to hold the trading price at or above the offering level. If any money is left from this component of the gross spread after these expenses, it is divided among the members of the underwriting syndicate on the basis of underwriting commitments; the lead investment banks will underwrite the largest number of shares and other investment banks will underwrite the remainder of the shares in decreasing amounts depending on their position in the investment banking hierarchy, a position, as we mentioned above, monitored and maintained by the syndicate desks at these investment banks. From the foregoing, it is apparent that just appearing in the syndicate may bring little or no compensation. The managing underwriters, who also sell most of the stock, enjoy the lion's share of the gross spread.

The managing underwriters also benefit from commissions on the heavy volume of trading in the first days and weeks following the offering, most of which will be directed through these firms because of the commitment they have made to the issuing company to act as market-makers. If demand for the IPO has been strong and the stock price continues to appreciate, the firms will also make trading profits on the positions which they take in the stock. On the other hand, if demand for the offering is weak, they will experience trading losses in honouring their commitment to be market-makers and therefore ready buyers of the stock.

The so-called 'quiet period' during which the issuing company and underwriters are prohibited from making statements about the company and the offering (apart from a narrowly drawn press release) continues for 25 days after the offering is effective. The managing underwriters' research analysts then typically release a report about the company's business, including estimates of future earnings per share for the business. These estimates are crucial to the way the stock is valued in the market and may be stated orally before the offering but will not have been printed for public distribution prior to the publication of these research reports. Since the securities laws in the United States require disclosure every three months from companies whose stock is publicly traded, research reports, which may simply be company updates, will typically appear every three months as well, but typically far enough in advance of public disclosure to avoid an inference that the analyst is a recipient and purveyor of material inside information.

In practice, however, the research analyst is a vital spokesperson for companies in their first few years of trading on the public markets. Quality research coverage is one of the main criteria for selecting an investment bank as a managing underwriter. The analyst gives the company publicity which keeps the market aware of smaller company stocks and helps to maintain the share price. For this reason, research analysts are equally important to buyers who are active in small-capitalization investing. As a company grows larger and trading volume becomes more substantial, more research analysts will follow the stock. This is because institutional buyers will direct trading in the stock through that firm, as a broker or market-maker, to reward the firm's analyst for the advice rendered or for the consistency of information which the institution values in making trading decisions.

## MATCHING INTERESTS OF BUYERS, SELLERS AND UNDERWRITERS

What may be apparent from this review of the initial public offering process is that there is a concurrence of goals among the seller (the issuing company), the managing underwriters and the buyers. The seller wants to receive the highest price possible for its stock on the initial public offering, yet this evident truth must be considered in relation to the specific interests of the stockholders in the initial public offering. These include management, who are generally themselves also shareholders and whose financial success is tied to the future performance of the company; investor shareholders, who in IPO companies in the United States are frequently venture capital firms; and members of the Board of Directors, who have a fiduciary responsibility to protect shareholder interests. If all existing shares in a company were sold in an IPO, new buyers could be found only with great difficulty because the sale would show a lack of conviction among the sellers in the future value of the stock, on which the selling presentation to buyers is predicated. Furthermore, most of the stock sold in an IPO is usually new stock to bring new money into the business to help fund its future growth. If too much of the stock sold in an IPO is existing stock, potential buyers will shy away from the offering as a 'bailout'. Therefore existing shareholders in the issuing company and those responsible for their interests must safeguard the price of the company's stock after the offering, since it is only later that these shareholders will be able to fully realize the value of what they own. Management must also protect the post-offering stock price as a vehicle for raising capital again in the future to finance the company's further growth.

If the IPO stock price is not defensible longer term in relation to the fundamentals of the business, the post-offering stock price will eventually fall below the IPO price; new investors will be disappointed and lose interest in the stock so that, even if they continue to hold the stock, trading volume will dry up. This loss of a following and corresponding loss of liquidity for new-issue, small-capitalization companies makes subsequent public offerings very difficult. Conversely, investors are satisfied if a stock steadily increases in price following an IPO, building confidence in the company and conditioning the capital market for future public offerings.

Investment banks managing IPOs stand between these interests of the seller and the buyer. A good investment bank will be able to convince the seller that its interests lie in appreciation of the stock price and that it should accept a realistic assessment of the level at which the IPO should be priced for this to occur. Investment banks competing for the position of managing underwriter are sometimes accused of 'buying the business' by promising the issuing company an IPO price that cannot be achieved or, if achieved, cannot be sustained in the aftermarket. Since credibility with an issuer and investors in the next IPO will be weaker, this strategy is unsustainable for building a leading position as an investment bank in IPO underwriting but may be followed by investment banks that engage in this activity only episodically without viewing it as a core business. Investment banks that have a track record of underwriting new issues that go up in price acquire 'brand name' recognition with investors, which immediately qualifies subsequent IPOs managed by them for investors' attention. Both issuer and investors expect managing underwriters to sponsor the stock through sustained research and market-making and those who do so further enhance their reputation with sellers and buyers.

Offerings managed by investment banks occupying a leading position in the IPO business typically possess certain characteristics that illustrate the investment bank's influence with the company issuing the stock and that reassure institutional investors that their concerns, some of which have already been referred to, are being addressed. Shares in the offering will typically not exceed more than one-third of all the company's shares outstanding after the offering. Of the shares in the offering, the shares sold by selling stockholders, as distinguished from new shares which will bring additional capital into the company, will not exceed one-third to one-half of the size of the offering. These characteristics taken together reassure investors that the company already has sufficient operating history and resources for the offering to add to but not dominate the value of the business; that the present stockholders have enough confidence in the company to want to retain a substantial part of their ownership; that the company is a high-growth business and therefore needs new capital to achieve that growth; and that a significant number of closely held shares remain for possible future sale as investors seek to increase their stakes in the business.

Institutional investors also look for offerings with share values not less than $20 million and aggregate post-offering values of the issuing company of not less than $60 million. This is because institutional investors want to make sure there is enough stock for it to be widely held so that there is active trading and therefore liquidity for buying and selling purposes. Institutional investors also want to be able to build a $5 million position in the stock if they plan to hold it in their portfolios, since managing smaller positions is equally time consuming with less potential aggregate return. At the same time, institutions are reluctant to have this position exceed 5 per cent of a company's stock since this requires filing special disclosure statements under the securities laws.

Finally, investors look for offering prices per share of between $13 and $20 since this balances a sense of substantiality and the possibility of further price increase. Setting the price at these levels simply requires splitting the stock into the correct number of shares in relation to the overall company value.

Investment banks depend on institutional buyers also to observe certain rules of conduct. At a minimum, institutions are expected to honour their pre-offering order indications, placed during the marketing period, when the offering becomes effective. Investment banks also look for institutional buyers who will help to nurture the new stock by holding on to the stock for a reasonable period of time after purchase, or at least until there is some fundamental disappointment in the issuing company's business which would give the institutional buyer a substantive reason to sell. Finally, investment banks will expect certain key institutions with which they regularly do business to follow up their order indications on the offering with purchases of additional stock in the aftermarket immediately following the offering. The managing investment bank's syndicate desk will 'cut back' order indications as a way of sending a signal to institutions to buy up to the amount of the orders in the aftermarket, thereby building follow-up demand into the offering. This predictability is important to the managing underwriter in controlling the volatility of the new stock while the float (shares in public hands) is still small and liquidity is thin. Dependability of buying behaviour forms the basis of a relationship in which institutions can expect to be favoured in the allocation of new issue stock by the managing underwriter.

Valuation of the company for purposes of an initial public offering also requires a good understanding of the investor's perspective. Institutional investors will compare the suggested offering price as a multiple of the earnings estimate per share for the year in which the offering occurs (the P/E) to the P/E of other public companies which might be considered 'comparables', that is operating in the same business or otherwise sharing similar operating fundamentals and growth characteristics. Companies with higher growth rates and stronger operating characteristics such as higher profitability levels and higher returns on equity will have higher P/E levels. Earnings per share calculations are based on weighted average shares outstanding for the year in which the offering occurs, based on pre- and post-offering share counts with some further accounting for option shares. The suggested offering price is a discount from the price arrived at by applying a defensible P/E level to the earnings per share estimate. This 'IPO discount' is typically 15 per cent and can be rationalized as a compensation to prospective buyers of the stock for the risk of purchasing stock in a company not previously tested in the public markets. This discount strengthens the price dynamics of IPOs because it generates demand for the stock following the offering at least up to the price that is considered its proper trading level. In the medium term, one might fear that buyers of the stock would be inclined to sell once this discount has been captured. As previously noted, however, institutions committed to IPO investing will lose their claim to favourable allocations in the better IPOs if they are perceived as 'flippers', that is as sellers of IPO stocks short term. These institutions also believe that real gains are linked to holding for the longer term.

This system of reciprocal courtesies between investment banks managing IPOs and institutional buyers has been criticized as a closed system prone to market distortions (see for instance *Forbes*, 18 Jan. 1993, pp. 66–9). Specifically, the large number of buy orders generated by road shows, the IPO discount, tacit restrictions on investor selling after the IPO and promotional research all combine to drive up the price of the IPO stock, which attracts investors independent of the logic of the stock price relative to the company's operating fundamentals or other opportunities in the investment market. Consequently the market appears 'overheated', meaning that price/earnings ratios in excess of 50x are frequently observed. In years when IPO momentum is particularly strong, the marketing and distribution dynamics of IPOs can cause unsustainable price appreciation, which is typically corrected within a year, as happened, for example, in 1983 and 1987. And as 1992 came to a close, some observers were fretting that the 1992 generation of IPOs was heading for a correction because in their opinion the average Nasdaq price/earnings ratio of 35 was too high compared with the S&P 500, which stood at 24.

## IPO GAMES IN PRACTICE

In the USA there is abundant evidence that in the short term IPOs perform better than the stockmarket as a whole, but in the long term they perform worse. The post-IPO price rise in the days following a flotation is technically known as 'underpricing', because, to finance theorists, it suggests that the initial pricing by the managing underwriter was below what the market was prepared to pay. To date, although at least half-a-dozen explanations – some more plausible than others – have been offered by finance theorists, there is no universally accepted theoretical explanation of the IPO underpricing phenomenon. But we do know that in practice underwriters deliberately employ techniques to levitate shares in the market immediately after an IPO. Here are some of the more common ones that were reported in the recent article in *Forbes* magazine cited above.

### Overstimulating demand

Underwriting syndicates put on huge road shows to promote investor interest before a flotation. As a typical IPO is usually for 5 million shares or fewer, it is not too difficult to generate a potential demand that far exceeds the supply. Sometimes the demand is red-hot, if not white-hot. For instance, when the Cheesecake Factory – a trendy US restaurant chain – went public with a 2.1 million share offering it is estimated that there were buy orders for 100 million shares. When an issue is red-hot, underwriters often promise an allotment to their best customers on condition that they make a commitment to purchase the remainder of their initial order in the open market after the shares have begun trading. That can create a buying frenzy, which drives up the price, on the first day of trading.

## Penalizing flippers

Underwriters sometimes take back a stockbroker's underwriting commission if the latter's customers sell their shares immediately after the offering. The practice has been known to continue for weeks or even months if the after-market for the shares is cold.

## Boosting the stock

It used to be that underwriters did not issue research reports until 90 days after an IPO – the so-called quiet period. In 1988, the SEC reduced that period to 25 days. Thus shares get a welcome shot from a favourable research report that boosts their price 25 days after the initial flotation.

## Stunting the shorts

When the price per share is perceived by some investors as too high, they sell it short, usually by borrowing shares from a stockbrokerage firm that is holding them for a client who bought them on margin. On many new issues, brokerage firms will not lend them out, thereby thwarting would-be short selling, which might drive the price down.

## Placing stock with friends

Underwriters prefer to sell shares to friendly customers who are going to hold on to them rather than sell them as soon as possible in the aftermarket.

## SUMMARY

Despite all those tactics aimed at driving up share prices after an IPO and keeping them up, the prices of the majority of new listings eventually start to fall relative to the general market. And, as we will see in the next chapter, in the long term they underperform the market. Hence investors on average get burned by IPOs – especially those who buy shares at high prices in red-hot markets and hold on to them for the long term. Individual investors are particularly vulnerable because they tend to be shut out of choice initial offerings, which are snapped up by institutions. Instead, individuals buy shares of choice companies in the price run-up in the IPO aftermarket. Or perhaps even worse, they buy IPOs that are readily available because of lack of institutional interest.

Not surprisingly, the euphoria engendered by red-hot IPO markets is followed by despondency as prices fall and the market becomes ice-cold. The US IPO market has experienced many hot-cold cycles, proving that the market has the resiliency to come back again and again. In contrast, European secondary markets, which are young and fragile, have no such history. They have yet to prove that they can recover from the despondency that now besets them.

In defense of the IPO process, however, the limited liquidity of new stocks requires a certain amount of sheltering and nurturing to make them attractive to investors at all. Otherwise, their price volatility would prevent this market from competing with other investment options. Second, the better investment banks committed to managing IPOs have less of a tendency to follow the price surges in the IPO market referred to above in setting offering prices than have those investment banks operating at the margin. Obligations to issuers require some observance of the high offering prices possible when these 'market windows' open, but good firms use these windows to capture higher prices for good companies rather than using the window to bring weak companies to market.

On balance, the IPO market in the United States has evolved into a sustainable vehicle for raising capital for the high-growth, small and medium enterprise segment of the US – and increasingly the global – economy.

## References

Allen, F., and Faulhaber, G. (1989). Signalling by underpricing in the IPO market, *Journal of Financial Economics,* 23, 303–23.

Barry, C., Muscarella, C. J., Peavy III, J. W., and Vetsuypens, M. R. (1990). The role of venture capital in the creation of public companies – evidence from the going-public process, *Journal of Financial Economics,* 27, 447–71.

Bartlett, J. W. (1988). *Venture Capital: Law, Business Strategies, and Investment Planning,* New York: John Wiley.

Bygrave, W. D., and Stein, M. (1989). A time to buy and a time to sell: a study of 77 venture capital investments in companies that went public. In *Frontiers of Entrepreneurship Research, 1989,* ed. N. C. Churchill et al., Wellesley, Mass.: Center for Entrepreneurial Studies, Babson College.

Dawson, S., and Reiner, N. (1988). Raising capital with initial public share issues in Germany 1977–1985, *Management International Review,* 28(1).

Gilardoni, A. (1989). *Un nuovo mercato mobiliare per piccole e medie imprese*, Milan: EGEA, Universita Bocconi.

Jenkinson, T. (1990). Initial public offerings in the UK, USA and Japan. Discussion Paper 427, Centre for Economic Policy Research, pp.1–26.

Ooghe, H., Manigart, S., and Fassin, Y. (1991). Growth patterns of the European venture capital industry, *Journal of Business Venturing*, 6(6), 381–404.

Paribas Belgique (1985). Le Second Marché de Bruxelles, *Notes Economiques*, no. 60, 2–12

Peyrard, J. (1992). Les bourses européennes, Paris: Vuibert.

Ritter, R. (1987). The costs of going public, *Journal of Financial Economics*, 19, 269–81.

Roland, M. (1986). Bourse: l'important c'est l'image, *Tertiel*, no 17, Sept.

Sahlman, W. A. (1990). The structure and governance of venture-capital organizations, *Journal of Financial Economics*, 27, 473–521.

Stein M., and Bygrave, W. (1990). The anatomy of high-tech IPOs: do their venture capitalists, underwriters, accountants, and lawyers make a difference? In *Frontiers of Entrepreneurial Research*, ed. N. C. Churchill et al., Wellesley, Mass.: Babson College.

Deloitte Haskins & Sells (1987). Fiscal environment of and corporate vehicles for venture capital in Europe. Paper.

# 3

## INITIAL PUBLIC OFFERINGS: PRICING AND PERFORMANCE

*Benoît F. Leleux and Sophie Manigart*

### INTRODUCTION

Whether regarded as the first step of private companies into the public domain or the last stage of entrepreneurial activity, where assets built up during the company's life cycle are harvested by its founders, initial public offerings of equity shares deserve a prime place in the financial and entrepreneurial Hall of Fame. The popular press has helped to draw attention to the claim of IPOs to such an illustrious position – warranted by the outstanding performance of some IPO stars of the 1980s in the United States. Names like Home Depot, Liz Claiborne, Microsoft and Adobe Systems have become flag-bearers for the bounties to be found in public equity share offerings. Indeed, a $100 investment in Home Depot at the initial offering in September 1981 would have grown to $12 031 at the end of 1991, or 3755 per cent better than an equal amount invested in the S&P 500 over the same period of time. Microsoft similarly gained 1786 per cent from its issue date on 14 March 1986 to the end of 1991, a still astounding 1188 per cent above the S&P 500. The 1990s have plenty in store as well, with the likes of Discovery Zone, Inc., an operator of children's play centres, which made its debut in the first week of June 1993 at $22 a share only to surge to $35.5 at the end of the first day's trading.

Less publicized, although nearly as resounding and definitely more numerous, are the dismal showings of such big-time losers as Mediagenic, underwritten in October 1983 by Morgan Stanley at the adjusted price of $60 per share and worth about $0.02 at the end of 1991, assuming you could even find a buyer at that price (see Hulbert , 1991, for some examples in that vein or Scherreik, 1993, for the latest on the IPO front).

The outlandish results obtained by IPO shares, in either direction, have of course generated enormous attention from the academic world, always in search of evidence supporting the next 'anomaly' in market and pricing theory. Under the combined scrutiny of investors, issuers and academics, IPO shares have been shown to exhibit at least three fundamentally interesting characteristics:

- The 'initial price reaction' phenomenon. When shares are first listed in the stock exchange, their early market prices are shown, on average, to be significantly higher than the price at which the shares were initially sold (also known as the issue price). In other words, if you were able to buy $100 worth of each IPO share issued during the period 1974–85 in the United States at their fixed offer price and sell them on the market a few days or weeks later, you would have received an average of $116 for them (based on Ritter's calculations see Ritter, 1991), or an annualized, almost risk-free return of around 800 per cent.

- The 'Hot Issue' phenomenon. Very distinct cycles have been outlined in both the number of issues being brought to market and the level of the initial price reactions.

- The long-run 'underperformance' phenomenon. IPO shares, when held over the long run (three to six years), seem to perform abnormally poorly compared to shares from comparable firms (same industries, same sizes) during the same periods.

In the following sections, we first introduce some generic facts about the going-public process then move on to analyse in greater detail each of the phenomena described above. The fundamental objective is to answer the following questions: (1) are the flotations correctly priced in the market? (2) Is there evidence of the possibility of 'timing' the issue to improve the proceeds obtained? (3) How are the IPO shares performing in the long run? We complete the review of the IPO question by a series of six minicases concerning respectively France, the United Kingdom, Belgium, Spain, Germany and Italy. A conclusion wraps up the arguments.

## GOING PUBLIC: SOME FACTS AND FIGURES

If quizzed on the topic, a large proportion of the chief executives in the industry will still probably recognize the IPO as a privilege of the larger, more established firms. The facts, on the other hand, draw another picture. A recent study by Fechtor Detwiler & Co. (reported by Bruce Posner for the magazine *Inc.* in February 1993) of the IPO market from 1989 to mid-1992 in the United States indicates that nearly one-third of the issuers during that period had revenues of less than $10 million and nearly a quarter made offerings of less than $10 million. The distributions of sizes of issuers and offers' sizes are reported in Figures 3.1 and 3.2.

Even though similar evidence on the European front is hard to come by, and could not be located at all for the purpose of this study, it seems fair to say that initial public offerings are relevant as financial options for a large number of smaller sized, high-growth firms. It is thus of prime importance

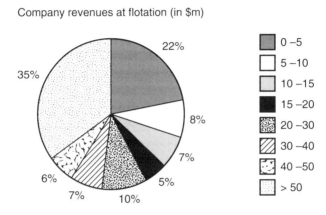

*Figure 3.1 Distribution of IPO proceeds in the US, 1989–1992*

(*Source*: Fechtor Detwiler & Co., Boston, June 1992; see Posner, 1993)

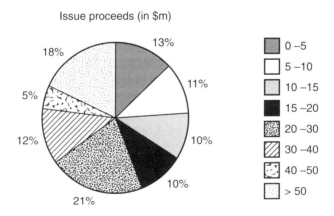

*Figure 3.2 Distribution of company revenues at flotation in the US, 1989–1992*

(*Source*: Fechtor Detwiler & Co., Boston, June 1992; see Posner, 1993)

to understand fully the mechanism of the forces at work in the issuing process. For this purpose, we summarize in the next section the available evidence on IPO pricing and performance and the theoretical models introduced to explain it.

## THE INITIAL PRICE REACTION PHENOMENON

The most intuitively appealing 'anomaly' in IPO pricing is the apparent systematic run-up in price observed in very early trading. IPO shares in the United States have been shown on average to gain some 16 per cent from their issue price to the first market price, a gain obtained with almost no risk and over just a couple of days or weeks at most (see for instance Ibbotson et al., 1988, for a good review of the literature). Obviously, this figure is only an average, with wide deviations observed for individual firms, some of them even exhibiting serious losses in early trades. Similar evidence has been gathered over the years for most stock exchanges of the world, with only the magnitude changing significantly between countries (see Leleux, 1991, or Loughran and Ritter, 1993, for a review of the international scene).

If one assumes that the market is efficient in setting security prices even when no history of public trade exists, then those unusually high returns occurring to the IPO investors immediately after the first listing of the stocks can be regarded as evidence that IPOs are substantially underpriced when issued, whether on purpose or simply by mistake (hence the more general description of the phenomenon as the 'initial underpricing', a terminology avoided here because of the causality model it underlies). A vast array of theoretical models has been generated to rationalize the initial behaviour of IPO share prices, of which only a handful are presented here. Some authors have argued quite convincingly that the underpricing is used by the underwriters as a means of reducing the probability of ending up with an unsuccessful issue and its consequential losses (Reilly, 1977). Ritter (1984) argues that some form of monopsony power exercised by the underwriters allows them to underprice the issues and selectively allocate the shares to privileged customers. In a related argument, Tinic (1988) postulates that the underpricing operates as an implicit insurance scheme against legal liabilities arising from the due-diligence process. Benveniste and Spindt (1989) show how underpricing can actually be used to induce truthful revelation of information from potential investors during the pre-selling period (during which underwriters attempt to determine the demand structure for the shares to be floated).

Dozens of other models have been introduced to account for the existence of the abnormal initial price reaction. Among them, we want to single out for description a generic class of models built around the concept of asymmetric information. It is now recognized that information is not homogeneously distributed among all market participants. For example, in a typical issue the underwriter probably knows more about the potential demand for the shares than the issuer itself, having gone through a pre-market process and having gained a lot of experience from previous issues. Baron (1982) uses this argument to justify the underpricing as a normal compensation for the use of the underwriter's privileged information. If the asymmetry of information is deemed to exist between different classes of investors, then it is possible to show, as Rock (1986) and Parsons and Raviv (1985) did, that the underpricing can come about as a means to counter the asymmetric rationing of the shares between informed and uninformed investors. In a sense, the underpricing is needed to 'bribe' the uninformed investors to the IPO market where their participation is required to fully place the issue.

It is also possible to present the argument more intuitively: informed investors only invest in 'underpriced' issues (those shares that will exhibit superb performances in early trades), leaving a disproportionate fraction of the 'overpriced' issue (which will perform very poorly) to the uninformed investors. This 'winner's curse' problem is very well described by Scherreik (1993): if a share is a really interesting investment, it does not need to be publicized and investors with good connections to the major brokerage houses will buy up all of the issue, leaving close to none for the amateur IPO investor. On the other hand, if a broker resorts to cold calls to place 'exciting' new issues, the major excitement will come from the ability to buy as many shares as you want. But expect a pretty nervous rollercoaster ride once the shares get listed.

The existence of the information asymmetries also creates opportunities for signalling and reputation games. In other words, if the quality of a particular offering cannot be easily observed, a lemons type problem, as in Akerlof (1970), is created in which firms of all qualities are pooled together and the average issue price is driven down to the point where the market could even disappear altogether. In such a context, incentives exist for firms to generate information about their quality and try to differentiate themselves from the mass in order to obtain higher valuations for their offerings. The problem is to make this information credible, which is to say that lower quality firms cannot mimic the signals of the higher quality firms, leading to a separating equilibrium. Investment bankers, auditors, underwriters, banking relations, venture capital backings, etc., have all been investigated as sources of quality certification (see for example Carter and Manaster, 1990;

Beatty, 1989; James and Wier, 1990; or Megginson and Weiss, 1991). A firm offered by a recognized underwriter, audited by a top accounting firm, to which leading bankers have made sizable loans and in which highly regarded venture capitalists have invested significant amounts generates a better quality image than one underwritten by an obscure underwriter, with qualified audits and no banking relations. With its credible image, the first company may not need to underprice as much as the second to attract investors to its initial offering.

## THE 'HOT ISSUE' PHENOMENON

A second interesting phenomenon is the existence of cycles in both the numbers of IPOs brought to market and the level of underpricing associated with the flotations. In other words, IPOs seem to come in cohorts and aggregate in calendar time. Ritter (1984) attributes the phenomenon to changing risks in the offerings. Loughran and Ritter (1993) pinpoint a more attractive explanation for the existence of cycles: issuing firms may time their offerings to be near market peaks in their respective industries. On evidence collected not only from the USA but also from a number of other European, Asian and South American countries, they show that private firms, and their advisers, appear to be able to time their IPOs to take advantage of 'windows of opportunities' proxied for in the study by the inflation-adjusted level of the stock-markets. A firm with an average timing ability is shown to be able to lower its cost of capital significantly (by as much as 800 basis points on average, according to the authors' figures), explaining the wide swings in the volume of IPOs for the 12 countries in the study. The cycles in the volume of IPOs are then partly due to firms timing their offerings to take advantage of changes in the cost of equity. A second and more dramatic consequence of this timing ability is examined in the next section.

## THE LONG-RUN UNDERPERFORMANCE PHENOMENON

The most enigmatic phenomenon so far in IPO pricing is the apparent underperformance of IPO securities in secondary trading. First highlighted by Stern and Bornstein (1985) and later analysed rigorously by Ritter (1991) and Aggarwal and Rivoli (1990), the long-term performance of IPO shares following their listing has been consistently shown to be dismal in the United States. Equal amounts of investment in all IPO shares in the first days of trading would on average generate returns inferior to the market's by about 25 per cent after three years (or about 8 per cent per year) and 38 per cent after seven years (Loughran and Ritter, 1993). Those long-term returns have been shown to depend on the issue year, the number of years the firm has been in existence prior to the IPO, the industry in which the firm operates and the number of firms going public during the same period of time. In still more graphical terms, Loughran and Ritter (1993) attempt to evaluate the various components of the underperformance for the stocks issued since 1968. They disaggregate the average annual return to investing in seasoned stocks with the same size distribution as the sample IPOs (which would have earned 15 per cent per year on average over the period considered) into 5 per cent due to the ability of IPO issuers to time their flotations and take advantage of market 'peaks' (because investing in seasoned stocks at the time of the IPOs generates average annual returns of only 10 per cent, compared to the 15 per cent earned on average on the same investments outside the IPO issuing dates) and another 8 per cent due to the underperformance effect (because investing in IPO shares at the time of the offerings creates average annual returns of only 2 per cent, compared to the 10 per cent earned on non-IPO share investments with the same timing).

A first comprehensive, pan-European study of IPO long-term performance was conducted by Leleux and Muzyka (1992). Using methodologies similar to Ritter (1991), they support the same general pattern of stock underperformance in the long run in each country analysed (France, United Kingdom, Germany, The Netherlands and Belgium). Strategies that consist in investing equal amounts in each initial public offering on the first day of trade generate consistently negative, market-adjusted returns in the three-year horizon following the listings. Those results are shown to be independent of the flotation method used (three flotation methods are available, for example, in Paris), the year when the listing took place and the market on which the introduction took place.

Figure 3.3 highlights the cumulative abnormal returns for IPO shares issued in Paris in the years 1988 to 1992 (from Leleux, 1993), using the three different flotation procedures available in France. It shows that independently of the flotation technique selected, the same general pattern of long-term underperformance can be observed, leading to a three-year return that is on average 30 per cent lower than the return obtained on the market index. The 'mise en vente' procedure seems to perform much worse than the other two procedures, but the sample size in that case limits generalizations. Figure 3.4 compares the IPO long-term performance results measured in the United States by Jay Ritter (1991) to those for Europe, estimated by Leleux and

Muzyka (1992). It is quite clear from the chart that the general pattern of long-term underperformance is present in both cases, the two settings diffe-ring mainly by the extent of the initial price reactions.

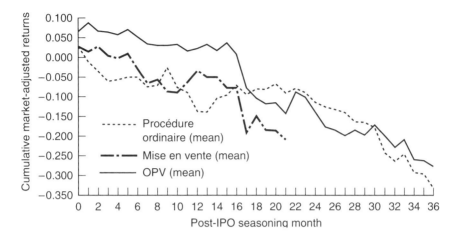

*Figure 3.3 Long-term performance of French IPO shares, 1988–1992  by three methods of introduction*

(*Source*: Leleux, 1993)

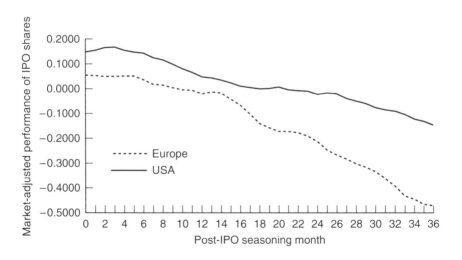

*Figure 3.4 Long-term performance of IPO shares, Europe versus USA*

(*Sources*: Leleux and Muzyka, 1992, for the European data – France, United Kingdom, Germany, Holland and Belguim; Ritter, 1991, for the US evidence)

## Minicase 1

### Does knowing who sells matter in IPO pricing? The French second market

An interesting extension of the information asymmetry model of underpricing is presented by Rémy Paliard and Bernard Belletante (1992), both researchers from the Groupe ESC Lyon in France. The argument centres around the distribution of knowledge about the IPO process itself among the participants. The authors hypothesize that shareholders who are in the finance industry are better informed than other actors (such as the company's managers, employees or owners) because of their prior experience with other offerings. Accordingly, if those better informed shareholders decide to part with some of their holdings in the initial public offering, they will also look to influence the timing and choice of issuing procedure to do what they can to limit the underpricing phenomenon. This hypothesis is translated into a distinct preference for 'hot' markets and 'price-driven' procedures (competitive or one-stage auctions, as opposed to the more standard American fixed-price offers) which have been shown to be related to lower levels of underpricing on average.

On a representative sample of 165 firms floated between 1983 and 1991 on the French second market, the authors do observe a prevalence of price-driven procedures in 'hot' issue markets, a significantly lower demand for shares offered in those high issue volume periods and lower underpricing overall. On the other hand, little evidence is gathered in support of a negative link between the proportion of equity in financial hands before the IPO and the level of underpricing. This may simply be due to the fact that the financial owners are not truly at stake when they sell only tiny fractions of their holdings or even none at all. Similarly, the nature of the financial owner does not seem to influence the propensity to go public in 'hot' periods or the choice of issuing procedure.

This minicase is particularly helpful in illustrating one significant problem with IPO pricing research so far. Most observers would agree that the pricing decision involves a considerable number of contributory factors: the nature of the owners, the complex contractual arrangements between all stakeholders, the ultimate objective of the issuer (guarantee liquidity to its holding? cash out and harvest?), etc. So far, most models of the pricing process are restricted by design or by pure mathematical necessity to a limited number of variables. In this way, we offer only two- or three-dimensional perspectives into what is most definitely a multidimensional question. Without denigrating the usefulness of such an approach, one also has to recognize the fact that analytical tractability comes at a cost: that of leaving outside the investigation some of the most important variables.

## Minicase 2

### Initial public offerings in the UK, 1984–1991

William Rees (1992) of the University of Strathclyde examines the phenomenon of the short-term underpricing of 489 initial public offerings in the period 1984 to 1991 on the London Stock Exchange, both on the Unlisted Securities Market (187 IPOs) and on the main market (302 IPOs), for both placings and offers for sale. He focuses on the information asymmetries and the signalling theories to explain underpricing in the UK. The percentage of equity retained by the pre-issue shareholder, the use of prestigious advisers, such as sponsors, brokers and accountants, and the choice of the Official List and the method of introduction are all hypothesized to be signals that cannot be replicated by inferior firms. It is expected that the use of the signals will lead, among others, to a lower underpricing percentage.

In line with a prior study of the Bank of England, which reports an average return in the first week of trading for IPOs in the period 1986–90 of 8.5 per cent for offers for sale and of 14.3 per cent for placings, the IPOs in the Rees's study also exhibit a significantly positive initial return. He finds furthermore that the use of a prestigious broker leads to a higher underpricing when the issue is introduced on the main market, while the same is true for a prestigious sponsor when the issue is introduced on the USM. On the other hand, the higher the proportion of equity retained by the initial shareholders – which is considered to be a positive signal to the outside world – the lower the underpricing for introductions on the main market and the higher the underpricing for introductions on the USM. These findings do not support the general implications of the signalling theory.

Rees further focuses on the determinants of the total post-issue value of the shares (after one week of trading), which is composed of the issue price per share and the initial return during the first week. The post-issue value is positively related to the proportion of equity retained, the choice of prestigious brokers and sponsors and issuing via the Official List, apart from the initial return. This might simply indicate that the shares with the highest value are effectively introduced on the official market and backed by the most prestigious brokers and sponsors.

## Minicase 3

### Mispricing of initial public offerings – evidence from Germany

Björn Hansson and Alexander Ljungqvist (Lund University and Nuffield College, Oxford, respectively) investigate the short-term and long-term performance of 163 IPOs on one of the eight German stock exchanges between 1978 and 1991 (Hansson and Ljungqvist, 1993). Introductions on both the main market and on the second market are included, as well as public offers and private placements. The public offers are always firm commitments, where the offer price and the number of shares are fixed.

On average, the shares are offered at a discount to their subsequent first-day trading value of almost 12 per cent (after corrections for the market movements between the offering date and the first day of trading). Only 25 of the 163 IPOs have an initial negative return. This overall positive initial return is not erased in the short term: the total return to an investor, corrected for the overall market movement, does not drop within the first 20 trading days. There seems to be no difference between the underpricing percentage in the main market and in the second market.

Contrary to the findings of Ritter (1991) in the US and of Leleux and Muzyka (1992) in France and the UK, the long-term performance of the German IPOs does not decline: the sample performed neutrally compared to the market index over the first 400 trading days. The high initial return of 12 per cent is thus, on average, not erased in the long run.

When taking the number of issues occurring during a certain year as a measure for a 'hot' or a 'cold' issue market, then 1986 and 1989 to 1990 were clearly 'hot' years. Although there is evidence that the underpricing varies heavily with year of issuance, it cannot be associated with hot or cold markets. There was significantly more underpricing in 1986, but underpricing in 1989 and 1990 was average. There is furthermore no evidence that a larger issue would be less underpriced than a smaller issue, contrary to the size effect found in the US (Ritter, 1984). However, the 10 per cent smallest of the issues have, on average, an initial return that is 11 per cent higher than the other issues.

A further surprising finding, contrary to the expectations of the signalling theories, is the fact that when the previous owners sell out all or part of the company (which is generally interpreted to be a negative signal), then the underpricing is lower, everything else being equal. Finally, the choice of the underwriter does influence the initial return to the investor. While one particular bank avoids significant underpricing on average, another one discounts its issues very heavily. However, no bank in particular could be associated with abnormal long-term performance.

## Minicase 4

### Underpricing of initial public offerings on the Milan Stock Exchange, 1985–1991

Umberto Cherubini and Marco Ratti (1992) of the Banca Commerciale Italiana study the IPOs on the main Italian stock exchange, the Milan Stock

Exchange (MSE), which represents 95 per cent of the total Italian market capitalization. There are three methods to get a share listed on the MSE: an offer for sale at a fixed price with a new share issue, an offer for sale at a fixed price without a new share issue; and an offer for sale by tender, which is less often used. A particular feature of the Italian stock exchanges is that there is a substantial time-lag between the expiry date of the offer for sale and the first official quotation: in this sample of 75 IPOs, the median time lag is 95 calendar days. In this context, initial underpricing is necessary to compensate for the capital cost and for the additional risk taken on by the investors. However, the shares may be quoted on the unofficial Over The Counter market during this time period.

The median underpricing between the offering and the first OTC quote is 14 per cent (corrected for variations in the market index), while it is 15.5 per cent between the offering and the first MSE listing. A hot-issue market seems to be accompanied by a higher level of underpricing. As in the German study, there is no evidence that either firm size or offering size affects the initial return percentage, or that prestigious underwriters lead to less underpricing. However, the following characteristics are associated with a larger initial return: a larger proportion of equity retained by the owners - again contrary to the expectations of the signalling theory; a larger oversubscription of the offering; and the fact that the firm has further recourse to the capital market to raise new equity or bank loans.

Some of these results are in line with the previous minicases but do not support the theoretical explanations. The fact that the oversubscription rate and the underpricing percentage tend to move together hints at the fact that the new investors are able to spot *ex ante* those issues that promise the highest short-term returns (remember that most offers come with a fixed price). Finally, the third explanatory characteristic of the level of underpricing, that is, the firm having further recourse to the capital market, may be explained by the fact that those firms want to leave a good taste in the mouth of the initial investors, hoping to recoup the cost of lower pricing in the initial offer by getting favourable terms on the next seasoned equity offering.

## Minicase 5

### Initial public offerings – the Spanish experience

The highest degree of underpricing in the six countries reported here is experienced by the IPOs on the Barcelona and Madrid stock exchanges in the period 1985–90, as reported by Ahmad Rahnema, Pablo Fernandez and Eduardo Martinez-Abascal of IESE, Barcelona (Rahnema et al., 1992). The average initial return to the investor who bought a share of each offering and sold it on the first trading day was 35 per cent for a sample of 71 IPOs. This average, however, is influenced by the extremely high initial returns in 1986 (65 per cent) and 1987 (49 per cent). Whereas 1986 was a 'cold issue' period in Spain, with a relatively small number of offerings in that year, 1989 was clearly a hot-issue period, with the number of issues more than double the number in any other year in the study; the level of underpricing in that year was nevertheless close to the average.

In the long term, however, there is a significant negative return for the investors in IPOs, compared with investors in the market portfolio. The best investment strategy is to invest in IPOs but to sell the investments after a period of 90 days.

Contrary to the findings reported for the other stock markets, the initial return is negatively related to underwriter prestige, so does not support what is theoretically expected under standard signalling models. It is furthermore lower when there is a public offering, versus a private placement, and when the firm is larger. The age of the firm, however, has no influence on the initial return. Finally, when the initial investors retain a larger percentage of the offer, this is a positive signal to the new investors, leading to a significantly lower underpricing. There also seems to be an industry effect in the Spanish market, with the level of initial underpricing very much related to the industry of the issuing firm.

## Minicase 6

### Empirical examination of the underpricing of IPOs on the Brussels Stock Exchange

Bart Rogiers and Sophie Manigart of the Vlerick School of Management, University of Ghent, study the short-term performance of the 28 initial public offerings on the major Belgian stock exchange, the Brussels Stock Exchange (BSE) between 1984 and 1990, both on the main and on the secondary market (Rogiers and Manigart, 1992). The average initial return from the offering price to the first trading day is estimated at 9 per cent and rises to 13 per cent after three trading days (net of the market return). This is an indication that the BSE is not efficient: the stock price rises significantly more than the market index during the three days after the issue. There is no relationship between the introduction method and the level of underpricing. The years 1986 and 1987 were clearly hot-issue periods, both in the number of IPOs and in level of underpricing. The initial return to an investor was 6 per cent higher during these two years than in the other periods.

There is a positive relationship between the *ex ante* uncertainty on the value of the issue and the underpricing percentage, but no relationship was detected with the size of the firm. The prestige of the underwriter(s) does not affect the level of underpricing, but the number of underwriters does: when there is more than one bank involved, the underpricing is 6 per cent higher than when there is only one bank involved. The level of underpricing is higher when the equity retained by the initial owners and the oversubscription rate are higher.

## CONCLUSION

What can be learned from all these country studies? To synthesize the principal conclusions and their implications for practitioners, we call back the initial framework provided by the three 'anomalous' phenomena outlined at the outset.

### The initial price reaction

Table 3.1 summarizes the various issue characteristics studied and their relationship with the level of underpricing (the initial short-term return), although one should be cautious with these comparisons, as different authors use different research methods. The first thing to be noticed is that the same characteristics have different consequences depending on the country in which the study is conducted. The first four characteristics listed in the table are under the issuer's control. The choice between the main or the second market does not seem to influence the level of underpricing – but the regional location of the second market does seem to be important in France – while the choice of the underwriter, the equity retained by the initial investor and the timing of the issue seem to have different effects in the different countries. It is thus important for the entrepreneur/issuer to know the particular behaviour of the stock market on which he plans to float the shares. The only thing that seems robust across countries is the existence of significant initial price reactions (underpricing), although the magnitude of the effect varies greatly between markets and in calendar time. The same conclusions hold for the investors, who can look at additional characteristics to assess their potential initial return. The size of the issuing firm has no influence in most of the countries, but a large firm IPO tends to exhibit less underpricing than a small firm IPO in Spain. A higher oversubscription rate leads to higher underpricing in Italy and Belgium, hinting that investors are able to distinguish *a priori* what issues are good for them.

**Table 3.1  Characteristics of IPOs and their relationship with the level of underpricing**

| Characteristics | Country | Relationship |
|---|---|---|
| Underwriter prestige | UK | Higher underpricing |
| | Italy | No relationship |
| | Spain | Lower underpricing |
| | Belgium | No relationship |
| Equity retained | UK | Lower underpricing (Official List) Higher underpricing (USM) |
| | Germany | Higher underpricing |
| | Italy | Higher underpricing |
| | Spain | Lower underpricing |
| | Belgium | Higher underpricing |
| Market choice | UK | No difference |
| | France | Higher underpricing in regional exchanges than in Paris |
| | Germany | No difference |
| Timing (hot issue) | France | Lower underpricing |
| | Germany | No relationship |
| | Italy | Higher underpricing |
| | Spain | No relationship |
| | Belgium | Higher underpricing |
| Firm size | Germany | No relationship |
| | France | Weak negative relationship |
| | Italy | No relationship |
| | Spain | Lower underpricing |
| | Belgium | No relationship |
| Oversubscription rate | Italy | Higher underpricing |
| | Belgium | Higher underpricing |

## Hot issue markets

The temporal changes in the volumes of IPOs brought to market have been outlined in each country separately. Overall, the post-1987 period has been characterized by a massive reduction in the number of shares floated on the European exchanges, with a slight rebound in the market at the end of 1992 and early 1993.

## Long-term performance

In the long run though, the performance of IPO shares seems to be less than satisfactory, implying either that issuers and underwriters alike have a superb ability to time their issuance close to market peaks or that investors exhibit an insatiable and irrational hunger for new issues they could not get through the initial offer, driving the prices in early trading to unsustainable heights unrelated to the intrinsic value of the shares. Based on average figures again, a strategy that consists in buying IPO shares in early secondary trading and holding on to them generates returns lower than a risk-free government bond, while assuming a much higher level of risk. Not exactly an investment to be placed on the most recommended list!

The fundamental lesson to be learned from the rapid overview of the literature and of the recent investigations into IPO pricing in Europe is to beware of oversimplification in what is obviously a complex phenomenon. No single factor could or will, by and of itself, explain the three basic empirical anomalies outlined above; issuing new shares involves too many actors and stakeholders (issuer, investment banker, underwriter, market authorities, investors with various degrees of sophistication and access to information, etc.), each with their own objective functions and potential effect on the flotation, to allow a one-dimensional explanation. What these studies offer though is a formalization of what many will consider common sense: issuers do try to make the most of the initial public offerings, bringing their firms to the market when they will be able to receive the largest amount of money for them. The initial underpricing is then only the manifestation of direct underwriter support (they do not want to see the price fall below the offer price, ruining their reputations), the need to reimburse the costs incurred by some investors in participating in the offer (such as information acquisition or capital costs), the irrational behaviour of frustrated investors (who did not get enough shares in the initial offering and decide to buy them immediately in the market, whatever the cost), or a combination of the three. Whatever the rationale for the initial price run-up, it is clear that deviations from the intrinsic value of the shares will need to be corrected in the marketplace, for the better or the worse. And the early stars may not shine long... Furthermore, the multiple lock-up agreements (by which some crucial participants in the IPO are required to hold on to their shares for some period of time) usually included in the issuing contracts may significantly affect the future performance of IPO shares. The signal sent to the outside world by insiders quickly unloading their shares is obviously not very positive about the future prospects of the company.

Despite the problems outlined above, IPOs remain one of the most attractive and sought-after harvesting mechanisms. If the US market has hit some new highs in 1993 in terms of the volume of new issues brought to market, the European markets are still very much in the doldrums, with the light only slowly brightening at the end of the tunnel. Such a leader of the 1980s as the London Third Market is dead and buried, with the Unlisted Securities Market about to follow in its footsteps. The second markets in Brussels and Amsterdam are in a state of dormancy bordering on brain death, offering basically few opportunities for new introductions. Such a situation obviously has serious implications both for individual investors and venture capitalists. With one of the most lucrative exit routes blocked, it is the whole investment process that needs to be questioned and reexamined.

# References

Aggarwal, R., and Rivoli, P. (1990). Fads in the initial public offering market? *Financial Management*, 19(4), 45–57.

Akerlof, G. (1970). The market for lemons: qualitative uncertainty and the market mechanism, *Quarterly Journal of Economics*, 84, 488–500.

Baron, D. P. (1982). A model of the demand for investment banking: advising and distribution services for new issues, *Journal of Finance*, 37(4), 955–76.

Beatty, R. P. (1989). Auditor reputation and the pricing of initial public offerings, *Accounting Review*, 64(4), 693–709.

Benveniste, L. M., and Spindt P. A. (1989). How investment bankers determine the offer price and allocation of new issues, *Journal of Financial Economics*, 24, 343–61.

Carter, R., and Manaster, S. (1990). Initial public offerings and underwriter reputation, *Journal of Finance*, 45(4), 1045–67.

Cherubini, U., and Ratti, M. (1992). *Underpricing of Initial Public Offerings in the Milan Stock Exchange*, 1985–1991, Rome: Banco Commerciale Italiana, Economic Research Unit.

Hansson, B., and Ljungqvist, A. (1993). Mispricing of initial public offerings: evidence from Germany. Working Paper Series 19/1993, Department of Economics, University of Lund.

Hulbert, M. (1991). Getting Taken, *Forbes*, 147(13), 216–20.

Ibbotson, R. G., Sindelar, J., and Ritter, J. (1988). Initial public offerings, *Journal of Applied Corporate Finance*, 1, 37–45.

James, C., and Wier, P. (1990). Borrowing relationships, intermediation, and the cost of issuing securities, *Journal of Financial Economics*, 28(1), 149–71.

Leleux, B. F. (1991). Initial public offerings: puzzles, anomalies and other models... Working Paper, European Institute of Business Administration (INSEAD), Fontainebleau.

Leleux, B. F. (1993). Post-IPO performance: a French appraisal. Working Paper, European Institute of Business Administration (INSEAD), Fontainebleau.

Leleux, B. F., and Muzyka, D. F. (1992). European IPO market: a comparative performance study. Working Paper, European Institute of Business Administration (INSEAD), Fontainebleau.

Loughran, T., and Ritter, J. R. (1993). The timing and subsequent performance of IPOs: the US and international evidence. Working Paper, University of Illinois at Urbana-Champaign.

Megginson, W. L., and Weiss, K. A. (1991). Venture capitalist certification in initial public offerings, *Journal of Finance*, 46(3), 879–903.

Paliard, R., and Belletante, B. (1992). Does knowing who sells matter in IPO pricing ? The French second market experience. Working Paper, Groupe ESC Lyon, France.

Parsons, J., and Raviv, A. (1985). Underpricing of seasoned issues, *Journal of Financial Economics*, 14(3), 377–97.

Posner, B. J. (1993). Equity: doing a small offering, *Inc*, Feb., 35.

Rahnema, A., Fernandez, P., and Martinez-Abascal, E. (1992). Initial public offerings: Spanish experience. Paper, IESE, Barcelona.

Rees, W. (1992). Initial public offerings in the UK: 1984–1991. Paper, University of Strathclyde, Glasgow.

Reilly, F. K. (1977). New issues revisited, *Financial Management*, 6 (Winter), 28-42.

Ritter, J. R. (1984). The 'hot issue' market of 1980, *Journal of Business*, 57(2), 215–40.

Ritter, J. R. (1991). The long-run performance of initial public offerings, *Journal of Finance*, 46(1), 3–28.

Rock, K. (1986). Why new issues are underpriced, *Journal of Financial Economics*, 15, 187–212.

Rogiers, B., and Manigart, S. (1992). Empirical examination of the underpricing of initial public offerings on the Brussels stock exchange. Working Paper, Vlerick School for Management, Ghent.

Scherreik, S. (1993). The pitfalls of initial stock offerings, *New York Times*, 12 June.

Stern, R. L., and Bornstein, P. (1985). Why new issues are lousy investments, *Forbes*, 136 Dec., 52–190.

Tinic, S. (1988). Anatomy of initial public offerings of common stock. *Journal of Finance*, 43(4), 789–822.

# 4

HARVESTING, LONGEVITY AND
THE LIFE CYCLE OF MANGEMENT
BUY-OUTS AND BUY-INS:
A FOUR-COUNTRY STUDY

*Mike Wright, Ken Robbie, Yves Romanet, Steve Thompson,*
*Robert Joachimsson, Johan Bruining and Arthur Herst*

## INTRODUCTION

The last decade has seen the development of a buy-out market in Europe, both building on techniques used initially in the US and developing new ones specific to individual countries (Wright et al., 1992). The backgrounds to improvements arising from buy-outs can be seen in consideration of both agency cost theory and entrepreneurship theory (Bull, 1988). The latter may have particular relevance to smaller buy-outs where management teams typically have majority equity stakes. While much attention has focused on large transactions, many US and especially European buy-outs are relatively small. Indeed, in the UK, the second most developed buy-out market after the US, some 92 per cent of transactions are completed for purchase prices of less than the approximate equivalent of $20 million.

As buy-out markets have developed, both in Europe and the US, key attention has focused on the longevity of such structures and the means and timing of harvesting of investments by the parties concerned. Considerable debate has arisen concerning the length of time over which buy-outs retain their initial structure, with there being conflicting views as to whether buy-outs are long-term or short-term phenomena (Jensen, 1989; Rappaport, 1990). Recent evidence from the US (Kaplan, 1991) and from Europe (reviewed and extended below) shows that the short term/long term debate is somewhat simplistic since buy-outs are very much heterogeneous organizations.

In essence a buy-out involves incumbent managers in acquiring a significant equity state, while a buy-in involves external entrepreneurs, as individuals with institutional support, acquiring control of the company.

Buy-outs and buy-ins involve a fusion of the different objectives of managers, financiers and the companies themselves. A major aspect concerns the long-term plans of managers and financiers for the company and how both parties can realize their investment in a manner optimum for themselves, which in turn may have implications for the optimum life cycle of the company itself. Although these issues may well have been addressed at the time of the buy-out, significant actual and potential conflicts of interest may remain, and they may be increased by financial and acquisition market conditions which are considerably different than those foreseen at the time of the buy-out and which significantly affect the ability of the parties concerned to effect a harvest at the time and by the means initially envisaged. Moreover, different conditions prevailing in buy-out markets in individual countries may have important influences on the timing and form of harvest.

This situation raises important questions concerning harvesting which are of direct relevance to management as the entrepreneurs, venture capitalists, bankers, professional advisers and indeed policymakers. The longevity of this form of organization is of considerable importance. If buy-outs represent a form of organization in which management have greater incentives to perform than hitherto and in which institutions exert considerable influence, then there are clear issues for each of these parties as to whether the resultant gains are sustained over long periods or are merely transitory and as to what the explanation might be of why some buy-out structures last a long time and why others do not.

The paper addresses these issues as follows. Section 2 discusses the conceptual issues concerning the nature and timing of harvest and the control devices available to influence harvesting. Section 3 outlines a general framework for the development of a buy-out market. Section 4 explains the sources of data used and the research methodology adopted. Section 5 briefly reviews the trends and characteristics of buy-out markets internationally, with special emphasis on the four markets examined in detail here: UK, France, Holland and Sweden. Section 6 analyses the quantitative evidence relating to harvest in each of the four countries, including differences in harvesting patterns between different types of buy-out and whether actual forms of harvest differ significantly from original intentions. Section 7 summarizes the evidence from detailed interviews with buy-out managers and financing institutions in each country, with particular attention addressed to the effectiveness and adaptability of control and incentive devices in achieving harvests which meet the objectives of the parties concerned. Section 8 presents some overall conclusions.

## BUY-OUT LONGEVITY

The classic buy-out candidate is often viewed as being in a mature sector with stable cash flow and modest investment requirements, but market trend analyses show the existence of a wide range of buy-out types (Chiplin et al., 1992) either in terms of sectors, control mechanisms or financing structures. In the US, where attention has focused primarily on very large debt-financed

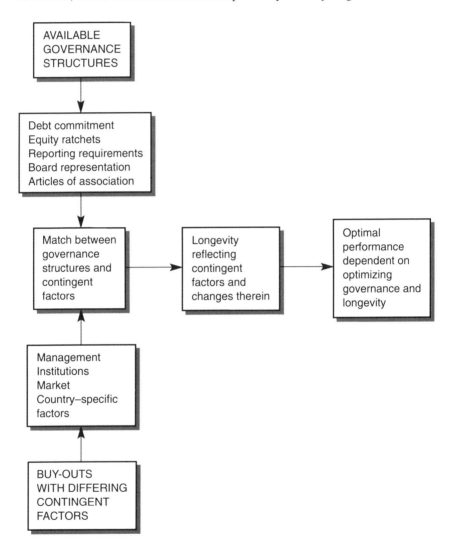

*Figure 4.1 General contingent model of the buy-out control process*
(*Source*: CMBOR)

transactions, venture capital has also played an important role in the buy-out market (Malone, 1989). This is even more true of European markets. These observations suggest the need to adopt a contingency perspective in analysing the link between governance structures, longevity and performance and that there may be good reasons why some buy-outs last a long time and why some do not. In general terms, a contingent model of the buy-out control process can be elaborated as shown in Figure 4.1. The need is to ensure an appropriate match between the buy-out's governance structure and the relevant contingent factors so that the life cycle of the bought-out company can move into the next stage at the appropriate time.

Evidence shows that the control structures in buy-outs are company specific and embrace mechanistic aspects to do with meeting interest payments, requirements to keep within debt covenants, board representation, levels of managerial equity stakes contingent on performance and regular detailed reports and meetings (see Wright et al., 1992). The overall governance of buy-outs involves a combination of structural mechanisms and a process by which adaptation to changing circumstances occurs (Green and Berry, 1991). These structures mirror similar ones identified for venture capitalist investments generally by Sweeting (1991) and MacMillan et al. (1989) but which also link with organizations specifically focused on buy-outs (Sahlman, 1990). Examination of the buy-out process suggests that for each individual transaction the interests of the three parties have to be satisfied before a buy-out can be completed – management, institutions and the company itself (Wright et al., 1991).

The influence of managers may be particularly important where the initiative for a buy-out is taken by management who perceive an entrepreneurial opportunity (Bull, 1988; Wright et al., 1992). To the extent that differences occur between types of deals and between countries in the degree to which management participate in the buy-out, different influences on longevity and control mechanisms may be expected. Where management have highly specific non-transferable skills, they may have little option but to remain with the firm into the long term and evidence from buy-outs suggests widespread long-term commitment to the firm (Wright and Coyne, 1985). By the same token, outside purchasers may be dissuaded from acquiring such a company where incumbent managers are reluctant to accept them. The extent to which managers may wish to continue to pursue an entrepreneurial career rather than exiting through becoming managerial employees again, or through retirement, also impacts on longevity. Ronstadt (1986) shows that for entrepreneurs in general, career exit rates are much lower than venture exit rates, but that entrepreneurs who start their entrepreneurial careers relatively late are more likely to have short entrepreneurial careers. Differences in the motivations of buy-out managers – such as reacting to a one-off opportunity versus proactive recognition of a chance to implement one's own growth strategy (Wright et al., 1992, p. 60) – may be an important element in this decision.

The buy-out markets in the four countries examined here involve a variety of institutional participants, ranging from local clearing banks, through various venture capitalists, to large specialist debt and equity providing close-end funds (Wright, 1991). Requirements for institutions to provide returns to shareholders in the short term will influence the type of buy-out in which they will invest and the speed of harvest they seek. Differences may be expected in the approaches of institutions who do not operate under this constraint, which may provoke serious control problems, particularly in syndicated deals.

Life cycle theories suggest that the most important company-related characteristics which are likely to influence the longevity of a given organizational form concern rapidly changing markets, a fast-growing company, concentration of markets where it is necessary to have a sufficiently large critical mass to survive, and relatively high levels of merger activity (Mueller, 1988). Although the classic buy-out is in a stable industry, unforeseen events may occur to change the appropriate life cycle and financing instruments are available to enable buy-outs to occur in less stable and predictable circumstances (Wright et al., 1991, ch. 8). Moreover, divestment buy-outs or those arising on privatization from the public sector which had been frustrated by parental constraints may grow rapidly initially when they are released but soon come up against new constraints and require to exit to continue to survive or develop (Green and Berry, 1991). Such pre-buy-out constraints on investment policies, new product development, appropriate managerial structures, etc., are frequently imposed by private sector parents (Jones, 1992; Singh, 1990) and the arguably greater degree of such constraints imposed on public sector divisions, particularly those whose parents were being prepared for privatization, are now well documented. Financing structures may attempt to allow for future growth but considerable uncertainty and underestimation of its extent may pose problems. In addition, where a division has been constrained and lost ground in a rapidly growing market it may be difficult to catch up, indicating that exit to become part of a larger group is warranted.

Individual country contexts may also be expected to influence both financing structures and longevity. Clearly, the relative development of stock-markets influences the extent to which an IPO is a feasible and attractive option for harvesting. In addition, outside the Anglo-Saxon context, the market for corporate control and corporate governance generally places less emphasis on complete ownership transfer and greater weight on investor influence in the running of a business (Franks and Mayer, 1990).

The discussion in this section suggests that differences in forms in which buy-outs are harvested may be expected both within and between buy-out markets. Within a given market, larger buy-outs and those where management have ratchet incentives will have a higher propensity to be harvested than smaller buy-outs where management have major equity holdings; buy-outs experiencing greater than expected investment needs and significant structural changes in their markets will be more likely to exist; and buy-outs which experienced the greatest pre-buy-out constraints and the greatest post-buy-out catching-up problems may also need to exit earlier. Differences in exits between markets may be related not simply to different levels of market maturity  but also to the different nature of stock and acquisitions markets, the different make-up of sources of buy-out and differences between the institutions funding buy-outs.

## GENERAL FRAMEWORK FOR DEVELOPMENT OF A BUY-OUT MARKET

The development of any buy-out market is conditional on the presence of a number of key conditions: generation of buy-out opportunities; an infrastructure to complete buy-outs; and routes by which investors may realize their gains (Figure 4.2).

### Generation of buy-out opportunities.

An entrepreneurial culture needs to be viewed both in terms of the attitude to risk of incumbent managers in divisions of groups or in family businesses (providing scope for buy-outs) and of external individuals seeking firms in which to invest and manage (providing scope for buy-ins). In some countries, highly qualified, well-remunerated managers may not be willing to take the risk of a buy-out. In others, managers may be willing to undertake the risk but there may be serious questions concerning their ability to own and manage an independent entity. International differences in entrepreneurial attitudes are examined in more detail in Chapter 7 below.

The extent and nature of takeover activity in an economy may be influenced by factors such as the relative size of the quoted company sector, the ease with which hostile bids can be made, the state of the stock-market, and the existence of willing sellers at prices buyers are prepared to pay. An active takeover market legitimizes the transfer of ownership of assets and encourages the development of a network of intermediaries. In some countries characterized by a relative high level of family-owned businesses there may be considerable resistance to the sale of businesses, although increasing

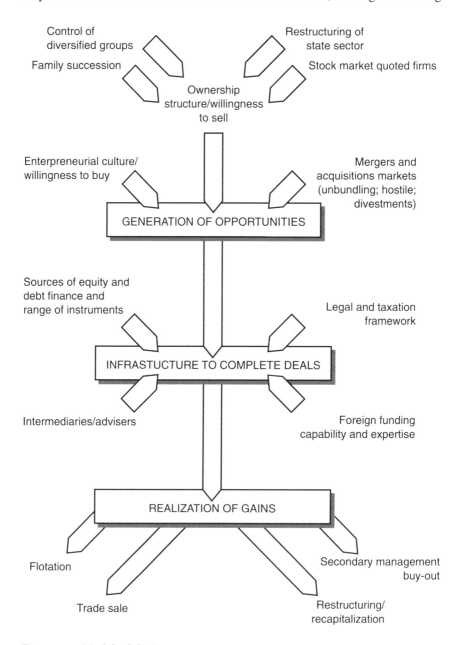

*Figure 4.2 Model of the buy-out process*

global competition and succession problems are provoking widespread changes in these attitudes. Buy-outs and buy-ins may be important means by which the independent status of family businesses may be maintained in the face of succession problems. The growth of privatization programmes internationally may also give rise to buy-out opportunities, especially where there is a need to restructure large state holding companies through the divestment of peripheral elements.

## Infrastructure to complete buy-outs

The nature of buy-outs outlined above indicates a need for specialist financing instruments and funding sources. Key roles are assigned to the attitudes and ability of banks to lend to buy-outs and to venture capital firms in differing countries. Banking attitudes towards buy-outs are influenced by the extent to which security can be obtained for loans, whether equity or only debt involvement is permitted, the closeness of relationships with industrial firms and past experience with risky investments in industrial firms generally or, since the late 1980s, the outcome of earlier experience with lending to buy-outs. Venture capital firms may be more willing to invest in buy-outs than the banks and provide the equity and quasi-equity capital necessary to meet the difference between purchase prices and the amount banks are willing to lend against secured assets. Marked variations in the state of development of venture capital industries seem likely to play a key role in explaining differences between buy-out markets. For European countries at least, evidence shows that investments in buy-outs generally account for insignificant proportions of emerging venture capital markets (Ooghe et al., 1991). The extent to which venture capital firms are owned by the banks may also be an important influence on their involvement in the buy-out market. At the smaller end of the market, private equity investors ('business angels') may have an important role to play, especially where formal venture capital is underdeveloped. Such investors may also provide managerial inputs.

The existence of a network of intermediaries able to identify targets and structure transactions is also important, with accounting firms, mergers and acquisitions brokers and lawyers filling these roles to greater or lesser extents in different countries. While there may be a number of ways in which buy-outs can be structured to take account of local legal and taxation regimes, several factors are of crucial importance. Tax consolidation may be important in buy-outs for tax-efficient servicing of financing where a *Newco-Target* structure is used to effect the transaction (*Newco* simply refers to the legal entity which is created specifically for the purposes of acquiring the target company). In such a situation, the revenue streams of the *Target* company can be paid as dividends in a tax-efficient manner to *Newco*, which borrowed the funds to finance the buy-out but which has no trading revenue of its own. A key element in fostering the development of a buy-out market is usually regarded as the ability of a company to provide financial assistance for the purchase of its own shares.[1] Significant variations exist between countries in respect of accounting and auditing rules and regulations. These differences may pose problems in terms of valuing companies and assessing their performance in some countries, making it difficult to identify suitable buy-out targets and making institutions reluctant to extend funding. Other relevant legal issues concern the extent of restrictions on the issue of different kinds of financial instruments with varying dividend and voting rights.

## Ability to realize gains

As noted already, the parties to a buy-out will at some stage wish to realize their gains. In addition, the life cycle features of the company itself may make it necessary to change the initial buy-out structure. In some cases, the necessity may be to become part of a larger critical mass in order to survive, so that sale to a third party is a preferred option. In others, stockmarket flotation may be the means by which growth opportunities can be realized. Differences between countries in the nature and extent to which gains are realized will depend on the degree of buy-out market maturity, the extent to which markets for corporate assets and primary and secondary-tier stock markets are developed and the timing of investment perspectives taken by management and financing institutions. Clearly, the timing and relative attractiveness of the above conditions will directly influence the rate of buy-out development in a particular country.

## DATA AND METHODOLOGY

The research discussed in this chapter has been carried out using the facilities of the Centre for Management Buy-Out Research (CMBOR), an independent research centre at the School of Management and Finance at the University of Nottingham, with associates in France, Holland and Sweden. The data are drawn from the authors' data base of over 6000 European management and employee buy-outs. In order to compile the data base several sources are used: a six-monthly survey of all known financing institutions and the major accounting participants in the UK buy-out market; a systematic search of online text data bases and financial news services covering

Europe; a systematic search of annual reports of major firms based in the UK; monitoring of the *London Gazette*; and a search of the other specialist financial press and other specialist publications across Europe. In order to examine the length of time that buy-outs survive in this form, analysis is carried out using data derived from a representative sample of 158 buy-outs completed in the period from mid-1983 to the beginning of 1986,[2] where it was possible to monitor subsequent harvesting or other forms of exits through CMBOR's regular monitoring of financial institutions and public sources of information. For purposes of the analysis which follows below, harvesting is identified as involving four types: sale to a third party, IPO (stock-market flotation), secondary buy-out/buy-in and receivership.

In the four countries of the UK, France, Holland and Sweden face-to-face interviews were held with senior representatives of the major financing institutions, selected to provide a cross-section of perspectives on buy-out exit. Interviews in the four countries were conducted on the basis of a common checklist of questions developed through discussions between the researchers in each country and generally lasted at least an hour.

## CHARACTERISTICS AND TRENDS

International trends in buy-outs in the period from 1989 to 1991 are shown in table 4.1. For space reasons, the table has trends only from 1989 (and it should also be noted that except for the UK and US, data prior to this period are less reliable); 1991 is the latest date for which comprehensive information is available. The data in the table include all types of buy-outs defined above. In terms of total value, the US until 1991 was clearly the largest buy-out market in the world. Much of this activity was accounted for by very large leveraged buy-outs of companies quoted on a stock market, although there is a strong level of smaller management buy-out activity in which venture capital firms play an important funding role. The UK is the second largest buy-out market in value terms but has become the largest in terms of the volume of transactions. As in the US, the value of the UK market has fallen sharply since 1989 as problems with large, highly leveraged buy-outs have made debt providers reluctant to fund further transactions. However, the volume of buy-outs remained high as opportunities to fund smaller transactions from groups needing to restructure or from failed firms proved attractive to venture capital and other providers of funds. Indeed, in the UK recessionary conditions of the early 1990s buy-out investment opportunities for venture capitalists shifted towards viable parts of failed firms. A fifth of buy-outs in this period involved firms in receivership.

**Table 4.1  Numbers and values of buy-outs and buy-ins in OECD countries, 1989–1991**

|  | Number | | | Value ($m) | | |
|---|---|---|---|---|---|---|
|  | *1989* | *1990* | *1991* | *1989* | *1990* | *1991* |
| Australia | 14 | 10 | n.a. | 326 | 449 | n.a. |
| Austria | 5 | 8 | 10 | 131 | 80 | 141 |
| Belgium | 13 | 8 | 9 | 129 | 172 | 183 |
| Canada | 36 | 43 | 22 | 705 | 460 | 405 |
| Denmark | 32 | 27 | 15 | 275 | 195 | 168 |
| Finland | 16 | 25 | 20 | 119 | 119 | 220 |
| France | 130 | 150 | 120 | 1391 | 3117 | 2783 |
| W. Germany | 25 | 36 | 28 | 794 | 519 | 607 |
| Ireland | 12 | 15 | 11 | 33 | 107 | 39 |
| Italy | 23 | 27 | 30 | 589 | 570 | 1115 |
| Netherlands | 45 | 37 | 57 | 345 | 160 | 600 |
| Norway | 8 | 10 | 5 | 20 | 234 | 58 |
| Portugal | – | 4 | 4 | – | 27 | 7 |
| Spain | 12 | 15 | 8 | 115 | 107 | 123 |
| Sweden | 32 | 40 | 19 | 1285 | 1385 | 857 |
| Switzerland | 21 | 13 | 18 | 164 | 369 | 437 |
| UK | 521 | 594 | 565 | 12 277 | 5524 | 4989 |
| US | 335 | 141 | 152 | 60 546 | 18 237 | 5596 |

Data converted from local currency using appropriate average year exchange rates.
*Sources:* CMBOR; *Venture Economics*; M&A Canada; Footscray University (Australia).

The development of the UK market is examined in more detail in the following chapter by Bleackley and Hay. The UK market was until 1990 as big as the rest of Europe combined both in terms of the value and volume of transactions. However, since then the picture has changed as a result of growth in buy-out markets in France, where companies with succession problems have provided considerably buy-out opportunities, and in Holland and Sweden, where the main buy-out opportunities are provided by divestments (see Table 4.2).

These four European markets, the focus of attention in this paper, may all be characterized as displaying several of the necessary conditions for buy-out development, especially a need to effect ownership transfer though not necessarily for the same reasons, a relative or absolutely important venture capital industry and a legal framework facilitating such transactions (Wright et al., 1992). Except for Holland, peak levels of buy-out volume occurred in 1990. While the UK market has seen a sharp decline from the peak level of 1989, only Sweden shows a similar shift. The dominance of the UK market is emphasized when values are deflated by gross domestic product, with the value of the UK market being twice that of France and Holland (Table 4.3). Countries with buy-out markets which display signs of development (after taking into account differences in GDP) are Italy, West Germany, Denmark, Finland, Switzerland, Canada and Australia. Countries with very little buy-out activity include Spain, Portugal, Norway, Austria, Greece, Japan and New Zealand.

Table 4.2  Sources of buy-outs and buy-ins in the UK, France, Holland and Sweden, 1989–1991 (per cent)

| Source | UK | France | Holland | Sweden |
|---|---|---|---|---|
| Receivership | 10.7 | 3.0 | 0.0 | 1.3 |
| Domestic divestment | 42.6 | 24.0 | 57.8 | 62.4 |
| Foreign divestment | 7.1 | 12.9 | 24.4 | 7.5 |
| Privatization | 3.0 | 2.1 | 1.1 | 2.5 |
| Family succession | 32.2 | 52.8 | 16.7 | 6.3 |
| Stock-market | 4.4 | 5.2 | 0.0 | 20.0 |
| Total | 100% | 100% | 100% | 100% |
| Sample size | 1648 | 233 | 90 | 80 |

*Source:* CMBOR.

A general indication of harvesting opportunities is provided by the sizes of stock markets and acquisitions markets in each country. The UK has by far the largest and most active stock and takeover markets. The French markets have become considerably more active in recent years but the capitalization of the domestic Dutch stock market is twice as large as that in France when deflated by GDP. There are also marked differences in the nature of takeovers in the four countries. Franks and Mayer (1990) in comparing France to the UK note the lower level of hostile takeovers, greater levels of protection for employees and managers, higher levels of restrictions on voting rights of shareholders and mutual cross-shareholdings between corporations, and extensive acquisitions of minority equity stakes and the key role played by the 'noyau dur' of shareholders in France. In Sweden, the takeover market has been particularly active in respect of smaller firms and quoted companies (Cooke, 1988).

**Table 4.3** Relative sizes of buy-out markets in OECD countries, 1991

|  | Gross domestic product ($bn) and ranking | Buy-out market value as % of GDP, and ranking |
|---|---|---|
| Austria | 162 (14) | 0.087 (13) |
| Belgium | 197 (13) | 0.093 (11) |
| Denmark | 131 (15) | 0.128 (8) |
| Ireland | 43 (21) | 0.091 (12) |
| Finland | 129 (16) | 0.171 (6) |
| France | 1192 (4) | 0.233 (3) |
| Germany | 1554 (3) | 0.039 (16) |
| Greece | 70 (19) | n.a. |
| Italy | 1134 (5) | 0.098 (10) |
| Netherlands | 285 (10) | 0.211 (4) |
| Norway | 108 (17) | 0.053 (15) |
| Portugal | 69 (20) | 0.010 (18) |
| Spain | 524 (8) | 0.023 (17) |
| Sweden | 235 (11) | 0.365 (2) |
| Switzerland | 230 (12) | 0.190 (5) |
| Turkey | 107 (18) | n.a. |
| UK | 1006 (6) | 0.496 (1) |
| US[1] | 5549 (1) | 0.099 (9) |
| Australia | 292 (9) | 0.154 (7) |
| Canada | 587 (7) | 0.069 (14) |
| Japan | 3363 (2) | n.a. |
| New Zealand | 42 (22) | n.a. |

[1]The sharp fall in the value of US buy-out since 1989, when it reached $66 billion, means that it has probably been more adversely affected by the recession of the early 1990s than any other country except for its neighbour, Canada.

*Source:* CMBOR/Barclays Development Capital Ltd/Touche Ross.

## HARVESTING OF BUY-OUTS AND BUY-INS: QUANTITATIVE EVIDENCE

The analysis in this section focuses principally on the UK, where quantitative information on harvests is most accessible.

### United Kingdom

The majority of UK buy-outs completed in the period 1981 to 1991 had been harvested by the end of December 1992, the latest date for which information is available. Only a quarter of the 3452 buy-outs completed in this period have been harvested by means of either IPO, trade sale, secondary buy-out/buy-in or receivership (Table 4.4) The most common form of harvest for buy-outs has been trade sale, followed by receivership. Less than 5 per cent of buy-outs have floated. Similarly, only almost a quarter (23.5 per cent) of the 510 private buy-ins completed between 1985 and 1991 (the period for which data on this form of transaction are available) have been harvested by any of these routes (Table 4.5). For private buy-ins, receivership has been the most common form of harvest. Less than 5 per cent of private buy-ins in this period have been the subject of a trade sale and only 10 (2 per cent) have taken the form of IPO.

**Table 4.4  Exits of management buy-outs in the UK, by year of buy-out**

| Year of MBO | Float[1] | | Trade sale | | MBO/MBI | | Receivership | | No exit[2] | | Total | |
|---|---|---|---|---|---|---|---|---|---|---|---|---|
| | No. | % | No. | % | No. | % | No. | % | No. | % | No. | % |
| 1981 | 17 | 11.8 | 24 | 16.8 | 4 | 2.8 | 14 | 9.8 | 84 | 58.8 | 143 | 100.0 |
| 1982 | 23 | 9.7 | 36 | 15.2 | 7 | 3.0 | 17 | 7.2 | 154 | 64.9 | 237 | 100.0 |
| 1983 | 26 | 11.1 | 35 | 14.9 | 4 | 1.7 | 18 | 7.6 | 152 | 64.7 | 235 | 100.0 |
| 1984 | 20 | 8.4 | 53 | 22.2 | 8 | 3.3 | 18 | 7.5 | 140 | 58.6 | 239 | 100.0 |
| 1985 | 24 | 9.2 | 42 | 16.0 | 7 | 2.7 | 23 | 8.8 | 166 | 63.3 | 262 | 100.0 |
| 1986 | 17 | 5.4 | 46 | 14.6 | 7 | 2.2 | 22 | 7.0 | 223 | 70.8 | 315 | 100.0 |
| 1987 | 16 | 4.7 | 52 | 15.1 | 8 | 2.3 | 39 | 11.3 | 229 | 66.6 | 344 | 100.0 |
| 1988 | 8 | 2.2 | 37 | 9.9 | 2 | 0.5 | 41 | 10.9 | 287 | 76.5 | 375 | 100.0 |
| 1989 | 2 | 0.5 | 18 | 4.8 | 2 | 0.6 | 43 | 11.5 | 308 | 82.6 | 373 | 100.0 |
| 1990 | 2 | 0.4 | 12 | 2.5 | 3 | 0.6 | 42 | 8.7 | 425 | 87.8 | 484 | 100.0 |
| 1991 | 1 | 0.2 | 5 | 1.1 | 2 | 0.4 | 14 | 3.2 | 423 | 95.1 | 445 | 100.0 |

[1] Includes Official USM, Third, OTC markets and reverse-ins and cases where primary exit was one of these but was followed at a later date by another form of exit.
[2] Includes refinancing.
*Source:* CMBRO/BDCL/Touche Ross.

**Table 4.5  Exits of private MBIs in the UK, by year of MBI**

| Year of MBI | Float[1] | | Trade sale | | MBO/MBI | | Receivership | | No exit[2] | | Total | |
|---|---|---|---|---|---|---|---|---|---|---|---|---|
| | No. | % | No. | % | No. | % | No. | % | No. | % | No. | % |
| 1985 | 0 | 0 | 1 | 4.3 | 1 | 4.3 | 3 | 13.1 | 18 | 78.3 | 23 | 100.0 |
| 1986 | 6 | 24.0 | 1 | 4.0 | 0 | 0 | 2 | 8.0 | 16 | 64.0 | 25 | 100.0 |
| 1987 | 0 | 0 | 7 | 14.9 | 0 | 0 | 4 | 8.5 | 36 | 76.6 | 47 | 100.0 |
| 1988 | 2 | 2.4 | 6 | 7.1 | 0 | 0 | 26 | 30.5 | 51 | 60.0 | 85 | 100.0 |
| 1989 | 2 | 1.7 | 6 | 5.0 | 0 | 0 | 29 | 24.4 | 82 | 68.9 | 119 | 100.0 |
| 1990 | 0 | 0 | 2 | 2.1 | 0 | 0 | 13 | 13.5 | 81 | 84.4 | 96 | 100.0 |
| 1991 | 2 | 1.7 | 1 | 0.9 | 0 | 0 | 6 | 5.2 | 106 | 92.2 | 115 | 100.0 |

[1] Includes Official USM, Third, OTC markets and reverse-ins and cases where primary exit was one of these but was followed at a later date by another form of exit.
[2] Includes refinancing.
*Source:* CMBOR/BDCL/Touche Ross.

Marked differences occur in the proportions of venture-backed and non-venture-backed buy-outs which have been harvested. To the end of December 1992, 27 per cent of the 1440 venture-backed buy-outs completed between 1985 and 1991 had been harvested, whereas this was true of only 13 per cent of the 1158 non-venture-backed buy-outs completed in this period.

Significant differences also occur in the proportions of large and small buy-outs which have exited (Table 4.6). To the end of June 1992, a sixth (16.2 per cent) of buy-outs completed for a purchase price below £10 million in the period 1981 to 1990 had been harvested by means of an IPO, trade sale or secondary buy-out/buy-in. In contrast, well in excess of a third (35.3 per cent) of larger buy-outs completed in this period, those with a transaction value of £10 million or more, had pursued one of these methods. Harvesting rates among larger buy-outs completed from 1988 onwards show a marked falling off in comparison to earlier deals.

Monitoring of harvests by differing sources of the original deal shows that buy-outs which were previously part of the public sector and those which were originally divestments from non-UK parents record by far the highest propensity to be harvested by means of an IPO, trade sale or secondary buy-out/buy-in (Table 4.7). Buy-outs from receivership are more likely to fail than buy-outs from other sources. Buy-outs of quoted compa-

**Table 4.6  Exits of buy-outs completed between 1981 and 1990 at end June 1992 (UK)**

| | Original transaction value less than £10m | | | Original transaction value £10m and over | | |
|---|---|---|---|---|---|---|
| | Exit by flotation, trade sale, secondary MBO/MBI | | All buy-outs in category | Exit by flotation, trade sale, secondary MBO/MBI | | All buy-outs in category |
| Year of MBO | No. | % of all MBOs | | No. | % of all MBOs | |
| 1981 | 42 | 29.8 | 141 | 2 | 100 | 2 |
| 1982 | 59 | 25.4 | 232 | 5 | 100 | 5 |
| 1983 | 59 | 26.0 | 227 | 6 | 75 | 8 |
| 1984 | 71 | 30.7 | 231 | 4 | 66.7 | 6 |
| 1985 | 51 | 21.0 | 243 | 18 | 90.0 | 20 |
| 1986 | 58 | 19.6 | 296 | 13 | 68.4 | 19 |
| 1987 | 55 | 17.4 | 316 | 18 | 64.3 | 28 |
| 1988 | 32 | 9.8 | 327 | 12 | 25.0 | 48 |
| 1989 | 14 | 4.4 | 316 | 4 | 7.0 | 57 |
| 1990 | 7 | 1.6 | 436 | 3 | 6.3 | 48 |
| Total | 448 | 16.2 | 2765 | 85 | 35.3 | 241 |

z-test of differences between total percentages existing in the two size categories in the period yields z = 7.37 (significant at 1% level.)

*Source:* CMBOR/BDCL/Touche Ross.

nies show the third highest propensity to be harvested, but this is little different from the overall exit rate. Table 4.8 shows the cumulative extent of harvesting post buy-out using a representative sample of 158 buy-outs completed in 1983-6 surveyed by CMBOR and whose harvests were monitored for seven years post buy-out. The proportion of buy-outs which have not been harvested declines steadily so that seven years after buy-out some 40 per cent of the sample had exited. The greatest increase in harvesting occurred in years 3 to 5 after buy-out. The principal indication from this evidence is that most buy-outs last a long time and a minority do not. Dividing the sample into size categories as defined by their original transaction value shows that the smallest buy-outs have a substantially higher propensity to remain as buy-outs within a seven-year period than do larger transactions. After seven years, 64.4 per cent of the buy-outs completed for an initial purchase price below £1 million had been harvested, 57.9 per cent of those with an initial purchase price of £1 million to £5 million and 42.1 per cent of those with an initial purchase price above £5 million. Actual harvesting patterns of the sample were also compared with their initial intentions as expressed in the survey questionnaire (Table 4.9). Of the 86 buy-outs in the sample expressing an intended exit route (54.4 per cent of the sample) only a fifth (17 buy-outs) had by June 1992 been harvested in this manner. The most notable differences between intentions and actual exit concern the low level of harvesting through secondary market flotation and the high level of trade sale.

**Table 4.7  Exit by source of buy-outs completed before the end of 1990 (UK)**

| Source of buy-out | Number exiting[1] | Total buy-outs | Exit as % total |
|---|---|---|---|
| Divestment (UK parent) | 266 | 1562 | 17.0 |
| Divestment (overseas parent) | 93 | 293 | 31.7 |
| Private/Family | 103 | 622 | 16.6 |
| Privatization | 45 | 140 | 32.1 |
| Receivership | 23 | 168 | 13.7 |
| Going private | 6 | 30 | 20.0 |
| Total | 536 | 2815 | 19.0 |

| z-tests | | |
|---|---|---|
| | Total v. divestment (overseas parent) | z = 5.20 (significant at 1% level) |
| | Total v. privatisation: | z = 3.97 (significant at 1% level) |
| | Total v. receivership: | z = 1.77 |
| | Total v private: | z = 1.41 |
| | Total v. going private: | z = 0.14 |
| | Total v. divestment (UK parent) | z = 0.0 |

[1] By means of flotation, trade sale or secondary buy-out/buy-in.
*Source:* CMBOR/BDCL/Touche Ross.

**Table 4.8  Cumulative exit status year by year of 158 management buy-outs completed in the period 1983–1995 (UK)**

| Age of MBO | No exit | | MBO/MBI | | Trade sale | | Float | | Receivership | |
|---|---|---|---|---|---|---|---|---|---|---|
| | No. | % | No. | % | No. | % | No. | % | No. | % |
| Year 1 | 157 | 99.4 | 0 | 0 | 0 | 0 | 1 | 0.6 | 0 | 0 |
| Year 2 | 149 | 94.3 | 0 | 0 | 4 | 2.5 | 5 | 3.2 | 0 | 0 |
| Year 3 | 136 | 86.1 | 1 | 0.6 | 8 | 5.1 | 12 | 7.6 | 1 | 0.6 |
| Year 4 | 124 | 78.4 | 3 | 1.9 | 15 | 9.5 | 14 | 8.9 | 2 | 1.3 |
| Year 5 | 112 | 70.9 | 4 | 2.5 | 22 | 13.9 | 15 | 9.5 | 5 | 3.2 |
| Year 6 | 98 | 62.0 | 5 | 3.2 | 28 | 17.7 | 16 | 10.1 | 11 | 7.0 |
| Year 7 | 95 | 60.0 | 5 | 3.2 | 29 | 18.4 | 16 | 10.1 | 13 | 8.3 |

*Source:* CMBOR/BDCL/Touche Ross.

**Table 4.9  Exits from buy-outs in the UK: intentions and actions**

| Actual exit route at June 1992 | Intended exit route at buy-out, 1983–6 | | | | | |
|---|---|---|---|---|---|---|
| | Multiple | Secondary market | Official list | Trade sale | None expressed | Total |
| Secondary market[1] | – | 3 | – | – | – | 3 |
| Official list[2] | 1 | 2 | 6 | – | 2 | 11 |
| Reserve in | 2 | – | – | – | – | 2 |
| Trade sale | 3 | 11 | 2 | 2 | 13 | 31 |
| MBO/MBI | – | 5 | – | 1 | 1 | 7 |
| Receivership | 2 | 7 | – | 1 | 6 | 16 |
| No exit | 4 | 19 | 5 | 10 | 50 | 88 |
| Total | 12 | 47 | 13 | 14 | 72 | 158 |

[1] 2 of the 3 buy-outs to enter the secondary market have subsequently been sold to other groups.
[2] 3 of the 13 buy-outs to enter the official list have subsequently been sold to other groups.
*Source:* Survey of 1983–6 buy-outs and data base analysis by CMBOR/BDCL/Touche Ross.

## France

In France harvesting rates have generally been well below those seen in the UK as investors have generally seen buy-outs as a longer term investment. IPOs have always been rare as a form of harvest, the only significant examples involving Fonderies Waeles, Le Creuset (IPO on the London USM) and Biopat. However, in June of 1991 the venture capital firm IDI came to the market four years after it was privatized in a FF1.6 billion management buy-out. For the most part, harvest has involved a trade sale and it is not unusual for sale to involve only a part of the equity, so bringing in an industrial partner to enable growth to occur, or enabling institutions to exit from the deal.

From the beginning of 1991 some notable problem cases involving restructuring and failure among French buy-outs and buy-ins can be identified (Wright and Desbrières, 1992) and recent cases have also involved the sale of partial equity stakes in buy-outs with long-term prospects but where the combination of initial high gearing and the recession has meant that necessary investment levels cannot be met.

## Holland

Available information suggests that of the 346 buy-outs and buy-ins estimated to have been completed in Holland between 1980 and 1991 almost a sixth (52 cases) were harvested initially through an IPO, trade sale or failure. The largest single form of harvest has been trade sale with some 26 being recorded, followed by IPOs (14) and bankruptcy (9). Of the IPOs, 10 occurred before the stock-market crash in 1987, with only four Dutch buy-outs coming to market since then.

## Sweden

Swedish buy-out harvests are shown in Table 4.10. The pattern of exits has fluctuated over the last five years and in contrast to the UK picture does not display a rising trend in the late 1980s and early 1990s. The most common form of harvest has been trade sale, with some 21 out of the total of 33 exits identified. Only two exits by IPO have occurred, the latest being in 1988.

**Table 4.10  Exits of Swedish management buy-outs and buy-ins, 1986–1991**

| Exit type | 1986 | 1987 | 1988 | 1989 | 1990 | 1991 | Total |
|-----------|------|------|------|------|------|------|-------|
| Flotation | – | 1 | 1 | – | – | – | 2 |
| Trade sale | 1 | 4 | 5 | 3 | 5 | 3 | 21 |
| Receivership | 1 | 1 | – | 2 | 1 | 5 | 10 |
| Total | 2 | 6 | 6 | 5 | 6 | 8 | 33 |

## INVESTOR AND MANAGERIAL PERSPECTIVES ON HARVESTING

The interviews conducted in the UK, France, Holland and Sweden with financing institutions and managers of buy-outs sought to identify commonalties and differences in attitudes, mechanisms and processes concerning harvest. The analysis in this section is presented in terms of the issues which arise, with the discussion highlighting behaviour on each aspect in the four countries.

## Preferences for different forms of harvesting

The rankings of the various forms of preferred harvesting method by country to emerge from our interviews with *institutions* are shown in Table 4.11. A key attraction of trade sale across all four countries is the ability to achieve actual realization of cash. Partial sale was less favoured than full because institutions essentially lose control of further exit. Similarly, trade buyers will also usually want control. An IPO in the short term involves only partial harvest by both institutions and management. In such cases the investor has to decide very carefully how long they will remain with the company as they no longer have the advantages of being insiders. In France, capital sales may typically involve management retaining an equity stake, in order to maintain their motivation, while institutions exit. In the UK the extent of one institution buying out another as a harvest form has hitherto been limited. This situation is less true in the other countries in the study. Differences in fee structures for restructurings and similar forms of harvest between the countries covered in the study, with the UK fees reportedly being less attractive, were noted as important influences on the relevant extent of such activities.

In the recessionary conditions of the early 1990s many institutions across the four countries report the delaying of harvest by trade sale because of the general absence of buyers. Where buyers can be found at what appear to be reasonable prices for firms within a distinctive competence, it is becoming

Table 4.11 Ranking of exit preferences of institutions in the UK, France, Holland and Sweden

| UK | France | Holland | Sweden |
|---|---|---|---|
| Trade sale | Trade sale (full) | Trade sale | Flotation |
| Flotation | Trade sale (partial) | Sale to other investors | Trade sale |
| Refinancing/ Secondary MBO | Secondary MBO | Share repurchase | Sales to financial investor |
| Share purchase | Private sale to new investors | Private sale through third market | Refinancing |
| | Refinancing | | Float/sale after building up group through acquisitions |
| | Flotation | Flotation | |

common practice to include 'no embarrassment mechanisms' to allow the venture capitalist to share in future gains within an agreed period.

While, in principle, IPO is the most preferred form of harvesting in Sweden it is not particularly common. Indeed recent changes in taxation regulations (see Joachimsson, 1991) have meant that the Swedish OTC market is no longer a viable harvest route. Other difficulties in Sweden in the general takeover market, which have meant that few trade buyers are available, have led to the development of a strategy to use a buy-out as a core company around which to build a group of significant size through subsequent acquisition. Once such a group has been assembled, harvesting through IPO or trade sale may be more feasible.

The harvesting form preferred may not be independent of size. IPO may be impractical for small companies, even in the absence of market constraints, and larger potential trade purchasers may be less interested in acquiring the smaller companies. In Holland, for example, the more likely form of harvest for smaller buy-outs is share repurchase by management, while the existence of participating dividends in the financing structure of UK buy-outs may put pressure on management to refinance or buy-out the institution. Problems with the liquidity of secondary-tier stock markets in France and the UK, in particular, pose difficulties in floating smaller buy-outs. In the UK, a minimum market capitalization of £25 million is now considered necessary before an IPO can occur. A particular issue identified in the UK is the investment behaviour of pension funds and insurance companies who currently tend to trade only in good companies with market capitalizations in excess of £100 million, thus further limiting harvest possibilities in smaller buy-outs.

The recessionary conditions of the early 1990s may seriously limit the ability of funds to harvest in the time-scale they need. Funds may have flexibility in that they can ask investors for an extension to the fund of up to two years, or alternatively (at least in theory) investments could be returned in specie. One possibility for providing increased liquidity for closed-end funds is by developing a secondary market whereby a new fund would buy the investments of limited life funds at whichever is the lower of cost or net realizable value. Any appreciations in the investments after being acquired by the new fund would be shared between the previous investors and the new ones on the basis of an agreed formula.

## Harvesting perspectives at time of buy-out

A common theme from all four countries was that it was unusual to specify precisely a form and type of harvest at the time of the deal, but it has become more common for at least some consideration to be given to harvest to ensure that management and investors have the same fundamental perspectives. In closed-end funds it is particularly important to consider harvest, but even where ratchets based on harvesting are set initially, changing conditions may advance (as in the late 1980s) or retard (as in the early 1990s) actual harvest. If there were exceptions to this view they were in respect of smaller buy-outs, including hand-ons (transmissions) of family firms, which were considered in general to have less need for harvest. This point was especially prevalent in France where, as seen in Table 4.2, this form constitutes the highest share of any of the four markets. In Holland, it is now considered that there is essentially little difference between actual and expected harvest, even though harvests are taking longer than was the case in the late 1980s. Rather, many buy-outs completed in the conditions of the mid-1980s were harvested two to three years sooner than had been anticipated.

## Harvesting control mechanisms

One of the most controversial harvest control mechanisms is the equity ratchet, whereby, as noted earlier, management's equity stake can rise (or possibly fall) if they meet (or fail to meet) harvest targets within a given period of time (see Thompson and Wright, 1991, for elaboration of the operation of ratchets). Among the four countries studied, ratchets have been most common in the UK, although there has recently been a sharp waning in enthusiasm among institutions. While it is still the case that it may be necessary to use a ratchet to enable a deal to be completed, the problems of disputes over its triggering and renegotiation have encouraged institutions to avoid them where possible. While the highly buoyant markets of the late 1980s caused problems with ratchets being triggered early, the recessionary conditions of the early 1990s frequently mean harvest is delayed and calls for further negotiations. In France, they are not common as management stakes are generally high given the predominance of smaller buy-outs and the requirements of the specialist buy-out legislation (see Heuze, 1991, and Wright and Desbrières, 1992, for details of the Rachat d'entreprise par ses salariés (RES) legislation). In Holland and Sweden, the existence of many buy-outs which are effectively investor led suggests less emphasis on this mechanism, and management equity stakes are usually considered large enough to provide adequate motivation. In Sweden, in cases where ratchets might be used, concern was expressed over the lock-up problem whereby management might try to block an early harvest by trade sale because the value of their ratchet would not be as great as it was likely to be in two to three years time.

Emphasis now appears to be switching to the redemption of financial instruments and the use of participating dividends. These are mechanisms whereby, as profits increase, institutions are available to participate in them by having the right to an increased dividend (see Wright and Coyne, 1985, for further details); they provide the institution with a higher yield as profits rise but in so doing put pressure on management to harvest their investment or find some means of paying-off the shares. Other institutions are also shifting preferences to sweet equity and options for management.

## Harvesting control processes

Besides formal control mechanisms built into the financing structure, controlling for harvest is also influenced by various processes involving the participants in the buy-out. Across the four countries, board representation was seen to play an important part in steering the company towards harvest. However, there was some distinction between countries on the roles played by management in determining the nature and timing of harvest. In the UK and France, where management have majority equity stakes in most buy-outs, it was seen as essential to obtain the agreement of management before harvest was possible. Even where management did not have a majority stake, their important role together with that of their advisers in creating the buy-out still meant that their views were of crucial importance. Hence, for example, it was reported that some IPOs of buy-outs in the UK in the early 1990s could have been trade sales but management would not cooperate. In Holland and Sweden, it was reported as more common for investors to lead the deal and to be majority owners and thus have greater control over the harvest process.

Harvesting control processes in syndications may be particularly difficult and may lead to attempts to avoid large syndications (as particularly observed in Sweden) or to the development of various syndicates between institutions with common objectives (as in Holland and the UK). In Sweden the delay and decision-making that can occur where each syndicate member has to consult his board has tended to lead to agreements for the syndicate leader to be able to *act* as a majority shareholder. The objectives of the minority participants may be protected by rules agreeing to let members exit from the deal if they wish after a specified minimum period of time has passed.

## Harvesting problem cases – refinancing 'living dead' and 'good rump'

The recessionary conditions of the early 1990s have brought into sharp focus the problem of having to deal with investments which seriously underperform. It is possible, in fact, to identify two problem cases. 'living dead' investments may be written down to a very low but realistic valuation so that it then does not matter significantly whether harvest occurs or not. However, such investments still risk involving a disproportionate amount of management time. Moreover, it may be difficult for the venture capitalist to implement change in such companies until a pressure point arises which cannot be relieved by other funding sources. More recently, active efforts may be made either to solicit an offer, which may be to sell for a nominal sum to a trade buyer, or, more likely, to persuade management to buy them. A further issue arises in respect of the role of management in such cases in large and small deals. In small buy-outs management may own the vast majority of the equity and a very small group of managers may carry out the major functions, thus making it difficult to remove underperforming management or enforce a trade sale. In larger buy-outs, no single manager may be indispensable. When sales do occur, because the possibility for a turn-around may still exist and lead to significant gains on a nominal purchase price, institutions may include 'no embarrassment clauses' to participate in future gains.

The second category, 'good rump', is distinguishable from the first in that these firms are viewed as capable of being turned round, but as yet the effects of restructuring have yet to be seen. Such cases may be underperforming because of general sectoral problems. In both cases the nature of the restructuring to be undertaken in order to turn round the business may be problematical and be heavily influenced by whether the institutions are controlling shareholders or not.

In Sweden, underperformance is likely to lead to a considerable increase in monitoring by the funding institution, including increased frequency of meetings and reporting. However, institutions in Sweden tend to be very cautious about changing management, unless underperformance is clearly their fault. In the UK, if institutions are a controlling shareholder, making changes is theoretically straightforward. However, because of the importance of management to the business, great care is needed in taking action. Institutions report that the principal strategy is to produce a consensus on necessary action, but it may be difficult to argue with UK managers over asset disposals or deferrals of capital expenditure programmes. A problem of refinancing is that it may be difficult to agree with other parties over what form it should take, and it may cause problems in the continued motivation of managers who, if they remain, have had their equity stakes greatly diluted. This problem was also noted in France, in particular. In syndicated investments, restructuring may be delayed or take a particular direction because of differences in the attitudes of syndicate members. In the UK, if management are seriously at fault and it is possible to enforce change, a management buy-in of a buy-out may be an option, especially if managers are available who match the requirements of the problem company. Occasionally such a route may also be used in Holland.

## Management after harvest

As noted earlier, if management are a key element in the buy-out, their longer term objectives and behaviour are crucial to both the timing of harvest and what happens thereafter. In an IPO, management for obvious reasons invariably stay with the firm for a reasonable period. In trade sales the patterns are more mixed. Typically management may be locked into the new parent on the basis of, say, a one-year service contract. Management may not wish to be contracted beyond this stage, at least initially, because of the uncertainty as to how the new owners will behave. Moreover, it may be difficult to motivate such individuals as employees now they have high levels of personal wealth. A few managers may choose the point of the trade sale to retire from the company, although not necessarily from their business career. Some managers in the team may not be required when the buy-out becomes part of a new parent. However, besides the longevity of the buy-out as an independent entity, the importance of management also raises the question as to the longevity of their entrepreneurial behaviour (Ronstadt, 1986).

Across the four countries, very few managers have exited from their companies, especially outside the UK. In the UK, three core activities for ex-buy-out managers have been identified. First, a small number may be used to lead new by-ins. However, there is some concern expressed that the second deal does not work as well as the first, partly for motivational reasons and partly because the buy-out manager is less familiar with the new situation. If buy-out managers are to be used in such instances, it is necessary to identify which members of the team are capable of leading a buy-in. Some members of the buy-out team may be good function directors but be unsuitable to lead a buy-in. Some managers with specialist finance and marketing functions (less so, production) may be placed in buy-outs and buy-ins where there are skills gaps. A second role for exiting buy-out managers is in undertaking the due diligence requirements in new deals, in preference to accountants, as the buy-out manager may have more commercial experience and hence produce higher quality work at lower cost. A third role is for ex-buy-out managers to become board representatives where the managers of the venture capitalist do not have the requisite skills for making a positive contribution to the monitoring of a buy-out investment. There appears to be as yet little active attempt to seek to place entrepreneurs in non-executive roles or in buy-ins in Sweden and Holland.

## CONCLUSIONS

This study has examined issues concerning the development of buy-out markets and the longevity of buy-outs in four European countries with the most developed buy-out markets. The principal conclusions to emerge which have direct implications for practitioners are as follows:

(1) European buy-out markets differ considerably, both from that in the US and between European countries, according to how well developed and favourable the necessary conditions for market growth are at a given point in time. The opportunities for completing buy-out transactions also vary between countries according to differences in ownership and industrial structures. Practitioners need to be aware of these differences and their implications for buy-out opportunities. The four countries examined here represent the most developed European markets, with divestments providing greatest buy-out opportunities in the UK, Holland and Sweden and family succession cases the greatest opportunities in France. In the UK, buy-outs of companies in receivership and buy-ins are also significant parts of the market.

(2) For institutions involved in cross-border investments, important differences between buy-out markets need to be appreciated. These differences relate both to expected time-scale to harvest and to the form that exit is likely to take. In all four countries most buy-outs have not exited, although a quarter have in the UK and a sixth have in Holland. The UK has the most developed exit market for buy-outs. Since the late 1980s, sales to third parties have replaced flotations as the most common form of exit, although more recently receiverships have come to prominence. In Holland and Sweden, despite a high level of interest in flotations, trade sale is also the most common exit route. In France, partial sales, often involving institutions selling either to other institutions or to industrial partners, are an important addition to the straightforward trade sale.

(3) In monitoring investee companies, flexibility and adaptability are key aspects in steering companies towards an appropriate harvest, rather than reliance simply on mechanistic devices such as ratchets.

(4) Initial harvest intentions are not commonly achieved, although giving some consideration to eventual harvest at the time of the deal provides a frame of reference for future discussions and reduces the possibility for potential conflicts between entrepreneurs and investors. In addition, there is a need for continual monitoring of the nature and form of harvest within the overall process of governance of buy-outs.

(5) Both the quantitative evidence and the results of our interviews with funding institutions and buy-out managers emphasize that buy-out longevity

is a heterogeneous phenomenon. Across the four countries, quick harvest appears generally to have been a feature of larger deals in the late 1980s, buy-outs from the public sector and buy-outs from troubled firms which fail to establish themselves as independent entities. In other cases, investors generally need to take a longer term perspective.

(6) The finding that the majority of buy-outs tend to last for longer rather than shorter periods, even in the highly buoyant period of the late 1980s, has major implications for closed-end specialist buy-out funds who need to realize their investments to achieve returns to investors.

(7) Problems in managing for harvest in larger deals may arise due to different perspectives by syndicate members and these have been accentuated in the UK, in particular, by extensive use of harvest-dependent ratchet mechanisms. This suggests a need to choose syndicate partners carefully and to simplify incentive mechanisms for management.

(8) In France and the UK, in particular, management have a key role to play in the timing and form of harvest, even in Holland and Sweden, where management and investor buy-outs tend to be more common, the views of management concerning harvest need to be taken serious account of.

(9) In adverse economic conditions, investors need to be alert to different harvest possibilities such as secondary buy-outs and buy-ins, buy-backs, partial sales and restructurings as an alternative to the more conventional trade sales and floats. The importance and feasibility of these alternative mechanisms, however, vary between countries.

(10) In terms of problem buy-outs, an important distinction needs to be made between 'living dead' and 'good rump' which has implications for the nature and feasibility of harvesting.

(11) Financial institutions have yet to develop a systematic strategy towards utilizing those managers who have achieved a successful harvest, especially those who display positive entrepreneurial characteristics, in new investments in buy-ins or to complete buy-outs where there are gaps in the team.

## Notes

[1] Financial assistance involves the giving of security to lenders on the assets of the company to enable the company to purchase its own shares to effect a buy-out. In the UK, Section 151 of the Companies Act 1985 prohibits such transactions as a generality. A charge may, however, be taken over the shares of the target company. Section 154 relaxes the provisions if the transaction is carried out by a private company, as long as appropriate declarations are made by the directors of the company and supported by the company's auditors as to the solvency of the company.

[2] See Wright et al. (1992) for detailed description of the sample. No significant differences were found between the demographic characteristics of the sample and the population of buy-outs

contained on the CMBOR data base. The sample excluded the relatively small number, at that time, of mangement buy-ins whereby an *external* team of individual managers together with external finanical support acquire a target company. These deals have become more significant in the UK since 1985 and have been the subject of a separate study (Robbie et al., 1992).

# References

Bull, I. (1988). Management performance in leveraged buy-outs: an empirical analysis, *Journal of Business Venturing*, 3(2), 263-78.

Chiplin, B., Wright, M., and Robbie, K. (1992). *UK Management Buy-outs in 1992: Annual Review from CMBOR*, Nottingham: CMBOR.

Cooke, T. (1988). *International Mergers and Acquisitions*, Oxford: Blackwell.

Franks, J., and Mayer, C. (1990). Capital markets and corporate control: a study of France, Germany and the UK, *Economic Policy*, April.

Green, S., and Berry, D. (1991). *Cultural, Structural and Strategic Change in Management Buy-outs*, London: Macmillan.

Heuze, C. (1991). Management buy-outs in France. *In Economist Guide to Buy-outs*, 6th edn, ed. M. Wright, London: Economist Publications.

Jensen, M.C. (1989). Eclipse of the public corporation, *Harvard Business Review*, Sept–Oct.

Joachimsson, R. (1991). Management buy-outs in Sweden. *In Economist Guide to Buy-outs*, 6th edn, ed. M. Wright, London: Economist Publications.

Jones, C.S. (1992). Accounting and organisational change: an empirical study of management buy-outs, *Accounting, Organisations and Society*, 17(2), 151–68.

Kaplan, S. (1991). The staying power of leveraged buyouts, *Journal of Financial Economics*, 29, 287–313.

MacMillan, I., Kulow, D., and Khoylian, R. (1989). Venture capitalists involvement in their investments: extent and performance, *Journal of Business Venturing*, 4(1), 27–47.

Malone, S. (1989). Characteristics of smaller company leveraged buy-outs, *Journal of Business Venturing*, 4(3), 349–59.

Mueller, D. (1988). The corporate life-cycle. *In Internal Organisation, Efficiency and Profit*, ed. S. Thompson and M. Wright, Oxford: Philip Allan.

Ooghe, H., et al. (1991). Growth patterns in the European venture capital industry, *Journal of Business Venturing*, 6(6), 381–404.

Rappaport, A. (1990). The staying power of the public corporation, *Harvard Business Review*, Jan.–Feb.

Robbie, K., Wright, M., and Thompson, S. (1992). Management buy-ins in the UK, *Omega*, 20(4), 445–56.

Ronstadt, R. (1986). Exit, stage left: why entrepreneurs end their entrepreneurial careers before retirement, *Journal of Business Venturing*, 1(3), 323–38.

Sahlman, W. (1990). The structure and governance of venture capital organisations, *Journal of Financial Economics*, 27(2), 473–524.

Singh, H. (1990). Management buy-outs and shareholder value, *Strategic Management Journal*, July–Aug.

Sweeting, R. (1991). Early-stage new technology-based business: interactions with venture capitalists and the development of accounting techniques and procedures, *British Accounting Review*, 23, 3–21.

Thompson, S., and Wright, M. (1991). UK management buy-outs: debt, equity and agency cost implications, *Managerial and Decision Economics*, 12(1), 15–26.

Wright, M., ed. (1991). *Economist Guide to Buy-outs*, 6th edn, London: Economist Publications.

Wright, M., and Coyne, J. (1985). *Management Buy-outs*, Beckenham: Croom-Helm.

Wright, M., and Desbrières, P. (1992). Buy-outs in France, *Acquisitions Monthly Buy-out Supplement*, Oct.

Wright, M., Thompson, S., and Robbie, K. (1992). Venture capital and management-led leveraged buy-outs: a European perspective, *Journal of Business Venturing*, 7(1), 47–71.

Wright, M., Thompson, S., Chiplin, B., and Robbie, K. (1991). *Buy-ins and Buy-outs: New Strategies in Corporate Management,* London: Graham & Trotman.

# 5

## MANAGEMENT BUY-OUTS AND THE ECONOMIC CYCLE: THE PATTERN AND DETERMINANTS OF ACTIVITY

*Mark E. Bleackley and Michael Hay*

### INTRODUCTION

Between 1980 and 1992 the UK economy went through a complete economic cycle: recession, recovery and growth followed by recession. During the same period, management buy-out activity also went through a clear cycle. The figures speak for themselves. In 1981 £180 million was invested in 143 MBOs; during the next three years the value of MBO investments increased by an annual rate of 30 per cent and the number of transactions by a rate of 18 per cent; between 1985 and 1989, as UK economic growth accelerated, so too MBO activity burgeoned, reaching a peak in value in 1989 when £3.9 billion was invested in 374 deals; during the early 1990s the market has contracted somewhat, with the total value of MBO investments in 1991 falling to £2.1 billion, some 55 per cent of the value of activity seen in 1989.

At first sight the strength of the MBO market and its pattern of activity would appear to be a direct function of the economic cycle. The MBO cycle tracking the economic cycle – intuitively the proposition makes good sense. It feels right. But is it? Are things really that simple?

The broad question then is: 'What is the relationship between the economic cycle and MBOs?' But it became clear that to answer this, we would also have to answer others:

- Where do MBOs come from?
- What impact does mergers and acquisitions activity have on the MBO market?
- What effect does the availability of debt have on the nature and level of buy-out deals?
- How do MBO exit patterns vary over the cycle?

In reviewing these questions we shall also compare MBO activity in the UK with patterns in the US market for small-company leveraged buy-outs. The answers we found can be distilled into five propositions:

1 Corporate restructuring is the major source of MBOs.

2 An increase in M&A activity is followed two to three years later by an upswing in MBO investments.

3 Bank lending is cyclical and the availability of debt has a major impact, particularly at the upper end of the MBO market.

4 There is a clear relationship between phases of the economic cycle and MBO exits.

5 The MBO market exhibits markedly different characteristics depending on the size of the transaction.

## METHODOLOGY

The research project investigates the nature and characteristics of buy-out activity in the UK since 1980 (the earliest date for which reliable data is available). The study does not address the performance of MBOs or investors. The methodology comprised a number of components and drew on a wide range of sources including: (a) analysis of publicly available data, notably that from the Centre for Management Buy-out Research at the University of Nottingham (CMBOR), supplemented where necessary by data collected from primary sources; (b) in-depth interviews with senior executives from 14 venture capital firms (accounting for 75 per cent of current MBO investment), with several of the banks most active in providing debt for MBOs, and with five large public companies which have actively divested businesses via MBOs in recent years (quotations below are taken from these interviews); (c) examination of the relationship between the economic cycle and MBO activity using statistical techniques, complemented by a descriptive analysis of the patterns observed at different points in the cycle.

## THE PATTERN OF MBO ACTIVITY IN THE UK SINCE 1980

In reviewing the historical pattern of MBO activity (Figure 5.1) we have identified three phases linked to different periods of the economic cycle and stages in the evolution of the buy-out industry.

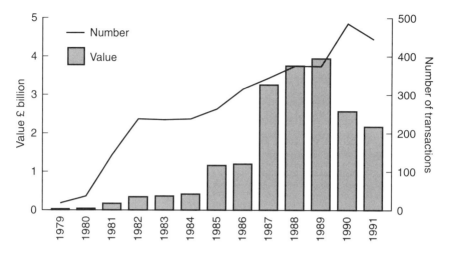

*Figure 5.1 UK buy-outs 1979–1991, value and number of transaction*

(*Source*: CMBOR)

## Phase 1: Initial development 1980–1984

A number of factors stimulated the development of the MBO market in the early 1980s after several years in which the acquisition of a company by its former managers had occurred in a modest way.

- *Change in political attitudes*: The government under Margaret Thatcher encouraged the small business sector as a response to the problems of the severe recession at the beginning of the decade, signalling a distinct change in political attitudes (Wright et al., 1992). Significant legislative and tax changes complemented this approach.

- *Opportunities for exit*: The formation of the Unlisted Securities Market in November 1980 gave impetus to the development of the UK venture capital industry and particularly the buy-out sector.

- *Role of institutions*: The buy-out became a more widely accepted means of corporate restructuring (Coyne and Wright, 1982) and an attractive investment vehicle for management and financial institutions. UK venture capital firms, which had cut their teeth on start-up and expansion finance deals in the 1970s, began to recognise MBOs as a profitable investment opportunity.

- *Entrepreneurial climate*: Managers became attracted by the possibility of making material capital gains. Corporate and personal income taxes were reduced progressively throughout the 1980s, and this was supplemented by a continuing improvement in the small business environment generally.

- *Availability of debt*: Banks became major providers of debt finance, particularly in the second half of the 1980s. In many cases they were able to earn higher margins when compared to other lending activities.

Between 1981 and 1984 there was a distinct rise in MBO activity served by an increasing number of venture capital firms. As Figure 5.1 shows, during this period the amount invested in MBOs increased by 124 per cent (to £403m in 1984) while the number of completed transactions increased by 66 per cent (237 transactions in 1984). By the end of 1984 the newly formed British Venture Capital Association (BVCA) had a membership of 50 firms, many of which invested in buy-outs.

## Phase 2: The growth years 1985–1989

The MBO market during the second half of the 1980s showed phenomenal growth. The general economic recovery that took place during this time, together with a resurgence in corporate profitability, stimulated growth in the stock market. In turn this fuelled the takeover market, with the increased use of paper to pay for transactions. As a result the competition from other bidders for buy-out opportunities increased substantially. This raised buy-out prices, yet the existence of an ever increasing number of banks and other financial institutions which were able to provide debt and mezzanine funding enabled MBOs to compete with outside bidders in many cases.

Apart from a brief hiatus after the stock market crash of October 1987, the market rose to a peak in value terms in 1989 when 3.9 billion was invested in MBOs, almost 10 times the level seen in 1984. This value of transactions was strongly influenced by a few MBOs, most notably Magnet (£631 million), BPCC (£265 million) and Allders (£224 million). The growth in buy-out activity can be largely attributed to the increasing number of large transactions – the average deal size increased from £1.7 million in 1984 to a peak of £11 million in 1989. In this year full membership of the BVCA reached 124 companies.

## Phase 3: Market contraction 1990–1992

Since the beginning of the current decade, the amount invested in MBOs has fallen substantially, although the number of transactions has increased. With economic conditions deteriorating, some of the larger MBOs, characterized by high gearing levels, underperformed and attracted considerable adverse press comment. The banks, suffering from an increasing level of bad debts generally, became more cautious in their approach to lending, particularly to large MBOs.

Significant buy-out opportunities continued to be generated as companies refocused on their core activities in response to the difficult economic climate. However, the more conservative approach by the lending banks, including the withdrawal of some from the market, together with poor prospects for economic growth in the short to medium term severely limited the number of larger transactions which could be completed.

The total value of MBOs fell 45 per cent from £3.9 billion in 1989 to £2.1 billion two years later. Over the same period the number of transactions rose 19 per cent from 374 to 444, demonstrating clearly the extent of the decline at the top end of the market. The number of transactions with a value of less than £25 million increased by a quarter between 1989 and 1991. Such transactions have accounted for between 90 per cent and 95 per cent of the total number each year since 1986. Larger deals have never represented a significant proportion of the sector by number, but they have heavily influenced the value of transactions, accounting for over 55 per cent of the sector value in 1991, for example.

## PRINCIPAL SOURCES OF MBO TRANSACTIONS

There are four major sources of MBOs: corporate restructuring (which consists of corporate divestment and receivership); government intervention; family-owned companies; and taking a public company private ('going private'). The contribution each makes to the number of transactions completed in any one year is shown in Figure 5.2. There are buy-out opportunities throughout the economic cycle but their nature varies.

### Corporate restructuring

Disposals arising from corporate restructuring are by far the most important source of buy-out transaction, accounting for 72.4 per cent of transactions (by number) in 1991 and 75 per cent by value (including receiverships). Since 1982 between 62.4 per cent and 86.7 per cent of MBOs (by number) in any one year can be attributed to corporate restructuring. The stated reasons for these disposals, from both UK and foreign companies, are many and varied, ranging from cash generation and the elimination of underperforming business to the refocusing of the business portfolio. Rather more

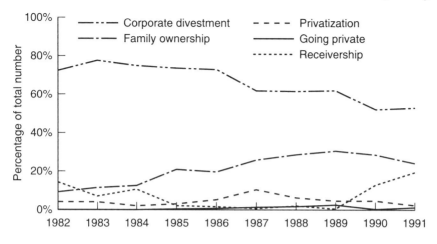

*Figure 5.2 Sources of MBO transactions in teh UK, 1981–1991*
(*Source*: CMBOR)

cynically, one interviewee commented that 'it is a means of showing their shareholders that the management is doing something!' (interview notes).

The nature of a particular divestment can be categorized as 'strategic', 'tactical' or 'distress' (Montgomery et al., 1984). Given the size and significance of those divestments that might lead to MBO opportunities, we are less concerned with the 'tactical' type and instead shall focus on two rationales which underlie corporate restructuring activity: strategic and financial distress. In many cases they cannot be disentangled from each other. Nevertheless it is clear that the dominant rationale changes at different stages of the economic cycle.

## Strategic rationale

This is used when a company wishes to refocus around one or a few businesses by disposing of non-core activities. These disposals may not necessarily be underperforming businesses; rather they may be the result of excessive diversification which no longer fits with 'what the company knows best'. The chief executive will often dispose of businesses and refer to the need to take the company 'back to basics' or 'back to its core'. This is not a new phenomenon. As one venture capitalist observed, 'there was a lot of focus on "return to core" in the early to mid 1980s. At this time companies were able to get as good a price from institutions by selling to the management as they could selling to a trade buyer' (interview notes).

An early example of refocusing a company through buy-outs is BICC, the cable, construction and engineering company which in 1982 sold two companies to its management. These were Rotunda, a leading manufacturer of self-adhesive tapes for the industrial and consumer markets, and Translight, a company involved in street-light maintenance and installation. A more recent example is Thorn-EMI which, over the last few years, has undergone a major refocusing exercise leading to the disposal of several non-core activities. The £68m buy-out of Kenwood, the kitchen equipment manufacturer in 1989 and the £103 million buy-out of the software company Data Sciences enabled Thorn to concentrate on its entertainment and retail business. In November 1992, Grand Metropolitan sold Express Foods to it management for £96 million, thereby completing its exit from the dairy business.

*Financial distress rationale*

This is used when a company encounters severe cash flow problems and is forced to sell businesses to release funds for the continued growth or survival of the remaining operation. An extreme case of this is receivership.

A good example of the financial distress rationale is the action taken by Svenska Cellulosa (SCA) following its acquisition of Reedpack. The paper and packaging company Reedpack was itself a £680 million buy-out from Reed International in 1988 and was subsequently bought by the Swedish multinational SCA for £1.05 billion in 1990. The acquisition took place at the peak of the market and SCA had to raise significant debt to fund the deal. The combination of this and adverse trading conditions in its major markets forced SCA to sell several businesses. The carton packaging businesses comprising Field Packaging and Cothorp Board Mill and the plastic packaging business Reedpack Plastics were each sold to their management in 1991 for £109 million and £34 million respectively.

Companies in receivership or administration are a significant source of buy-outs and buy-ins. These companies might be part of a much larger corporate group or independently owned. The number of companies in receivership is heavily influenced by the prevailing economic climate. From close to zero between 1986 and 1988, the number of buy-outs from receivership has increased rapidly as the economy has moved into recession, reaching a record 19.4 per cent (by number) of total buy-outs in 1991. A similar trend occurred in the years of low economic growth in the early 1980s when between 7 per cent and 14.3 per cent of all buy-outs (by number) from 1981 to 1984 came from receiverships.

Examples here are the failure of the Coloroll group in 1990 which spawned seven buy-outs and one buy-in, including Kosset Carpets, Staffordshire

Tableware, Fogarty and John Wilman; and the receivership of the financial services group British & Commonwealth in 1991, which led to a total of seven buy-outs of different parts of its business, including Bricome Industries, MW Marshall and Toplis & Harding (Chiplin et al, 1991).

## Government intervention

Political and regulatory changes can stimulate a period of corporate activity leading to a significant number of MBO opportunities. The Thatcher government's privatization programme in the 1980s generated a number of buy-outs, initially from previously nationalized industries and subsequently from local authorities and other public sector entities.

An early example of privatization generating an MBO was the transport company National Freight corporation, which was sold to its management in 1982 (Wright and Coyne, 1985). The privatization of the bus companies (National Bus Company, Scottish Bus Group and various local authority bus companies) has led to over 50 management-led employee buy-outs. As part of efficiency and cost-cutting programmes, local authorities have been contracting out cleaning, maintenance and food supply services, several of these to buy-out teams.

The timing and number of privatizations is influenced by political as well as financial considerations, making their connection with the economic cycle more tenuous – although, in the absence of other priorities, one would expect the government to make such disposals when it can obtain reasonable prices. Since 1982 an average of 4.3 per cent of all buy-out transactions has been generated from privatizations. The maximum in any one year was 10.4 per cent in 1987 at the height of the government's privatization programme.

Regulatory changes can also generate buy-out opportunities. The 1992 Single Market Programme has been a catalyst for much corporate activity in Europe in recent years. Closer to home, rulings form the competition and regulatory authorities may lead to forced disposals by companies under investigation. For example, the recent Monopoly and Mergers Commission judgement on the drinks and brewing industry triggered corporate activity which included the disposal of a chain of public houses, owned by Bass to a buy-in team – Enterprise Inns – for £60 million in 1991.

## Family-owned companies

The sale of a family business to its management might be prompted by an owner's retirement, conflict among family shareholders or the personal requirements of a major shareholder. Since 1982 family businesses have accounted for between 9.2 per cent and 30.5 per cent of the total number of transactions in any one year.

In the UK most buy-outs of family-owned businesses are much smaller transactions than in continental Europe, particularly France, Germany and Spain, where family-owned businesses are a significant feature of the market. Many companies on the continent were set up after the Second World War by founders now approaching retirement, and have been able to grow in the absence of well-developed takeover markets.

The actual flow of deals generated in this way over the economic cycle is difficult to determine. According to one venture capitalist, 'On the one hand in poor economic times the family may delay selling on the company in the hope that prices might improve; on the other, the family owners may be close to retirement and feel less able to pull the company through a recession. They may have little option but to sell the business' (interview notes).

## Going private

Public companies that have been taken private have accounted for an average of 1.4 per cent of the number and 11.7 per cent of the value of by-out transactions since they first occurred in 1985. These deals were particularly prevalent in the late 1980s when bank finance was more readily available, and they reached a peak of 30.5 per cent of the total value of deals in 1989. Generally of a material size, in recent years these deals have included the buy-outs of The Really Useful Group for £77 million 1990 (majority share subsequently bought by Polygram) and Virgin for £248 million in 1988 (the company was listed publicly in 1986).

## DETERMINANTS OF THE SUPPLY OF MBO OPPORTUNITIES

Economic conditions are a major influence on corporate activity and company performance and their acquisition and disposal programmes can be markedly different from one part of the cycle to the other. Whether companies dispose of businesses through a trade sale or a buy-out is a decision influenced by both financial and non-financial considerations.

## Economic conditions

Economic conditions play a strong part in determining both the source and number of buy-out transactions. In a direct sense, crisis conditions brought on by a prolonged recession can lead to forced sales, often at substantially discounted prices (the financial distress rationale). The contract distribution side of LEP (Swift Transport Services) was bought out by management for £19 million at a price to earnings ratio of 9.8 in 1992; by comparison the sector P/E at that time was 24.9.

This is supported by comments from the venture capital community: 'The recent merger and acquisitions wave was characterized by an exchange of assets leading to a refocusing on core business. Consequently coming into the current recession companies have already cut much of the fat and to cut any more would necessitate a forced sale' (interview notes).

More indirectly, poor economic conditions can highlight management mistakes. On several occasions this has led to the resignation of the chief executive office. It is not uncommon for the new incoming CEO to conduct a thorough strategic review of the business, which can often lead to disposals – maybe via an MBO – soon after.

## Mergers and acquisitions

Merger and acquisition activity has been strongly pro-cyclical (Scouller, 1987). Several MBOs over the last decade can be traced to the disposal of business from previous M&A activity. In some cases only part of an acquired business are attractive and so the remainder is divested (Wright, 1985), often significantly offsetting the costs of acquisition. Alternatively, the viability of acquired companies may be thrown into doubt due to changes in external circumstances (such as a prolonged period of economic recession), and divestment of the previously acquired company or parts of it may follow.

Previous research has shown distinct waves of M&A activity (King, 1989), with the last major boom taking place in the late 1980s. These periods can be linked to relatively high economic growth. The acquisition boom years of 1986–9, when around £80 billion was spent on acquisitions in the UK, can be compared to previous peaks of 1968 and 1972. A distinctive feature of the 1986–9 boom was that it was characterized by a few large acquisitions rather than many small ones.

Thus evidence found in our study of a relationship between growth in M&A activity and MBO investments some two to three years later would also suggest a correlation between the economic cycle and the level of MBO investment activity. The extent of this lagged effect is dependent on the duration and depths of the recession since companies, where possible, will await better times, when increased valuations can be realized on divestment.

## Disposal patterns over the economic cycle

The sources of MBO opportunities from divestments are many and varied. This makes it difficult to predict the flow of MBO investment opportunities at different phases of the economic cycle. However, our research suggests that a significant number of MBO opportunities occur as a result of financial distress or receivership during periods of economic decline, recession and at the early stages of economic growth when access to working capital facilities is limited.

As the economy picks up, the strategic rationale for disposals becomes more apparent and a significant trade incorporate assets takes place in the name of 'enhancing the core business' or 'disposing of non-core activities'. Further disposal may take place at or just past the peak as companies strive to rationalize their portfolios while sale prices remain high.

To evaluate the implications of these disposal patterns for MBO activity it is necessary to understand the reasons why corporate divestors sell to buy-out management teams in preference to trade buyers. When submitting a bid, prospective MBO teams can be at a disadvantage to trade buyers, many of whom are willing to pay more for the perceived synergies that an acquisition offers. Price and the extent of competition from trade buyers are therefore major factors.

Certain non-financial objectives might also have an impact on the divestment decision. From the vendor's point of view an MBO can be 'quicker and cleaner' (interview notes). The management itself may be a significant part of the value of the business and the threat of them leaving or not cooperating might reduce the price which can be obtained from an external buyer (Wright, 1985). In addition the vendor may not wish to sell to a potential competitor or encourage bad publicity by selling to a hostile third party. In the words of one active corporate divestor, a vendor may have 'some kind of loyalty towards its management' (interview notes). Among the companies interviewed there was no overriding preference between divesting via a buy-out or trade sale. Each company preferred to deal with the issue on a case-by-case basis.

As the economic cycle proceeds towards its peak, it becomes more difficult for MBO teams to compete with trade buyers who have easier access to debt and equity markets. During a recession or periods of low growth the competition from trade buyers for corporate disposals is less intense, with the companies being more preoccupied with the maintenance of their existing business. During these periods buy-out teams are in a better position to compete and relatively more buy-outs are transacted. A significant feature of the recession of the early 1980s was that many buy-outs were undertaken in the absence of significant competition from corporate buyers.

## The influence of bank attitudes on MBO activity

The attitudes of banks are influenced by general economic conditions and their perception of the risk of lending to different sectors. As most MBOs are structured with considerable levels of debt, these attitudes impact on MBO activity.

Bank lending exhibits cyclical behaviour in line with the economic cycle, although there is some evidence of a lagged effect. Bank lending increases (along with a reduction in fees and margins charged) as the economy shows strong growth, but the growth in lending may continue some time after the peak in the economic cycle. Banks similarly appear reluctant to increase their lending until they see definite signs of the economy emerging from a recessionary period.

The banks' commitment to the UK buy-out market reduced dramatically during the recession of the early 1990s (Beresford, 1992). This contrasts sharply with the 1987–9 period when there was a plethora of banks eager to participate. Underpinning this shift has been increasing concern with restoring capital ratios, making adequate bad debt provisions and reducing exposure in general. Moreover, concern over the performance of highly leveraged large transactions such as Magnet, MFI and Gateway has done little to help bankers' sentiment.

A senior bank executive observed: 'At the back end of the 1980s prices rose as the aspiration of the vendors was very high. Much of the gap between asset value and sale price was covered by the huge growth in mezzanine finance. The emphasis was more towards leveraged buy-outs (LBOs) rather than management buy-outs where the deals were done more for financial engineering reasons than for business reasons. Much of this was fee driven and the deals that caused the greatest trouble turned out to be those LBOs where the strategic rationale was not present' (interview notes).

With a different perspective, one venture capitalist commented: 'In this recession banks have been very cautious. A few large, heavily leveraged transactions have been one of the contributory factors. If there had not been these problems we would be getting a better reception in the banking halls!' (interview notes).

The cautious attitude of the banks is more evident in respect of larger transactions, and many foreign banks, in particular, which used to participate in syndicated senior debt factories have withdrawn totally from the market.

In the depressed economic climate the average debt commitment and the number of banks in a syndicate are now much smaller.

## FINANCIAL STRUCTURE OF MBOs

In periods of economic growth it becomes easier to raise a larger proportion of the total funding through bank debt and mezzanine finance; at the same time the strong trading performance of a company provides comfort to the lenders that capital repayments can be made and interest charges covered satisfactorily. During such periods large as well as small transactions have relatively easy access to equity and bank debt.

As economic conditions deteriorate and the economy moves into recession, the financial structures of buy-outs become more conservative, with both banks and equity providers taking a more prudent view of deal structures. Often the venture capital investors have to provide a larger proportion of the total finance package, both by way of equity and by preference shares and/or debentures. The number of larger transactions, dependent on a higher level of debt financing, is restricted under these conditions.

Figure 5.3 depicts the trend in gearing levels on large buy-outs (defined by KPMG Peat Marwick McLintock as over £10 million) since 1981. There is a lagged relationship with the economic cycle, with the highest gearing

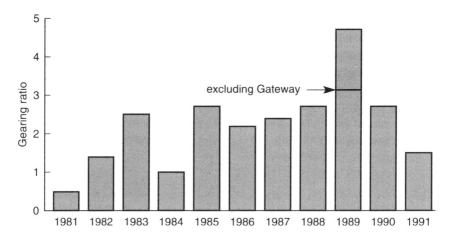

*Figure 5.3 The gearing ratio fo MBOs over £10 million in the UK, 1981–1991*

(*Source*: KPMG Peat Marwick McLintock)

ratio occurring in 1989 as the economy begins to cool down.[1] The 1989 figure incorporates the £2.2 billion Gateway transaction, which had a gearing of almost 11 to 1. Excluding this deal, the average gearing form 1989 was 3.2, more in line with the preceding few years. On this trend, gearing levels in the early 1990s appear low but not way out of line when compared to the early 1980s.

The financial structure of smaller transactions differs from that of larger deals, as is demonstrated in Table 5.1. Generally smaller transactions do not require the level of debt associate with larger one; with a more conservative financial structure (Chiplin et al., 1992), such deals are better placed to weather recession. Consequently the number of smaller transactions completed remains relatively static in an economic downturn.

Table 5.1  Financial structure of UK MBOs (amount of equity as a proportion of total financing, per cent)

| Size of buy-out | 1988 | 1989 | 1990 | 1991 |
|---|---|---|---|---|
| Less than £10m | 39.0 | 32.5 | 33.6 | 43.2 |
| £10m and over | 25.4 | 17.4 | 24.8 | 24.0 |

*Source:* CMBOR

## PREFERRED METHODS OF REALIZATION

Realizations, as well as investments, need to be considered within the context of the general economic environment. While the management team and investors might have their preferences, the most appropriate exist route is often dictated by economic conditions or by opportunities such as an approach from an interested acquirer, which may present themselves. In general, venture capitalists prefer to realize investments via trade sales, primarily because the proceeds are often greater and received in cash (Chiplin et al., 1989).

Management is typically more ambivalent, sometimes preferring to retain its independence via a flotation. In addition, the strategic requirements for the business might influence the appropriate mode of realization; for example, in the 1992 flotation of the kitchen equipment company Kenwood Appliances, Mr Timothy Parker, the chief executive, commented: 'The listing would allow Kenwood greater flexibility to expand through acquisition of capital investment and would reduce the likelihood of constraints on future product development' (*Financial Times*, 18 June 1992).

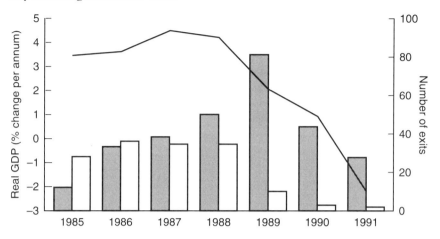

*Figure 5.4 Method of realization and the economic cycle, 1985–1991*

(*Source*: CMBOR)

Trade sales have been the most common exit route, outnumbering flotations by a factor of 2 to 1 since 1985. In the case of smaller transactions, their size often limits the feasibility of exiting by a flotation, and so trade sales predominate. The preferred exit early in the economic cycle, when P/E ratios are rising, is by way of a flotation (see Figure 5.4). Indeed in 1985 flotations accounted for 70 per cent of all realizations. However, as M&A activity increases and buyers are prepared to pay premium prices, trade sales dominate. By 1989, 88 per cent of exits (excluding receiverships) were via trade sale. There is therefore a clear link with the economic cycle.

## THE APPROPRIATE TIME TO INVEST AND REALIZE

The returns made by institutional investors in MBOs are very much dependent on the timing of both the investment and the realization. Even though some companies have had disappointing trading results, they have still provided excellent returns to investors because the company was acquired cheaply and sold to a trade buyer at the top of the cycle.

Normally the best time to invest in MBOs is towards the end of the recession and at the beginning of the growth phase, when prices are lower, potential gains greater and maximum advantage can be taken of the gearing effect. The recession of the late 1980s and early 1990s was noted for P/E ratios remaining relatively high, and certainly not falling to the levels seen in the recession of the early 1980s. A venture capital executive commented: 'During a recession companies do their spring cleaning. The need to generate cash and their assessment of when the recession will end determines their asset sale strategy. This particular recession has been longer than expected. Companies are not interested in selling their businesses at the beginning of recession for fear of not getting a realistic price. Later on in the recession, they may hold on to the businesses thinking that the recession may soon be over. It is only when things are really bad that forced sales take place. The last year of a recession may be the ideal time to invest in buy-out companies (interview notes).

On the other hand, returns are maximized by exiting when P/E ratios are high. This is often effected by flotations as the stock market rises during the recovery phases, and subsequently by trade sales as M&A activity increases towards the top of the cycle. Many venture capitalists are placing greater emphasis on a realization strategy for companies in their portfolio. As one commented: 'We have learnt from our mistakes. In the past, realizations were not created – they used to happen – and if you missed the window of opportunity your returns suffered. We now work closely with management to ensure that all parties maximize their gains. This extends to investments which might encounter trading or financing difficulties; it is to everyone's advantage that they are sold before their value suffers unduly' (interview notes).

This does not mean that investments and realizations at other times in the cycle will necessarily underperform. What we have shown is that the characteristics of buy-out opportunities at alternative points in the cycle will be different and the venture capital investor should take this into account when evaluating the investment. For example, nearing the peak of the cycle, buy-out opportunities may come from companies divesting parts of previously acquired businesses. Prices may be higher as a result of increased competition with trade buyers and a rising stock market. MBO investments at this stage in the cycle are generally held for a shorter time period.

## THE IMPACT OF THE ECONOMIC CYCLE ON THE MBO MARKET

The research indicates that trends in investment in buy-outs and in their realization are associated with different stages of the economic cycle. In the following the stages are treated as distinct to aid descriptive analysis, but in effect the cycle progresses from one stage to another in a continuum. In particular:

- *Recession (declining or negative rate of growth)*. Early on in the recession, companies might resist the financial pressures to sell businesses hoping for a quick upturn in the economic cycle. This is particularly true of large buy-outs where vendor price expectations remain high. Should these conditions persist, more and more companies have to dispose of businesses for reasons of financial distress. Levels of leverage fall as banks tighten their credit parameters. Realizations also decline, and what few there are (Chiplin et al., 1992) are normally via a trade sale.

- At the bottom of the cycle there are significant buy-out opportunities arising from the financial distress of public companies and an increased number of receiverships. Few of these transactions would be considered large MBOs. Levels of leverage continue to fall as the banks take a cautious approach. Realizations are few and far between.

- *Recovery (increasing rate of growth)*. At the early part of the growth phase the financial rationale remains prominent because companies are still forced into making disposals to fund the working capital needs of their business. As growth continues, the number of transactions rises as corporations focus on their core businesses for more strategic reasons and dispose of peripheral activities. Debt becomes more widely available as banks ease their credit restrictions, resulting in higher acceptable gearing levels and a relative increase in the number of larger transactions. With a stronger stock market, realizations via flotations become more common, although trade sales remain the dominant exit option, fuelled by the rise in M&A activity.

- At the top of the cycle the average deal size, level of gearing and the number of MBOs all reach their peak. These trends are interconnected with the wider availability of debt, which enables larger transactions to be completed. Realizations, the majority of which are trade sales, also peak – in line with the high level of M&A activity.

## THE US EXPERIENCE

Much of the academic research and business commentary in the United States is focused on the larger end of the leveraged buy-out market. A few researchers have investigated the characteristics of smaller LBOs. Kelly et al. (1986) introduced the concept of an entrepreneurial leverage buy-out (E-LBO), where ownership is concentrated in the hands of relatively few investors. For the purposes of this classification E-LBOs were defined as having an upper valuation limit of $50 million. A study by Malone (1989) investigated the characteristics of smaller-company LBO investments between 1981 and 1987, during what was a prolonged period of economic growth. He recognized that the long-term viability of these companies had not been sufficiently tested because most of his sample had not faced an economic recession.

The smaller-company leveraged buy-out is the nearest to a management buy-out in UK terminology. Between 1981 and 1992 42 per cent of all LBO investments in the US (where value is disclosed) have been under $50 million. The pattern of US LBO investments over the economic cycle shows a similar pattern to the one in the UK market (Figure 5.5). The number of large deals has fallen significantly in the last three years, while the number of smaller LBO investments has shown a much more consistent pattern culminating in a 28 per cent increase in the number of investments in 1992 over the previous year.

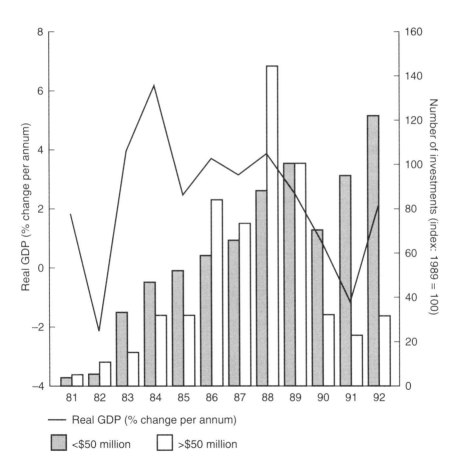

— Real GDP (% change per annum)

&#9632; <$50 million    &#9633; >$50 million

*Figure 5.5 LBO investments and economic growth in the US, 1981–1991*

(*Source*: Securities Data Company, Inc.)

## CONCLUSION

At the start of this paper we raised a central question. What impact does the economic cycle have on MBO activity? Our answer will be summarized and implications drawn from it.

1 There is a clear relationship between MBO activity in the UK – in terms of both the total number and value of MBOs – and the economic cycle. Phases in the economic cycle are associated with identifiable phases in the MBO market. Small company LBO activity in the US exhibits similar characteristics.

2 The link between the economic cycle and MBO activity operates at the level of both investments in – and realizations of – MBOs.

3 MBO activity does not precisely coincide with the economic cycle. This study provides clear evidence of a relationship between growth in M&A activity, which is strongly pro-cyclical, and MBO investments some two to three years later; in part this is a function of the disposal, post-acquisition, of the unwanted parts of an acquired business.

These relationships are, perhaps, not surprising. Intuitively they make sense. They are, moreover, well supported empirically. However, care must be taken in interpreting these results. Whilst they hold true for MBOs as a whole their effect varies in different segments of the MBO market. Hence our final conclusion.

4 The MBO market exhibits a marked 'two-tier' effect. It is evident that the buy-out market demonstrates different characteristics depending on the size transaction. The economic cycle strongly influences the level of activity of the buy-out market, but this influence varies with the size of the transaction. Larger deals in the UK, generally those above £50 million in value, have been strongly influenced by changes in the economic cycle, while smaller deals – those up to £25 million – have been relatively unaffected by macroeconomic changes (Figure 5.6). As a consequence, the amount invested in buy-outs and their average size vary considerably more than the number of transactions over the economic cycle.

### Implications

A number of implications flow from these conclusions which are, we believe, of significance for researchers and practitioners working in the venture capital industry. In essence these can be summarized as follows:

First, MBO investment opportunities will improve as the economy starts to move out of recession. A significant proportion of new MBO opportunities

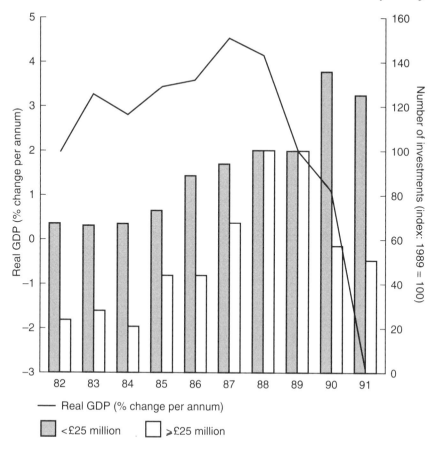

*Figure 5.6 Buy-out investments and economic growth in the UK, 1982–1991 – the two-tier effect*

(*Sources*: CMBOR; Central Statistical Office; London Business School)

will arise from the disposal of businesses by companies requiring cash to finance their increasing working capital requirements and vendors will dispose of businesses in the expectation of being able to secure a higher price than would have been possible during the economic trough.

Second, the spectacular growth in the level of buy-outs that occurred between 1986 and 1989 was the result of a combination of several factors: a sustained period of economic growth, increasing M&A activity, a buoyant stock market and the willingness of banks to provide debt financing. At the same time, the attractive returns of the mid-1980s encouraged a significant number of new entrants into the venture capital industry. One venture capitalist observed: 'Coming out of the last recession in the early 1980s it became practically impossible not to make money from buy-outs because many companies were for sale and there was minimal competition from trade buyers; prices were undemanding; trading conditions were wonderful with strong economic growth; exit conditions were tremendous with a buoyant stock market and the buy-outs were able to gear up with the willingness of the banks to lend.... I don't believe that we will see these conditions again. Rather than take the shot-gun approach of the past where we couldn't fail to miss we shall have to make better judgements in order to get the good returns' (interview notes).

In the early 1990s the buy-out market has reached a level of maturity prompting one interviewee to remark that the 'gravy train of the early 1980s' was unlikely to recur. Above-average returns, however, will be generated by those venture capitalists who demonstrate proficiency in the timing, selection and management of their MBO investments and realizations, that proficiency being underpinned by a clear understanding of the way in which the economic cycle and the different sectors of the MBO market interact.

Third, the competition to raise buy-out funds and seek buy-out opportunities will continue to grow. The number of opportunities is unlikely to keep pace with the level of investment funds available, particularly those earmarked for the larger transactions. This places additional emphasis on the development of in-house industry expertise and corporate networks.

Fourth, the average life-cycle of an MBO investment will lengthen, as a function both of a more elongated economic cycle and a more flexible attitude on the part of venture capitalist and their investors towards the holding pattern of their investment.

## Note

Gearing ratio can be described as a debt to equity ratio and is defined as the total of debt plus mezzanine finance divided by equity, i.e. $(D + M)/E$. It is a means of assessing the strength of a company's capital structure. Mezzanine finance is a term of high-yielding unsecured loans provided by certain financial institutions.

## References

Beresford, C. (1992). The maturing MBO market, *Director*, June.

Chiplin, B., Wright, M., and Robbie, K. (1989). Realizations from management buy-outs: issues and prospects. CMBOR executive briefing.

Chiplin, B., Wright, M., and Robbie, K. (1991). *UK Management By-outs in 1991: Annual Review from CMBOR*, Nottingham: CMBOR.

Chiplin, B., Wright, M., and Robbie, K. (1992). UK management buy-outs in 1991 and the first quarter of 1992. CMBOR, March.

Coyne, J., and Wright, M. (1982). Buy-outs and British industry, *Lloyds Bank Review*, Oct., 15.

Kelly, J.M., Pitts, R.A., and Shin, B. (1986). Entrepreneurship by leveraged buyout: some preliminary hypotheses. In *Frontiers of Entrepreneurial Research*, Wellesley, Mass.: Babson Centre for Entrepreneurial Studies.

King, M. (1989). Economic growth and the life-cycle of firms, *European Economic Review*, 33 (Mar.), 325–34.

Malone, S.C. (1989). Characteristics of smaller company leveraged buyouts, *Journal of Business Venturing*, 4, 349–59.

Montgomery, C.A., Thomas, A.R., and Kamath, R. (1984). Divestiture, market valuation and strategy, *Academy of Management Journal*, Dec., 830–41.

Robbie, K., Wright, M., and Thompson, S. (1992). Management buy-ins in the UK, *Omega*, 20(4), 445–56.

Scouller, J. (1987). The United Kingdom merger boom in perspective, *National Westminster Bank Quarterly Review*, May.

Wright, M. (1985). Divestment and organizational adaptation, *European Management Journal*, 3(2).

Wright, M., and Coyne, J. (1985). *Management Buy-outs*, Beckenham: Croom Helm.

Wright, M., Thompson, S., and Robbie, K. (1992). Venture capital and management-led leveraged buy-outs: a European perspective, *Journal of Business Venturing*, 7(1), 47–71.

# 6

## ANALYSIS OF THE TRADE SALE AS A VENTURE CAPITAL EXIT ROUTE

*Kaj-Erik Relander, Antti-Pekka Syrjänen and Asko Miettinen*

### INTRODUCTION

The current pace of technological development shortens the time during which certain technologies are viable. As noted by Merrifield (1988), any corporation that does not develop, adapt or acquire new technologies will lose its competitive edge. Large multitechnology corporations need to update technologies which support their core technological competencies. New technologies which are unfamiliar to them will keep emerging, often from small entrepreneurial firms. Connel (1987) points out that small firms constitute a major proportion of new US ventures. Although multitechnology corporations update their technologies through internal research and development, other means, including acquisitions of smaller technology-based companies, have become increasingly important in maintaining technological competence.

Recent statistics from the European Venture Capital Association indicate the importance of trade sales for venture capital divestments in Europe. In 1991, trade sales accounted for some 32 per cent of exits by number and 41 per cent of all exits by value, as shown in figure 6.1. The figure also shows the detailed geographic breakdown in Europe. By comparison, in the United States (Devlin, 1992) mergers and acquisitions accounted for 36 per cent of the total number of exits by venture capitalists from venture-backed companies in 1991. The trade sale is and will probably remain an important means of harvesting the value of a venture in Europe. For this reason the venture capital community would benefit from a better understanding of the trade sale process. The objective of this study is to analyse the whole process, including the views and strategies of all parties involved in a trade sale.

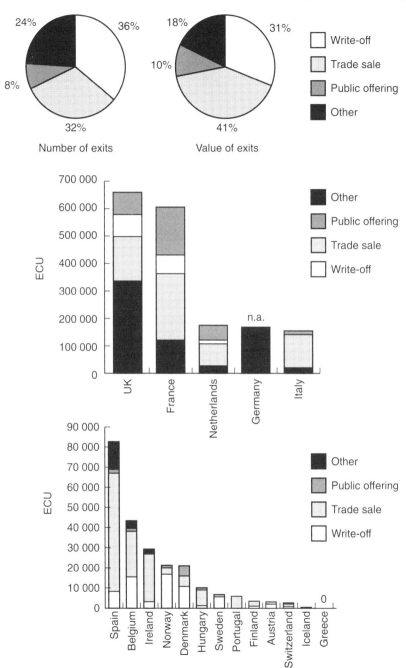

*Figure 6.1 Divestment statistics for 1991 from the European Venture Capital Association (all Europe; countries with volumes of divestments over ECU 100 000: countries with volumes of divestments under ECU 100 000)*

*(Source:* EVCA, 1992, pp. 37–40)

## Agency theory as a frame of reference

A lack of theoretical frameworks is often typical in small business research. Agency theory is a potentially valid and useful approach in this respect in directing attention to the problems that occur when cooperating parties have different goals and division of labour. More specifically, the agency theory focuses on the relationship in which one or more persons (the principal(s)) engage another person (the agent) to perform work on their behalf. Agency theory attempts to describe this relationship using the metaphor of a contract (Jensen and Meckling, 1976).

The basic premise of agency theory is that both principals and agents are rational maximizers of economic benefit. The unit of analysis is the contract between the principal and the agent. The contract is assumed to specify the rights of the agent and performance criteria on which agents are evaluated (Fama and Jensen, 1983). The theory tries to determine the most efficient contract governing the principal–agent relationship.

Agency theory is further aimed at resolving the problem of risk sharing that arises when the principal and agent have different attitudes towards risk. The second problem may arise when the goals of the principal and the agent conflict, and it becomes difficult or expensive for the principal to verify what the agent is actually doing.

Agency theory has its background in information economics. There are two major strands of the theory: positivist and principal–agent research (Jensen, 1983). The two strands share a common unit of analysis and the same focus on minimizing agency cost. Positivist research is less mathematically oriented, however. The principal–agent line is more empirically oriented and more focused on a general theory of the principal–agent relationship (Harris and Raviv, 1979).

In her analysis of the present state and development trends of agency theory, Eisenhardt (1989) outlines some recommendations for future advances. She recommends the use of a broader spectrum of possible contracts to expand the theory. Agency theory seems to be particularly relevant for situations in which contracting is problematic, such as situations where there is (1) substantial goal conflict between principals and agents, (2) sufficient outcome of uncertainty, and (3) unprogrammed jobs in which evaluation of behaviour is difficult. She sees studies on small firms as providing significant scope for agency theory.

Barnea, Haugen and Senberg (1981) have indicated that agency problems tend to arise in small firms because the level of asymmetric information – of differences in information available to the entrepreneur and outside investors – is greater and the agent has the capacity and incentive to affect wealth transfers between different parties. The greater the asymmetry of information in the entrepreneur's favour, the easier it is for the entrepreneur to take actions detrimental to the interest of other parties. This problem may be getting worse in the small firm because information about small firm managers who engage in such activities may be less subject to control through the managerial labour market (Pettit-Singer, 1985).

## Technology as an engine of a trade sale

The majority of the technologies used by corporations are of external origin. As Lewis and Linden suggest (1990, p.65), large corporations need to continually scan the technology development outside their companies. Michael Radnor (1991, p.131) has developed a graphic view of the scanning of technologies, as illustrated in Figure 6.2. Radnor divides relationships to technologies into regions. A company's basic technology domain is described as its core region. Within that core region is a subregion A, which represents the technologies the company recognizes as part of the core technologies needed for product and process development. These technologies are not owned by the company, but they are recognized. The company wants to develop them through internal research and development or by acquiring them. Subregion B represents technologies that also belong to the basic core domain, but they are not recognized as such by the corporation.

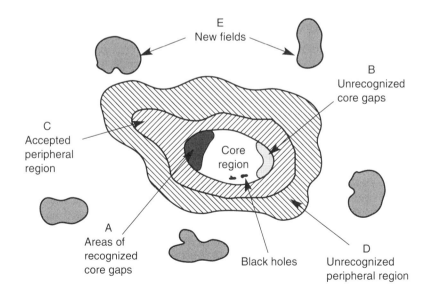

*Figure 6.2 Technology regions*

(*Source*: Based on Radnor, 1991)

Black holes represent technologies yet to be developed in the core region. Failure to recognize technologies in subregion B can pose a threat to a corporation's growth. Area C represents a peripheral region around the company's core technology. Surprises may be caused by technologies which show up within peripheral region D or in region E, new fields outside a company's technological domain.

The practical implications of this notional map are that companies need to identify their core technologies. When a company has a valid assessment of its core technologies and technology gaps, it is easier to identify potential sources of new technologies and to be proactive. MacMillan and McGrath (1992) have developed an approach to the graphic display of technological design barriers which corporations should identify and shift. A specific example of the application of such a diagram is given in Figure 6.3.

The current technological design barriers of an aircraft engine limit the overall performance of the engine. By pushing the technological design barriers towards the area designated 'dominant design', an engine manufacturer is able to attain a dominant position and lure customers interested in the two design attributes of thrust and speed. Large corporations should look at the technological design areas that are critical in moving their design barriers. A venture capitalist invests in ventures that enable design barriers to be moved. If a shift in a design barrier is a major advance, the technology-based venture

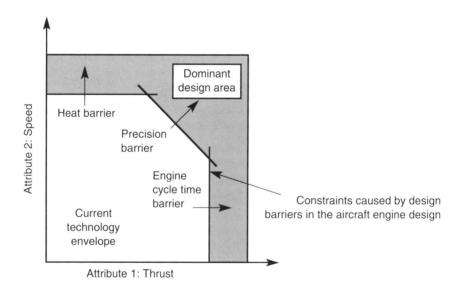

*Figure 6.3 Design space for aircraft engines and the dominant design area*

(*Source:* MacMillan and McGrath, 1992)

stands a good chance of growing into a firm which can have a successful initial public offering. At times, the shift in design barriers is difficult to exploit without a large corporate partner. Under these circumstances a trade sale can provide the best results for all parties.

Small companies are important and effective sources of innovations. Bleicher and Paul (1987) note that according to many studies the major share of innovations developed in the United States from 1953 to 1976 emerged from small companies. In his study Biggadike (1979) showed that new, independent businesses reach profitability in half the time required for businesses developed internally by corporations. Bleicher and Paul cite studies by the National Science Foundation which show that large corporations spend their research and development money four times less efficiently than small companies. Though technology-based ventures continue to provide new innovations and move critical technological design barriers after their acquisition by a corporation, there may be a decrease in innovation capability. According to studies by Granstrand and Sjölander (1990), however, the capacity to innovate can be preserved within an acquired company if the venture receives proper organizational handling.

The authors presume that technology-based ventures increasingly fill the technology and product gaps for large corporations. This is particularly true for companies whose ventures push technological design barriers outwards but who are unable to take sufficient advantage of these advances on their own.

## Exiting venture capital investment

Although exiting venture capital investments is important in realizing value, up to now only a few studies have addressed this issue. The problem has lain in finding patterns in this highly case-dependent phenomenon. Rind and Muskin (1987) have grouped acquisitions as defensive, operations-related or finance-related, according to corporate motivations. Defensive acquisitions take place in response to challenges presented by the target company. Operations-related acquisitions are more proactive and are intended to fill gaps in product lines or markets. Finance-related acquisitions will not be reviewed here. Understanding corporate motivations helps in identifying potential buyers. Clarke and Gall (1987) have formulated a business unit divestment model for large corporations which also aids in locating buyers. Potential acquirers can be identified by studying their balance sheets, their objectives and their public statements on expansion, as well as their internal economics and familiarity with acquisitions. Studies of management buy-outs and trade sales (Houlden, 1990; Wright et al., 1990) point to the increasing importance of trade sales as compared to flotation.

There have been few studies done on the trade sale phenomenon and they contribute little to our understanding of the research problem. The best and most current information for the venture capital community on trade sales comes from interviews with experienced venture capitalists and consultants. John Lyon (1992) stated recently that venture capitalists should identify trade sale exits at the due diligence stage and attempt to bring large corporations alongside investments as early as possible. The authors expect identification of exit potential, networking and corporate contacts to have a considerable impact on exiting through trade sales.

## Needs of technology-based ventures

Trade sales need to benefit all parties in order to function well as an exit route. A venture's development is as important as the needs of the venture capitalist or the acquiring corporation. Small companies need resources to grow. In their study of Silicon Valley company acquisitions, Bruno and Cooper (1981) found that mergers or acquisitions were motivated by a need for capital, for an additional product line or a need to cope with expanding markets. Based on data gathered at Babson College in Massachussets, Ronstadt (1986) determined that the reasons entrepreneurs exited in 31 per cent of the cases were purely financial.

A trade sale can provide sufficient resources for ventures and even improve their overall performance. In a study by Granstrand and Sjölander (1990), the problems of small, non-acquired companies were centred on financing and managing international marketing, financing and managing the development of a second major product generation and bridging a subsequent generation shift in the top management team. Data from Swedish acquisitions demonstrates how acquired companies grow faster. The authors assert that strategic complementary unions, such as the technology of a small venture and the resources of a large firm, provide a solid basis for a successful trade sale.

## METHODOLOGY AND THE RESEARCH PROCESS

Unlike related studies, our research has endeavoured to understand the whole trade sale process. There is, however, more emphasis on the views of the venture capitalist. The authors seek to create hypotheses for future studies, to illustrate the approaches of venture capitalists to the trade sale exit route and to provide the tools for successful exiting. The research methods used in this study were:

- interviews with 27 venture capitalists in 24 venture capital firms, located in 11 European countries, concerning their approach to exiting technology-based venture capital investments, especially through trade sales;
- case studies of five trade sales of European or US origin which track technology-based venture-capital-backed companies sold to large corporations primarily for their technology;
- additional interviews and discussions with industrialists, corporate venturing experts, merchant bankers and academics.

Over 80 per cent of the venture capitalists interviewed had significant experience in technology-based ventures. The combined capital under management was approximately ECU 5 billion in 1991. Half the interviews were conducted in person. The ventures sold in the trade sale cases were selected to represent different industries.

Several factors affect the reliability, the structure and the external and internal validity of this explorative and analytical study. The subject is a delicate one to all parties in a trade sale. The reliability and the validity of the study were strengthened by presenting a research plan to the interviewees, by using analytical generalizations and by utilizing multiple interviews and research sources.

## INTERVIEWS WITH VENTURE CAPITAL FIRMS

Results from the venture capitalist interviews are presented in Table 6.1. The 32 questions are listed, each followed by the most important or interesting answers. After each answer the percentage of venture capital firms with the same response is indicated if the percentage is 10 per cent or over. Due to their lack of time, some venture capitalists did not respond to all the questions. Some interviewees also gave more than one answer. Unstructured interviews were conducted to identify a large variety of ways in which exiting can occur. Better ways to structure future surveys will be developed from these efforts.

In order to determine the key issues for exiting a venture capital investment, we closed each interview with a request for further comments from the interviewees. The answers varied widely, covering almost all aspects of exiting through trade sales. Among other things, the venture capitalists emphasized that:

- networking was important when seeking buyers;

- many investors are good partners in the investment phase, but problems appear later, in the exit phase;
- the main problem is to find a buyer;
- too much time is spent on reviving lemons;
- negotiation time influences the internal rate of return;
- the entrepreneur is the key to trade sales, and entrepreneurs should be selected only if they are interested in selling the company;
- the company will sell if it is good;
- profitability must come first – the venture capital industry overestimates the importance of technology and underestimates the importance of profitability;
- no strict requirements should be set for the venture holding period;
- making a proper exit analysis is essential before investing in the venture;
- exiting to Nasdaq, the National Association of Securities Dealers Automated Quotations system, is increasing.

**Table 6.1 Interviews with venture capital firms: questions and answers**

**1  Some venture capitalists build exits whereas some do not. Do you sketch paths of development for ventures in advance?**

| | |
|---|---|
| Exit possibilities influence the investment | 25% |
| Exit analysis is part of investment analysis | 20% |
| Having an idea is important, but there is no plan | 10% |
| No development paths are sketched | 10% |
| Deal structure improves exit possiblities | |
| Several realistic exit routes are required before investing | |
| Five potential buyers are named before investing | |

**2  What exit mechanisms has your company had experience in? What have been the main exit mechanisms? Are there differences in the average return on equity?**

| | |
|---|---|
| All important exit routes are used | 50% |
| The main exit route is a trade sale | 30% |
| Trade sales are used | 10% |
| Initial public offerings are very profitable | 10% |
| Trade sales can be very profitable | |
| No experience with exits | |

**3  Has your company preferred certain exit mechanisms over others?**

| | |
|---|---|
| Initial public offerings are preferred | 35% |
| No preference or having a preference does not make sense | 35% |
| Trade sales are preferred | 15% |

**4  When is a trade sale used as an exit method? Is it only a question of price or opportunity?**

| | |
|---|---|
| When the threshold for initial public offering has not been reached | 20% |
| It is an opportunity-driven situation | 10% |
| Public market conditions are difficult | 10% |
| If strategic fit or potential synergies exist | 10% |
| When there is a consensus for it | 10% |
| Corporations buy poor ventures for turnaround | |
| Other exit routes are not good | |

**5  Are there differences in exit strategies for different industries?**

| | |
|---|---|
| No difference | 35% |
| Company and industry size are important | 15% |
| Public offerings are for technology ventures | 10% |
| Biotechnology-based ventures go public | 10% |
| A trade sale is for traditional industries | 10% |

**6  Do you actively scan the corporate strategy and the technology strategy of the potential buyers of a venture? How do you do it?**

| | |
|---|---|
| Potential buyers are monitored | 15% |
| That is the chore of the venture management | 10% |
| Not actively | 10% |
| Networking is essential to get exits | 10% |

**7  What will the situation be in the future? Are trade sales going to be the main exit strategy for cashing out in Europe?**

| | |
|---|---|
| Trade sales remain the main exit route | 70% |
| Initial public offerings are temporarily rare | 10% |
| Management buy-outs are also important | |

**8  In general, do you have alternative plans to develop a venture to an IPO or a trade sale?**

| | |
|---|---|
| It is a clear which exit route will be taken | 15% |
| Depends on the entrepreneurial team | 10% |
| Alternative plans exist | 10% |

**9  What are the criteria that make certain buyers appealing to you?**

| | |
|---|---|
| Price | 60% |
| Synergy or strategic fit | 35% |
| Acceptability to venture management | 15% |
| Name and reputation | 15% |
| Consistency in the industry and strategy | 10% |

**10  Does your company build a potential buyer base or do you do it by increasing your contacts within the venturing community? What is the role of intermediaries?**

| | |
|---|---|
| Contacts are made through networking | 60% |
| Intermediaries are important in finding buyers | 40% |
| A database is used | 10% |

**11  How is the actual contact with possible buyers made? How are they contacted and by whom?**

| | |
|---|---|
| Direct contact by the venture capitalist | 30% |
| Intermediaries are used | 25% |
| Venture management makes the contact | 15% |

**12  How is the actual decision to sell the firm made? How do you decide when the price and time are right?**

| | |
|---|---|
| When a consensus is reached | 10% |
| There are no exact methods | 10% |
| Waiting would not raise the internal rate of return | 10% |
| Venture is in a transition stage | 10% |
| Absolute and relative returns are compared to future expectations | 10% |
| Our strategy is followed | |
| Organic growth possibilities have weakened | |
| The venture or the fund have matured | |
| A threshold or critical mass has been reached | |

**13  What other criteria besides the price influence the trade sale decision?**

Consistency
Management interests
Deal structure
Credibility of the buyer

**14  Who usually participates in the negotiations?**

Lawyers
Venture capitalist
Entrepreneurial team
Shareholders
Intermediaries

**15  How long is the negotiation period from the initial contact to the signing of the sale's documents?**

| | |
|---|---|
| 1–3 months | 25% |
| 3–6 months | 25% |
| Over 6 months | 10% |
| Not possible to say | |

**16  How is the value of the firm determined? What are the roles of cash flow, technology, products, etc.?**

Strategic fit with the buyer

Value for the buyer
Quality of the entrepreneurial team
Cash flow, assets, profitability, price to earnings

**17  Do you have a minimum price under which you would not sell the firm? How is it determined?**

| | |
|---|---|
| Determined by a feeling | 20% |
| We have a walk-away price | 10% |
| Internal rate of return determines it | 10% |

**18  How is the final price reached?**

By making offers and counteroffers

**19  Are the escrow arrangements or other special arrangements that influence price used often?**

| | |
|---|---|
| No | 25% |
| Sometimes | 10% |
| Maximum of 10% of price is allowed to depend on future | 10% |
| Liabilities are limited to one year | 10% |

**20  How do the buyers evaluate the technology of the acquisition target?**

| | |
|---|---|
| They do it on their own | 50% |
| External consultants are used | 10% |
| They do it on their own, it is a security problem | 10% |

**21  Do you stay in contact with corporations which have bought a company from you? Does the buyer comment on the success of the acquisition later?**

| | |
|---|---|
| No | 50% |
| Critically important | 10% |
| Sometimes | 10% |

**22  In your view, how successful are acquisitions of venture capital backed companies to corporations?**

Mixed
Not possible to answer
European Venture Capital Association should study it
Not a relevant question

**23  How successful are trade sales for your company? (Compare the results to the objectives set at the time of the initial investments and to the objectives set for the trade sales.)**

| | |
|---|---|
| Successful | 15% |
| Satisfied | 15% |
| Not good | 10% |

24  **Under what conditions can a trade sale be recommended as a venture capital exit vehicle?**

When threshold for public offerings is not reached                                        10%
During financial difficulties or of a transition stage                                    10%
See answers to question number 4

25  **How would you, as an experienced venture capitalist, advise one to harvest an investment (in Europe, through a trade sale)? How should one proceed?**

Note the importance order of efforts: survival, profitability, growth, exit
First try NASDAQ, then local initial public offering, then trade sale

26  **In a trade sale, do you sell the whole company and its stocks?**

We sell it all

27  **How is the price paid, in cash, stock or on an earnings base?**

Cash and shares                                                                            60%
Cash                                                                                       40%

28  **Who usually prepares the legal issues on the contract?**

Venture capitalist (or his lawyers)                                                        10%
Buyer (or his lawyers)                                                                     15%

29  **What are the main legal issues in such deals?**

Warranty issues                                                                            40%
Tax issues

30  **Starting from the time of the initial investment, when should the exit take place?**

In 3 to 5 years
In 5 to 7 years

31  **How long does it take to prepare for a trade sale? How long is the trade sale process?**

6 months
2–3 months
6–12 months

32  **Has the timing for previous trade sales been advantageous?**

We did not think about it later
We should have waited
Timing has been correct

## OVERVIEW OF THE CASE STUDIES OF BUYERS OF TECHNOLOGY-BASED VENTURES

Of our five case studies, three can be used as examples of degrees of success from the venture capitalist's point of view, illustrating an unsuccessful, a successful and a moderate-profit trade sale. Corporations and venture capitalists do not like to discuss particular trade sale cases in detail, which has made research more difficult. Parties can end up in contention after the sale, and they sometimes agree to not discuss sales with outsiders.

The first case, which was unsuccessful for the venture capitalist, involved a technology-based start-up venture that was sold for its technology to a large corporation which was not in direct competition with the venture. The venture had created a new printing industry product that was more efficient and less costly than previous products. This venture's shift of the technological design barriers was significant, but due to insufficient resources and conservative markets the venture did not prosper. The venture capitalist did not have alternative exit plans and he was forced to exit quickly at a loss.

The successful trade sale case involved the later stage financing of a highly innovative firm in a pharmaceuticals-related industry. The venture's success was a product of good venture management. The sellers had several potential buyers. Contact with the final buyer was made through the venture capitalist. Since the offer was good and the venture was in need of financing, the deal was closed.

The moderate-profit case involved the trade sale of a technology-based venture manufacturing measuring equipment. The company was growing fast and its technology was threatening the markets of its eventual buyer. The venture was sold to the buyer because the offer was considered good and further refinancing would have been expensive. The high entry price of the venture capitalist, complementary effects and the potential for synergy determined the final, moderate-profit price.

The last two case studies focused on ventures in the computer industry and in the display manufacturing industry. In the first case, the quality of the venture increased the number of buyer candidates. In the second case, organizational problems slowed the integration of the venture into the buyer.

The case-study corporations all chose to acquire technology-based ventures though the acquisition process is complicated and it takes time to obtain the desired results. They made this important decision for various reasons: for some the acquisition was opportunity driven, for others it was in accordance with corporate strategy. The corporations interviewed generally considered that internal product development was either uncertain or too expensive. Equivalent companies offering licensing opportunities did not exist either. Purchase of the technology was the way to move their design barriers. In some cases, the corporations actually felt jeopardized by the new technology or business concept.

The large firms interviewed had been involved in acquisitions before and had developed systems of evaluating acquisition targets. Finding the acquisition target was usually done informally; in some cases a formal search for acquisition candidates was also used.

The case-study corporations recommended that potential acquirers develop clear objectives for any acquisition. Problems may appear when entrepreneurs become unit leaders. The cultural differences between a corporation and an entrepreneurial venture are very good reasons for not acquiring a venture. Finally, it takes time to realize the synergy effects.

The cases are discussed more thoroughly in their own section below.

## ATTITUDES TO EXIT AMONG EUROPEAN VENTURE CAPITALISTS

The interviews revealed two basic patterns among venture capitalists when it came to exiting, although neither pattern appeared in its pure form. One pattern we call the 'path sketcher', the other the 'opportunist'. Path sketchers are genuinely interested in exit problems. They do not plan the exit, but try to increase the probability of exiting successfully. They are aware that the majority of successful exits take place through a trade sale. They analyse thoroughly the business and exit possibilities of an investment target and the exit possibilities influence the deal structure. At times this kind of venture capitalist, together with the entrepreneur, is able to identify potential buyers by name simply by looking at corporations that could benefit from the improvements made by the venture as it overcomes technological design barriers.

Opportunists trust their management skills and the concept of the investment target. Before making an investment, these venture capitalists do a thorough business analysis and may also map out some exit opportunities, but these have little influence on their investment decisions. The main exit target route for them is an initial public offering. Figure 6.4 illustrates these two approaches.

The venture capitalists interviewed were all variations on these two types. It is difficult to say whether it is better to be a path sketcher or an opportunist. A venture capitalist's exit approach is influenced by numerous factors. Skills in evaluating technology and people, in selling firms, making

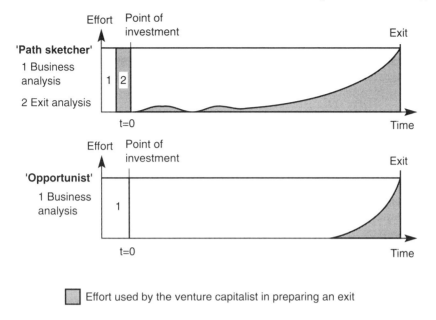

Effort used by the venture capitalist in preparing an exit

*Figure 6.4 Two approaches to exiting venture capital investments*

personal contacts, understanding a geographical region and accumulating money in the stock market are only a few of the important factors which may have an impact on an individual's choice of a successful exit route. Venture capitalists should determine their strategic objectives and combine them with their skills to craft an exit approach which suits their particular needs.

The difference between the path sketcher and the opportunist highlights the need for the temporal structuring of uncertainty. In the path sketcher approach, exit planning is seen as an essential part of the overall deal procedure, while the opportunist structures the temporal aspects of the deal in the short run and after the investment.

The issue of the importance of efficient scheduling for a structural analysis of temporal uncertainty is not a new one. It was Thompson (1967) who emphasized the issue of making the procedure more predictable to reduce the uncertainty over the availability and timing of resources. His notions about 'pooled, sequential, and reciprocal interdependence' could be applied here in terms of coordinating the efforts of the actors through standardized regulations, planning and ongoing mutual adjustment.

The principal–agent relationship and structure is a bit more complicated here than in usual applications of agency theory: the venture capitalist is the agent for the corporation on the one hand, and the principal for the entrepreneur on the other hand. This 'double-loop agency relationship' gives a rather broader spectrum of contacts and can be a potentially useful way to expand agency theory; it takes it beyond a partial view of cooperative efforts that, valid as it is, may leave out quite a lot of the complexity of the real business world.

## IMPLICATIONS FOR PRACTITIONERS

### Implications for buyers

Acquisitions are problematic for corporations, and yet they provide unique opportunities to improve technological skills and enlarge product range. The implications for corporations planning to buy technology-based ventures can be gleaned from the case studies.

**The buyer must have a clear appreciation of his acquisition objectives and be aware of any organizational problems**

A clear statement of a corporation's strategic objectives can help that company determine the means of achieving them though an acquisition. Acquiring products is different from acquiring a product development team. When acquiring technology, a buyer needs to be careful not to disturb the entrepreneurial culture of the venture. Technology acquisition calls for retaining key persons. Developing synergies takes time. Combining different cultures is necessary for achieving results, but it often cannot be hurried.

**The entrepreneur will not necessarily be the best subsidiary manager**

The role of an entrepreneur changes in a venture after its acquisition. For various reasons, an entrepreneur will not work as keenly with a project as the nature of the task changes. The acquiring corporation should be prepared for this eventuality, and it must be ready to establish an organizational structure which is best for all parties after the acquisition. The entrepreneur is necessary for the venture during the transition period; afterwards, tasks should be suited to the entrepreneur's particular talents.

**The buyer should network with the venture capital community to ensure access to a flow of acquisition candidates**

A corporation which is in the market to update its technological skills or product range needs contacts with the venture capital network. The potential technology acquirer should also be prepared to delineate its corporate and technology strategies so that the quality of the acquisition candidates provided by the venture capital community is maximized.

## Implications for venture capitalists

The study confines itself to pointing out certain important factors in exiting, rather than separating successful strategies from unsuccessful ones. Some implications of these findings for venture capitalists are the following:

### The venture capitalist should make a rigorous analysis of the exit possibilities before investing

It is important to try to predict the most probable exit route. If the venture develops into a very profitable corporation, selling the firm will not be difficult. Problems can appear if a venture's technology is appreciated by only a few companies and the technology has not yet proven exceptionally profitable. A thorough analysis can reveal potential risks. The best potential buyers are those who would benefit from the shift in design barriers.

### The venture capitalist should network actively to create an 'exit flow' for ventures, just as there is a deal flow for investments

Bygrave (1988) notes that networking is vital in the venture capital industry. If the probable venture capital exit route seems to be a trade sale, then involvement in networks increases the possibility of finding good buyers. It is always possible that an intended initial public offering may not succeed and the venture may need to be sold. There are always some lemons to be divested. It takes a lot longer to exit a venture than to invest in it.

### The selling negotiations should not be left to the entrepreneur

The entrepreneurs or any other equity holders have different objectives for an exit. The venture capitalist needs to ensure that the negotiations are a joint effort and that the entrepreneur does not negotiate with the buyer behind the venture capitalist's back.

## Implications for the entrepreneurial team

The conclusions drawn on behalf of the entrepreneurial team are based on the case studies and interviews. They basically favour the trade sale as a way to develop the venture, but they warn about changes after the acquisition.

### A trade sale may be very rewarding for the entrepreneur

A trade sale is not a second-class exit route when compared with an initial public offering. Even if the trade sale is not considered successful by the venture capitalist, it may be very rewarding for the entrepreneur. Running one's own business is, however, very different from running a subsidiary. The time for the entrepreneur to negotiate his reward is before the acquisition.

### Acquisition can provide valuable resources for the venture

Acquisition can provide necessary financial resources for a venture's development. The synergies that develop when a venture's technology joins with the acquiring corporation's market credibility, distribution system and managerial resources can be even more important than the financial resources that are gained.

## SCHEMES FOR EXIT BY TRADE SALE

Exiting venture capital investments is a diffuse phenomenon. Numerous factors influence the exit route, and foreseeing the future is next to impossible.

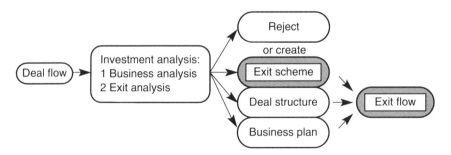

*Figure 6.5 The investment decision process*

The investment decision is, however, the first step towards the exit. Figure 6.5 illustrates a somewhat ideal investment decision process.

The creation of an effective investment is best done by a venture capitalist who is keenly aware of having unique skills and goals. At least half of the effort spent on an investment analysis should be targeted at exit questions. Assumptions about the state of national economies and stock markets at the expected time of exit will influence an investment decision. The venture capitalist must also take into consideration the important influence of information about the technology in question, the role of intermediaries, available financial and managerial resources, networking, and the number of corporations facing similar technological design barriers.

A thorough exit analysis aids the venture capitalist in structuring the deal with the entrepreneur. An exit analysis provides an exit scheme for the venture. One exit scheme planning strategy could be developed by starting with the target exit the venture capitalist expects to use and back-filling the milestones which would most likely precede that exit. Finally, criteria for re-evaluation in other divestment situations should be determined. Figure 6.6 illustrates the structure of building an exit scheme.

The scheme could shed light on several possible exit routes, to maximize options. The plan *per se* is not important, but planning is. For example, each exit option can be weighed against the risk of keeping the venture, the cost of additional investments, the internal rate of return objective, the relative and absolute return of divestment and the maturity of the investment and funds. These alternatives need to be analysed because the exact nature of an exit cannot be predicted.

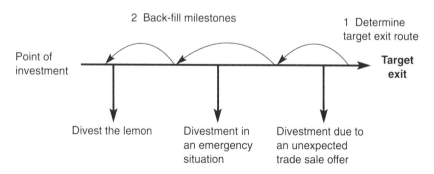

*Figure 6.6 Building an exit scheme*

# A FRAMEWORK FOR ANALYSING TECHNOLOGY-BASED VENTURES AND PLANNING EXITING ACTIONS

We close this discussion by presenting a framework for analysing and developing successful strategies for exiting technology-based ventures. These steps are illustrated in Figure 6.7. We have identified three main classes of exit route for the portfolio companies: initial public offering class, trade sale class and question mark class. It is often possible to predict which type of exit is the most probable for a certain venture. The first two classes are considered successful. The question mark class includes exit routes involving mainly financial structuring, as well as write-offs and liquidations. The dynamics of the venture development may change the exit class of the venture, as the arrows in Figure 6.7 indicate. Each class of venture goes through three development phases: investing, adding value, and exiting. In each cell of the matrix there are key actions which can aid in building a more successful exit for the investors.

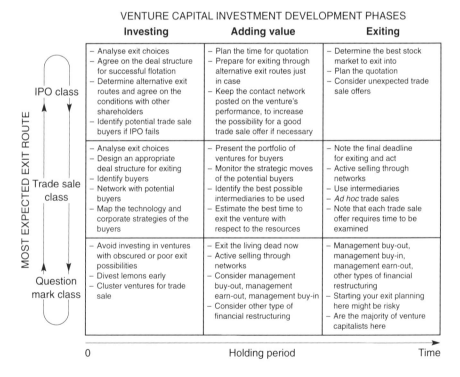

*Figure 6.7 A matrix for analysing and developing successful strategies for exiting technology-based ventures*

The framework should be used to help venture capitalists think through the critical actions necessary for exiting portfolio companies. Refining and testing it are left for future studies. We do believe that the key elements a venture capitalist needs in order to build a successful exit strategy are included, especially with respect to exiting through trade sales. Besides the framework, a venture capitalist also needs an understanding of technological design barriers and the strategic objective of other parties in a trade sale in order to exit successfully.

## CONCLUSION

The trade sale phenomenon is influenced by many determinants. The venture capitalist sees it as the main exit route for harvesting the value of a venture. The entrepreneur has similar goals but lacks the experience with trade sales and often has to rely on the experiences of a venture capitalist. For the technology buyer, it is an interesting tool for rapid product acquisition, but it can be problematic in terms of corporate culture confrontations.

The need to identify the best partners for a trade sale is of critical importance. Ideally a technology-based venture should contribute to the technology skills of the buyer. On the basis of this study we argue that a venture capitalist will contribute to the internal rate of return in a trade sale if corporations with specific technology needs are brought together with technology-based ventures which have proven their profitability while moving critical technology design barriers.

Trade sales continue to be an important part of the economic structure; they are critical to the venture capitalist and an opportunity for the buyers. To function well, the trade sale process demands international contacts and intensive networking.

We have also suggested that agency theory provides an empirically testable perspective on problems of cooperative efforts that may be applied to exit actions, with their principal–agent structure; however, the theory's partial view of processes like these needs to be extended to enable it to master the complexity of venture capital exit routes.

Additional perspectives and the use of multiple theories could help to capture the complexity. Our frame of reference and types of approaches to exiting the investment give some evidence about the possibility of combining institutional and agency theories. The institutional emphasis on tradition could complement the efficiency emphasis of agency theory, resulting in a better understanding of the potential benefits to the whole venture capital community in exiting particular venture capital investments.

## CASE STUDIES

## Case Alpha

---

Alpha was a small firm which provided high quality technology-based systems for the printing industry. The business started quite promisingly. The entrepreneurial team knew the industry well. Although the industry was a rather conservative one, the firm was successful in getting its first important customers. In order to grow and reach larger markets, it needed to expand abroad. Therefore, a subsidiary was established in the company's largest target market area. Alpha's problems began when one of the company's key financiers withdrew. The search for replacement financing took too long. Difficulties also surfaced in marketing. Although sales were increasing rapidly, the introduction of Alpha's product line was more difficult than expected. Conservative customers still remained very loyal to their existing production processes, workers, machinery, and work habits. Alpha lacked credibility.

### *Venture capitalist and exit scheme*

It was soon realized the Alpha would require strong financial support to penetrate the markets. After some unforeseen financial problems, Alpha turned to the venture capital firm Zeta for funding. Zeta became Alpha's major source of funds. The original plan of the venture capitalist and the entrepreneurial team was to have the founders of the company sell company shares. The sale would take place either by listing the company or setting up a trade sale. Some miscalculations and unexpected events resulted in financial problems, which caused Alpha to drift into an exit at a poor time. Exiting a year earlier would have been much more advantageous for the sellers. The chairman of the board and the founder of the company contacted several firms in search of a buyer. A potential buyer had to have adequate financial resources, sufficient delivery channels, an ability to move fast with the acquisition and a business which operated in related technologies.

### *Buyer and motivations for buying*

Lambda is a multinational corporation which produced products similar to Alpha's. It was doing well financially and its top management was well aware of the new technologies introduced by Alpha. Lambda's business strategy was to make acquisitions which supported existing business; technology-based ventures with good product lines and research and development capabilities had already been acquired. Lambda's top management knew that Lambda's core business was maturing. It did not make its move until one of the other market leaders introduced products similar to those of Alpha. Then Lambda's top management decided that something ought to be done to obtain this new technology. Lambda had two choices: either acquire Alpha or begin internal development of the new technology and products. It seemed probable that a new subsidiary would have to be established, so that the development process might take too long.

## Integration

The first contact was made by Alpha's chairman of the board. The offer to buy the whole company was considered interesting and a letter of understanding was signed. Alpha became a research and development department within Lambda. Alpha's brand name was retained and its products were marketed separately from Lambda's product line. Immediately after the acquisition Lambda chose to introduce a new financial control system; otherwise Alpha was free to continue to operate as it desired. Alpha's unique company culture was retained.

## Results and conclusions

The venture capitalist did not profit from investment in Alpha. From the buyer's point of view, it is still too early to judge the value of the acquisition, but sales have risen and more employees have been hired by Alpha. The trade sale did not produce significant wealth for the entrepreneurial team. The key factor illustrated by this case is that risks always exist. It is time consuming to sketch out alternative scenarios in advance, so if one particular scenario does not succeed, then a fall-back plan is available and can be applied. Although the venture itself was good, the resources for its development were insufficient and the timing of the exit was therefore disturbed. From the buyer's standpoint, the objectives of the acquisition will determine the corporation's post-acquisition strategy. The current management of Alpha answered our questions on behalf of the entrepreneurial team.

## Case Beta

Beta's core product line was in technology related to the pharmaceutical industry. Although Beta was experiencing financial and managerial difficulties, it was not for sale. The company's management, however, did recognize that something ought to be done. The venture capitalist, Eta, worked with

Beta's managers for nine months to devise a plan for the company's development. Within three years sales had quadrupled, and the company had become
an important leader in its market niches.

## Venture capitalist and exit scheme

Eta was an experienced venture capitalist and industrialist. The original
intention of the venture capitalist was to go public with Beta; however, the
financial situation at the stock exchange was not favourable for public offerings. The exit possibilities had already been listed at the initial investment
phase. Although Beta was doing very well, there were some problems. The
company's growth was requiring increased capital. The venture capitalist
was planning to increase its investment in the company. The amount of
money needed, however, for the company's next development steps was
large. The owners were not capable of increasing their investments in the
company substantially, and the venture capitalist was close to the limit of the
major equity position. The main reason for Eta's divestment of Beta was the
offer received from the future buyer, Omicron. Both the investor and Beta's
management were prepared to develop the firm further, but it was simply
less complicated to divest.

## Buyer and motivations for buying

Beta's eventual buyer, Omicron, was a non-European corporation, which
was interested in extending its operations globally. Omicron was well aware
of Beta's product line and technology. There were several other potential
buyers; however, these companies were not seen as the most important candidates for purchasing Beta, and two of them were excluded when a letter of
understanding was signed with Omicron. The buyer was doing well financially and producing products similar to Beta's, though its customer groups
were slightly different. Omicron's attempts to penetrate Beta's market areas
had been unsuccessful. Beta's technology was simply superior to that of the
buyer's. There was a good fit between the two companies, their technologies
and their product lines.

## Negotiations and integration

The initial contact with the potential buyer was made directly at the top
level. The negotiation period was quite short, lasting only two weeks. The
deal was closed when a consensus was reached on price, deal structure and
the future of Beta. The deal included an escrow arrangement. The idea of the

corporate buyer was to preserve the unique company structure of Beta. Beta was capable of operating on its own and had good managerial resources.

## Results and conclusions

From the venture capitalist's point of view the sale of Beta to Omicron was successful. There was a strategic fit between the two companies so selling the firm was considered better than postponing the exit. It is still too early to judge the success of the acquisition from the buyer's standpoint, but the requirements for success are present. For the original equity owners of Beta, the deal was a success. As this case demonstrates, selling a good company is easier than selling an unsuccessful one. The timing and the availability of other buyers and exit routes worked well for the sellers. Although the researcher investigating this case was not allowed to interview the parties participating in the trade sale, this should not affect the findings.

## Case Gamma

---

Gamma was founded as a garage company to produce measuring equipment. The product was superior because it incorporated new technology that permitted simultaneous online measurement of many different substance levels. Gamma's sales stimulated high growth. A complete product line was created. The venture's development was hindered by a lack of sufficient funds from Theta. A large part of the investment made by Theta was used up in buying shares from a seed capitalist and was therefore not available for developing the firm. Additional managerial skills were needed to guide the company as Gamma grew. A management expert was hired as chairman of the board. Annual sales grew from ECU 14 to 30 million.

## Venture capitalists and exit scheme

Gamma's case involves two venture capital firms. Initially, Gamma received money from a seed venture capitalist and from Theta, a venture capital firm specializing in financing growth. Given its technology, Gamma was not the type of firm that could be taken public. The most probable exit route would be a trade sale. Sigma, the eventual buyer of Gamma was known to the entrepreneurs. They did not, however, see Sigma as a potential buyer until it approached the entrepreneurs and stated its interest in buying Gamma.

Gamma's development was hampered by market and customer-related factors. To continue growing, Gamma needed back-up and financing to build its marketing systems. At this point, Gamma was approached by Sigma's top management. The entrepreneurs wanted credibility for Gamma, a future for themselves in the company and cash for their efforts. The development of Gamma as an independent unit was ensured, and Sigma also agreed to retain the original business culture of Gamma. The final decision to sell was made by Theta. The price was not a good one, but it was in line with objectives to accept a modest profit in exchange for realizing immediate value.

### Buyer and motivations for buying

Sigma was a technology-based venture which was founded as a spin-off from a larger parent corporation. The parent company was a large, quoted conglomerate. Prior to acquiring Gamma, Sigma had made two acquisitions to improve service to its customers. Sigma wanted to continue to acquire companies that would fill technology gaps and extend their markets, thereby providing growth and better customer service. Sigma was looking at companies with a particular product profile, fully developed products, an existing management team, a growth rate of 20 per cent or higher and sales up to ECU 7 million per year. The venture capital network was told about their requirements for new acquisition targets. During an exhibition, contact was made between the top managers of Sigma and Gamma. Only through acquisition of Gamma could corporate and technology strategy objectives be fulfilled.

### Negotiations and integration

A base target price was established by estimating the expected cash flow for the next five years. The price and the future of Gamma's personnel were the main issues under negotiation. The venture capitalists would be paid in cash; the entrepreneurs in stock loans and cash. The founders would be obliged to work for Gamma for the next five years. Gamma's entrepreneurial culture was not to be destroyed. It almost seemed that Gamma would be left to run on its own, though a new financial control system was put in place.

### Results and conclusions

The trade sale was deemed acceptable by the venture capitalists and the entrepreneurs. All Sigma's objectives other than the sales objectives were met. This case illustrates the importance of networking. The buyer, the entrepreneurs and the venture capitalist did pursue contacts during the development of Gamma. The contact was finally made through the venture. In order for the trade sale to take place, it was important for the buyer to have clear objectives and a sense that the firm to be acquired would fit strategy. The trade sale also met the needs of Gamma and the venture capitalists. The commission paid to the negotiating chairman of the board was a catalyst for the negotiation process. In general, selling a firm can take so much time that the process can endanger the management of the company.

## Case Delta

The business idea of the technology-based venture in this fourth case, Delta, was to manufacture and market high-precision visualization equipment for high-end users. Delta was founded in the United States in the early 1980s. Delta's key customers required the best quality products with the highest reliability. Delta's sales had developed satisfactorily, but it did not seem possible for them to reach the level necessary for going public.

### Venture capitalist and exit scheme

The venture capitalist Iota was a private, American venture capital firm which specialized in investing in technology-based ventures. A trade sale was considered the most probable exit route. The divesting of Delta and its sale to Tau were the result of the desire of the venture capitalist and other equity holders to realize their investment. The eagerness of Tau to buy the firm provided the final push for signing the deal.

### Buyer and motivations for buying

The buyer, Tau, is a Western European corporation. Since its founding, Tau has been involved in making acquisitions as a means of achieving strategic goals. Tau's criteria for selecting acquisition candidates were clearly defined. Any company under consideration needed to fit Tau's overall strategy. It also needed to have a market niche with potential to grow. A company should not be too dependent on just a few important people. It should be in a field of activity related to Tau's but not a direct competitor. Its financial position was not considered that important. Tau even explains its strategy to important intermediaries and it generally receives one acquisition proposal a week. Tau's acquisition of Delta was the result of a search for a subsidiary abroad. Tau desired a company with local status in its country so that it could provide products to all important customer groups. The other criterion was for the company to possess a high-level technology. Delta was acquired.

*Integration*

During the first six months after an acquisition, it is Tau's practice for the person responsible for the long-term realization of synergies and for the success of the acquisition to spend one-third of their time at the acquired company's location. The company is tied financially to the parent company. Delta's president was required to stay with the company for three years, but this proved to be too long. After the first year there, he was interfering with the developing synergies rather than working for them.

*Results and conclusions*

At the moment it is too early to adequately evaluate the results. Integrating Delta into Tau has taken longer than expected, and the costs have been higher. Involvement of both Tau and Delta personnel in creating the synergy has been necessary. It has been difficult to draw final conclusions about the venture capitalist's exit success and behaviour, because the researcher of the case was denied interviews with all the parties participating in the trade sale, resulting in a lack of data in some areas.

## Case Epsilon

Epsilon specialized in designing and manufacturing computer hardware and software. It was established in Central Europe in 1984. Epsilon enjoyed a 20–30 per cent increase in sales per year. Epsilon's growth meant that it was sufficiently large and important to consider selling. When its sales reached approximately ECU 13.5 million, it was time to divest the venture from Kappa's portfolio.

*Venture capitalist and exit scheme*

The venture capital firm Kappa was considered an experienced venture capitalist both in investing in and exiting from technology-based ventures. From the start Kappa had felt that the best exit route for Epsilon would probably be a trade sale. Epsilon's business made it dependent on large industrial corporations. The actual corporate or technology-oriented strategies of the potential buyers for Epsilon were not assessed. Kappa did, however, have a detailed history of their previous strategic moves. The reasons for selling Epsilon centred on two factors: first, the venture had reached the threshold for selling; second, the entrepreneurs felt that it was time for the company to forge an alliance with a strong industrial partner. Four companies were contacted by Kappa to explore the possibility of a trade sale. Eventually one of the buyer candidates proved interesting, and negotiations to sell Epsilon were initiated.

*Buyer and motivations for buying*

Epsilon's buyer, Omega, was a subsidiary of a multinational firm which specialized in several electronics industries. Omega was contacted for several reasons. First, Omega appeared to have sufficient funds to pay for Epsilon's technology. Second, the technological fit between Epsilon and Omega was evaluated and deemed promising for both parties. The overall industrial, financial and human factors favoured selling Epsilon to Omega. A team of scientists and engineers from Omega conducted a technological audit of Epsilon to assess its technological know-how.

*Negotiations and integration*

The final price for the venture was decided by Omega's determination to buy Epsilon. The market share, technological know-how, commercial presence and present and future profitability of Epsilon certainly influenced Omega and enhanced its willingness to buy the venture. The deal included an escrow arrangement which tied the closing price to Epsilon's performance for the next two years. All of Epsilon's stock were sold to Omega, and the deal was paid in cash. Epsilon had a capable management team of its own, which made its purchase less risky for Omega.

*Results and conclusions*

Currently it is too early to comment on the success of integrating Epsilon into Omega's operations. The sellers realized a good price for the venture. The business merited that purchase price because it had a strong management team, a competitive advantage based on its technological edge in the market and technology that was properly protected by patents. Despite a lack of detailed exit planning, the exit was successful. Since the venture was profitable and not risky, there were several candidates ready to buy it. Buyers are easy to find when a venture is good. While the researcher of the case was denied interviews with all the parties of the trade sale, this should not affect the results.

## General case comments

The venture capitalists in all these cases tended more to the opportunist than the path sketcher pattern. However, the more successful ones had a clearer vision of the exit. The venture capitalists in each case considered an exit scheme useful and desirable. Keeping the acquisitions objectives in mind was important. The buyers networked with venture capitalists, and while this was not useful in these particular cases, it was considered important. For the entrepreneurs and the ventures *per se*, the trade sales were beneficial.

# References

Barnea, A., Haugen, R., and Senberg, L. (1981). Market imperfections, agency problems and capital structure: a review, *Financial Management*, Summer, 7–22.

Biggadike, H.R. (1979). The risky business of diversification, *Harvard Business Review*, 57 (May–June), 103–11.

Bleicher, Knut, and Paul, Herbert (1987). The external corporate venture capital fund: a valuable vehicle for growth, *Long Range Planning*, 20 (6), 64–70.

Bruno, Albert V., and Cooper, Arnold C. (1981). Patterns of acquisition in Silicon Valley start-ups. In *Frontiers of Entrepreneurship Research*, ed. Karl H. Vesper, Wellesley, Mass.: Babson College.

Bygrave, William, D. (1988). The structure of the investment networks of venture capital firms, *Journal of Business Venturing*, 3(2), 137–57.

Clarke, Christopher J., and Gall, François (1987). Planned divestment: a five-step approach, *Long Range Planning*, 20(1), 17–24.

Connell, David (1987). Bridging the gap between the academic researchers and industrial corporations, *Industrial Management and Data Systems*, Jan.–Feb., 19–24.

Devlin, Kathleen (1992). M&A no match for powerful IPO market, *Venture Capital Journal*, 32(2), 27–31.

Eisenhardt, K.M. (1989). Agency theory: an assessment and review, *Academy of Management Journal*, 28, 548–73.

EVCA (1992). *Venture Capital in Europe: 1992 EVCA Yearbook*, Zaventum: EVCA.

Fama, E., and Jensen, M. (1983). Separation of ownership and control, *Journal of Law and Economics*, 26, 301–25.

Granstrand, Ove, and Sjölander, Sören (1990). The acquisition of technology and small firms by large firms, *Journal of Economic Behaviour and Organization*, 13, 367–86.

Harris, M., and Raviv, A. (1979). Some results on incentive contracts with application to education and employment, health insurance, and law enforcement, *American Economic Review*, 68, 20–30.

Houlden, Brian (1990). Buy-outs and beyond: motivations, strategies and ownership changes, *Long Range Planning*, 23(4), 73–7.

Jensen, M. (1983). Organization theory and methodology, *Accounting Review*, 56, 319–38.

Jensen, M.C., and Meckling, W.H. (1976). Theory of the firm: managerial behaviour, agency costs and ownership structure, *Journal of Financial Economics*, 3, 301–25.

Lewis, William W., and Linden, Lawrence H. (1990). A new mission for corporate technology, *Sloan Management Review*, 31(4).

Lyon, John (1992). Look for an industrial partner from the very start, *Start-Up, the Newsletter for Europe's Seed Capital Network*, June, 8.

MacMillan, Ian C., and McGrath, Rita G. (1992). Technology strategy, market structure and executive teams. Unpublished working paper, Wharton School, University of Pennsylvania.

Merrifield, D. Bruce (1988). Industrial survival via management of technology, *Journal of Business Venturing*, 3(3), 172.

Myllyniemi, Tuija, Kauranen, Ilkka, Autio, Erkko, and Kaila, Martti M. (1990). *The Growth of New Technology-based Companies*, Helsinki: SITRA.

Radnor, Michael (1991). Technology acquisition strategies and processes: a reconsideration of the 'make versus buy' decision, *International Journal of Technology Management*, special issue on the role of technology in corporate policy, ed. Bela Gold.

Rind, Kenneth W., and Muskin, Martin (1987). 'Exiting' by disposition: negotiating an acquisition of your portfolio company. NASBIC Management Institute, July.

Ronstadt, Robert (1986). Exit, stage left: why entrepreneurs end their entrepreneurial careers before retirement, *Journal of Business Venturing*, 1(3), 322–38.

Thompson, J. (1967). *Organizations in Action*, New York: McGraw-Hill.

Wright, Mike, Chiplin, Brian, Thompson, Steve, and Robbie, Ken (1990). Realisations of venture capital investments: the case of management buy-outs in the UK, *Service Industries Journal*, 10(3), 499–520.

# 7

## REALIZING VALUE IN EUROPE: A PAN-EUROPEAN PERSPECTIVE

*William D. Bygrave and Daniel F. Muzyka*

### INTRODUCTION

Entrepreneurs' perceptions and attitudes are central to the issues raised in the preceding chapters on realizing the value of investments, and certain questions recur. First, what are the exit routes open to entrepreneurs and how do each of the specific methods of realization operate throughout Europe? Second, how do entrepreneurs view these alternative approaches for realizing enterprise value, and what assessments do they make of the advantages and disadvantages associated with a particular exit route – for example, initial public offerings, trade sales, management buy-outs, etc.?

Little or nothing has been known in a systematic way about how entrepreneurs in each of the European countries perceive the alternative methods available to them for realizing value in their businesses. Such material that we have had has been largely anecdotal and has lacked comparative dimensions – for example, comparisons among countries, comparison of IPOs with acquisitions.

A pan-European team was formed to study the key issue of entrepreneurs' perceptions of how to realize the value that they have created by funding and developing a successful enterprise. More specifically, eight leading European business schools, under the auspices of the European Foundation for Entrepreneurship Research (EFER) and Europe's Venture Capital Association (EVCA), examined the attitudes of venture-capital-backed entrepreneurs' to a number of crucial issues including:

- their preferred choice of funding (bank, individual investors, venture capital companies, etc.);
- the advantages and disadvantages of selling a business to its management or to an outside management;

- the case for and against seeking to raise financing or to exit via an initial public offering;
- The role that might usefully be played by a pan-European stock market targeting the needs of smaller companies offering stock to the public for the first time;
- the pros and cons of selling ownership to another operating company.

The names of the researchers who collaborated in this study, their schools, and the countries they covered are shown in Table 7.1. The project was coordinated at INSEAD, France.

Table 7.1  Research teams for the pan-European survey

| | |
|---|---|
| • **Pan-European:** | **INSEAD**, France – coordination |
| | *William Bygrave, Daniel Muzyka, Benoît Leleux* |
| • **Benelux:** | **Vlerick School of Management**, Belgium |
| | *Hubert Ooghe, Yves Fassin, Sophie Manigart, Bart Rogiers* |
| • **France:** | **Groupe ESC Lyon** |
| | *Rémy Paliard, Yves Romanet* |
| • **Germany:** | **Dortmund University** |
| | *Heinz Klandt, Bjorn Manstedten, Kai Thierhof* |
| • **Italy:** | **Bocconi University**, Milan |
| | *Sergio Pivato, Anna Gervasoni* |
| • **Scandinavia:** | **Linkoping University,** Sweden |
| | *Clas Wahlbin, Christer Olofsson* |
| • **Spain and Portugal:** | **IESE**, Spain |
| | *Ahmad Rahnema* |
| • **United Kingdom:** | **London Business School** |
| | *Michael Hay, Mark Bleackley* |

## GENESIS OF THE PAN-EUROPEAN STUDY

Concern among European venture capitalists about exit opportunities – especially flotations – at the beginning of the 1990s was the genesis of our pan-European study. At the EFER 91 Forum in Berlin, a group of venture capitalists (including both a former and a future chairman of evca), institutional investors, entrepreneurs and people involved in public policy issues met to plan a conference on realizing investments in private companies. One of us, Bill Bygrave, accepted an invitation to be Academic Chairman of the

EFER 92 Forum entitled Realizing Enterprise Value: IPOs, Trade Sales, Buy-backs, MBOs, and Harvests, which was subsequently held at the London Business School in December 1992. The practitioners felt that there was a need to understand European entrepreneurs' attitudes towards the financing and harvesting of their companies. It was agreed that a survey would be made of venture-capital-backed entrepreneurs throughout Europe and the results would be presented at the EFER 92 Forum.

## METHOD

The study itself took the form of an attitude survey administered to entrepreneurs in each participating country. The same questionnaire, translated into the appropriate language, was used for each country. The first entrepreneurs to be surveyed were identified by venture capital firms in each country. The initial sample was limited to venture-backed companies in order to restrict it to only high-potential ventures. A prototype questionnaire was circulated to a number of leading venture capitalists to get feedback on the questions from practitioners. Their feedback was used to modify it. Next it was tested on a number of entrepreneurs in each of the nations involved in the survey. Then it was modified again. The final survey instrument, shown in the Appendix to this chapter, contained approximately 100 questions. For most of the opinion questions, the survey used a 5 point Likert scale: Strongly Agree, Agree, Indifferent, Disagree, Strongly Disagree, plus a Don't Know.

The questionnaire was mailed in September and October 1992 to CEOs of venture-capital-backed companies whose names and addresses were supplied by venture capital firms in each of the countries in the study, and 322 usable replies were received. To guarantee their anonymity, entrepreneurs were allowed to return the questionnaires without their name and address. Hence it was not possible to pursue those who did not respond to the initial mailing. Of the 322 records in the data base, 30 per cent were from France, 18 per cent the U.K., 13 per cent Scandinavia, 12 per cent Germany, 8 per cent Spain, 8 per cent Italy, 8 per cent Belgium and 3 per cent The Netherlands.

## RESULTS

This is an ongoing study that encompasses a broad range of issues. In this chapter, we are focusing on the key issues from a pan-European perspective, but there are glimpses of national differences. Subsequent articles will delve into more detail, especially from the perspective of individual nations.

## Characteristics of the companies

Of the companies 61 per cent were in manufacturing industries, 24 per cent service, 9 per cent distribution and 6 per cent retail/wholesale. They had an average of 277 employees (see Table 7.2). They were rapidly growing companies with an average growth rate of turnover from 1990 to 1991 of 18 per cent. On average, 38 per cent of their turnover was exported.

Managers and relatives owned or effectively controlled just under 50 per cent of the shares of the companies; venture capitalists were the next largest shareholders, with 27 per cent; followed by other companies, with 10 per cent (see Table 7.3).

When asked how they came to be in charge of their firm, 37 per cent of the CEOs said that they founded it, 12 per cent that they bought it, 12 per cent that they inherited it, 34 per cent that they were appointed CEO, and the remaining 5 per cent said by other means (Table 7.4). The CEOs have a significant portion of their net worth tied up in the firm (53 per cent on average). Put differently, their personal fortunes depend to a large extent on the financial success of their firms. Hence it seems reasonable to expect that this group of CEOs is knowledgeable about realizing value in their companies.

## Financing their companies

For long-term capital the first choice of our sample CEOs is to use retained earnings, followed by borrowing money from financial institutions, banks and venture capitalists (Figure 7.1). Next choice is an initial public stock offering, then selling equity to venture capitalists, financial institutions, another company and wealthy individuals, in that order. Thus they prefer to borrow rather than sell equity to finance their companies. However, their answers showed that they have a strong aversion to borrowing from family or friends, with more than 70 per cent disliking each of those two sources. Nor do they like to raise money by selling equity to family and friends (more than 70 per cent disliked those two sources).

In general, our group of CEOs prefer to use formal sources (banks, financial institutions, venture capitalists) of outside capital rather than informal ones (angels, family, friends). And they would rather not give up any equity to get their capital.

For advice on financial matters they turn most often to their bankers, then their directors, investors, managers, and accountants (Figure 7.2). More than half of the respondents have never sought financial advice from fellow entrepreneurs, or lawyers, or consultants, or friends, or family, or public agencies. Last and definitely least used as a source of financial advice are academics, ignored by 86 per cent of our CEOs.

**Table 7.2  Characteristics of the companies in the pan-European survey, 1992**

| | Questionnaires | | No. by sector of activity | | No. of full-time employees | | Turnover growth rate for previous year | | Real industry growth rate for previous year | | | | | | % turnover exported | | Founding year of companies | |
|---|---|---|---|---|---|---|---|---|---|---|---|---|---|---|---|---|---|---|
| | No. | % of total | (1) | (2) | Mean | Median | Mean % | Median % | < 0 | 0–5 | 6–10 | 11–20 | 21–30 | > 30 | Mean % | Median % | Mean | Median |
| Belgium | 24 | 7.5 | 8 | 16 | 301 | 130 | 23.7 | 17.5 | 3 | 8 | 4 | 5 | 1 | 3 | 69.9 | 77.5 | 1954 | 1966 |
| France | 96 | 29.8 | 30 | 66 | 222 | 120 | 14.0 | 10 | 11 | 39 | 22 | 13 | 6 | 4 | 29.9 | 20.0 | 1957 | 1966 |
| Germany | 37 | 11.5 | 13 | 23 | 146 | 90 | 26.6 | 25 | 0 | 5 | 14 | 13 | 3 | 1 | 23.8 | 17.5 | 1967 | 1980 |
| Italy | 27 | 8.4 | 6 | 21 | 182 | 182 | 0.6 | 0.5 | 5 | 10 | 6 | 1 | 2 | 3 | 34.6 | 30.0 | 1972 | 1976 |
| Netherlands | 11 | 3.4 | 4 | 7 | 674 | 270 | 28.6 | 11 | 0 | 2 | 6 | 2 | 0 | 1 | 59.6 | 60.0 | 1963 | 1982 |
| Scandinavia | 43 | 13.3 | 13 | 30 | 185 | 70 | 15.7 | 15.5 | 6 | 15 | 6 | 6 | 2 | 6 | 48.4 | 52.0 | 1968 | 1983 |
| Spain | 25 | 7.8 | 20 | 4 | 200 | 40 | 19.8 | 10 | 1 | 7 | 7 | 7 | 0 | 1 | 21.5 | 1.5 | 1975 | 1985 |
| United Kingdom | 59 | 18.3 | 30 | 29 | 457 | 200 | 22.8 | 10 | 16 | 25 | 4 | 5 | 2 | 6 | 37.0 | 30.0 | 1973 | 1984 |
| Total | 322 | 100.0 | 124 | 196 | 277 | 123 | 18.0 | 10 | 42 | 111 | 69 | 52 | 16 | 25 | 37.7 | 30 | 1965 | 1979 |
| % distribution | | | 38.8 | 61.2 | | | | | 13.3 | 35.2 | 21.9 | 16.5 | 5.1 | 7.9 | | | | |

(1):  Service/distribution/retailing or wholesaling.
(2):  Manufacturing.

Scandinavia: Sweden, Norway, Finland, Denmark

**Table 7.3 Ownership distribution of companies in the sample (per cent)**

| | | Distribution of company share ownership[1] | | | | | | Shares effectively controlled by CEO and relatives |
|---|---|---|---|---|---|---|---|---|
| | Owner-manager | Owner-managers' families | Company employees | Other individuals | Banks | Venture capitalists | Other companies | |
| Belgium | 37 | 10 | 0.8 | 4.0 | 0.5 | 26.3 | 20.7 | 24.7 |
| France | 49 | 11 | 5.7 | 3.9 | 4.7 | 18.9 | 6.1 | 71.3 |
| Germany | 39 | 13 | 1.1 | 6.5 | 0.7 | 24.1 | 8.7 | 59.6 |
| Italy | 17 | 28 | 0.3 | 4.3 | 11.5 | 8.5 | 0.0 | 62.8 |
| Netherlands | 20 | n.a. | 4.6 | 2.9 | 10.0 | 51.4 | 7.7 | 22.2 |
| Scandinavia | 31 | n.a. | 2.6 | 9.1 | 3.8 | 36.0 | 13.5 | 29.8 |
| Spain | 39 | 26 | 2.2 | 10.6 | 5.4 | 1.5 | 26.8 | 45.9 |
| United Kingdom | 28 | 1 | 3.2 | 5.2 | 3.3 | 51.5 | 7.2 | 23.5 |
| Overall | 36.1 | 8.9 | 3.2 | 5.7 | 4.3 | 27.2 | 9.8 | 49.2 |

n.a. stands for missing data or sample size lower than 5 for the category

[1] The sum does not reach 100% because the 'other' category is not reported in the figure. Individual respondent errors lead to figures larger than 100% for Spain.

**Table 7.4 Involvement with their firms of CEOs in the sample**

| | Number of years in charge of the firm | | Method used to gain control of company[1] | | | | Per cent of personal net worth tied up in the firm | |
|---|---|---|---|---|---|---|---|---|
| | Mean | Median | Founded it (%) | Bought it (%) | Inherited it (%) | Appointed manager (%) | Mean (%) | Median (%) |
| Belgium | 8.7 | 8.0 | 29 | 14 | 19 | 33 | 39.4 | 25 |
| France | 11.9 | 10.0 | 35 | 17 | 17 | 30 | 65.5 | 70 |
| Germany | 9.7 | 7.5 | 53 | 3 | 20 | 20 | 57.4 | 50 |
| Italy | 7.4 | 5.5 | 23 | 14 | 27 | 36 | 47.5 | 50 |
| Netherlands | 6.0 | 5.0 | 33 | 11 | 0 | 44 | 47.6 | 30 |
| Scandinavia | 6.2 | 5.0 | 27 | 5 | 2 | 56 | 45.5 | 35 |
| Spain | 5.1 | 5.0 | 60 | 0 | 8 | 32 | 50.4 | 50 |
| United Kingdom | 5.7 | 4.0 | 40 | 19 | 0 | 29 | 40.9 | 30 |
| Overall | 8.4 | 6.0 | 37 | 12 | 12 | 34 | 52.5 | 50 |

[1] Excludes the 'other means' category so figures do not sum to 100%.

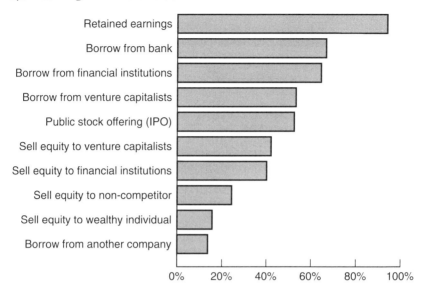

*Figure 7.1 Entrepreneurs' preferred sources of long-term capital (per cent of sample)*

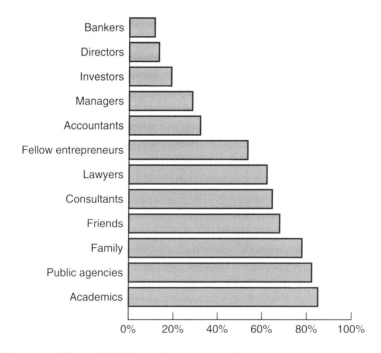

*Figure 7.2 Financial information: sources the entrepreneurs never consulted (per cent of sample)*

## Trade sales

Of the CEOs 75 per cent would consider selling shares in their companies to another firm; 79 per cent would consider selling all their company to a non-competitor firm; and 70 per cent would consider selling it to a competitor. They were aware of the risks of being replaced after a trade sale: 54 per cent agreed that selling out to another company might lead to the CEO and managers being replaced, as against 20 per cent who disagreed (Table 7.5). But they were also aware of the advantages of a trade sale versus an initial public offering: 75 per cent thought that a trade sale was easier than an IPO (as against 9 per cent with the opposite opinion); 78 per cent agreed that a trade sale was cheaper than an IPO (as against 2 per cent who disagreed); and 49 per cent felt that a trade sale involved fewer dealings with the financial community than an IPO (as against 23 per cent who disagreed). They were split as to whether a trade sale would place a higher value on their companies than an IPO, or vice versa (33 per cent agreed that it did, 25 per cent disagreed, and 30 per cent were indifferent).

## MBOs and MBIs

An overwhelming majority of the sample of CEOs had the opinion that MBOs reinforce motivation of the managers and the performance of the firm – 78 per cent versus 6 per cent (Table 7.6). But it appears that their convictions about outcomes are not nearly as strong because only half of them disagreed with the statement that MBOs are rarely successful (versus 21 per cent who agreed, and 18 per cent who were indifferent).

CEOs who did not believe that an MBO placed a higher valuation on a company than an IPO made up 40 per cent (versus 14 per cent who believed that it did). And very similarly, 38 per cent did not believe that an MBO valued a company higher than a trade sale (versus 15 per cent who believed that it did).

In response to questions about the types of firms that are suitable targets for MBOs, 73 per cent disagreed with the statement that only large firms were suitable candidates for IPOs (only 9 per cent agreed); they were divided as to whether only very profitable firms were suitable candidates for leveraged buy-outs (38 per cent agreeing and 35 per cent disagreeing); and 64 per cent agreed that MBOs can solve succession problems (13 per cent disagreed). So there was an overwhelming sentiment that smaller firms were fitting targets for MBOs, and that MBOs can solve succession problems.

These CEOs recognized that a company acquired by an MBO was quite likely to be sold in the future to another company (50 per cent agreed whereas 22 per cent disagreed).

**Table 7.5  Attitudes of CEOs in the sample towards trade sales as an exit route**

| | Strongly agree | Agree | Indifferent | Disagree | Strongly disagree | No opinion |
|---|---|---|---|---|---|---|
| It is easier to sell shares to another company than to float on the stock market | 52 (16.5%) | 185 (58.5%) | 35 (11.1%) | 24 (7.6%) | 4 (1.3%) | 16 (5.1%) |
| The expenses associated with selling shares to another company are less than those of a stock market flotation | 69 (24.8%) | 169 (53.5%) | 36 (11.4%) | 6 (1.9%) | 0 (0.0%) | 36 (11.4%) |
| Another company would place a higher valuation on my firm than a public stock flotation would | 20 (6.3%) | 83 (26.3%) | 95 (30.2%) | 72 (22.9%) | 8 (2.5%) | 37 (11.7%) |
| I would not have to spend any time dealing with the financial community if I had a company rather than the public invest in my firm | 29 (9.2%) | 126 (40.1%) | 63 (20.1%) | 62 (19.7%) | 9 (2.9%) | 25 (8.0%) |
| By selling stock to another company, my firm could get strategic assistance | 51 (16.1%) | 169 (53.5%) | 53 (16.8%) | 21 (6.6%) | 3 (0.9%) | 19 (6.0%) |
| If I sold a minority share of my firm to another company, I would have less managerial control than if I get a stock market listing | 24 (7.6%) | 85 (26.9%) | 62 (19.6%) | 99 (31.3%) | 23 (7.3%) | 23 (7.3%) |
| If I sold a majority interest in my firm to another company, I would be concerned that my managers and I might be replaced | 50 (15.9%) | 121 (38.5%) | 61 (19.4%) | 50 (15.9%) | 13 (4.1%) | 19 (6.1%) |

Exactly half of the CEOs of non-MBO companies would consider an MBO/MBI for their companies.

There were some very striking national differences in the answers by CEOs to the MBO/MBI questions, most noticeably between the UK and France, which have the highest level of MBO/MBI activity in Europe (Table 7.7). In general, it seems to show that the French have more reservations about MBOs than the British.

## IPOs

Our group of CEOs appeared to be quite well informed about the pros and cons of raising capital through an initial public offerings (Table 7.8). Here are what they considered to be the cons:

- Fees and commissions associated with stock-market flotations are too high (59 per cent agreed, 12 per cent disagreed);
- Managers of listed companies are forced to manage for short-term profits (54 per cent agreed, 24 per cent disagreed);
- It is difficult to maintain investor interest in small companies after the initial listing on the stock market (59 per cent agreed, 12 per cent disagreed);
- In general, investment banks neglect small company shares after the initial listing (57 per cent agreed, 6 per cent disagreed);
- Listed companies are vulnerable to unfriendly takeovers (51 per cent agreed, 19 per cent disagreed).

And here are their pros:

- A company gains considerable prestige by being listed on a public stock market (67 per cent agreed, 8 per cent disagreed);
- In general, a listed company can raise capital more easily than a non-listed company (65 per cent agreed, 13 per cent disagreed);
- A stock-market listing in more than one country strengthens a company's competitive position (45 per cent agreed, 11 per cent disagreed);
- In general, a stock market flotation places the highest valuation on a company (35 per cent agreed, 25 per cent disagreed).

The last pro appears to conflict with the response to an earlier question on trade sales that stated, 'Another company would place a higher valuation on my firm than a public stock flotation would.' (where 33 per cent agreed and 25 per cent disagreed, see Table 7.5). We think the explanation lies in the wording: the IPO question refers to companies in general, whereas the trade sale question refers to the CEO's own company.

**Table 7.6  Attitudes of CEOs towards MBO/MBI as exit routes**

| | Strongly agree | Agree | Indifferent | Disagree | Strongly disagree | No opinion |
|---|---|---|---|---|---|---|
| MBOs and MBIs are rarely successful | 7 (2.2%) | 60 (19.0%) | 56 (17.8%) | 117 (37.1%) | 40 (12.7%) | 35 (11.1%) |
| MBOs often result in the firm subsequently being sold to another company | 18 (5.7%) | 141 (44.8%) | 45 (14.3%) | 63 (20.0%) | 6 (1.9%) | 42 (13.3%) |
| It is difficult to find a group of managers inside the firm who are able and willing to buy the firm | 29 (9.2%) | 115 (36.5%) | 53 (16.8%) | 75 (23.8%) | 24 (7.6%) | 19 (6.0%) |
| MBOs are a good way to solve the succession problem | 45 (14.3%) | 158 (50.2%) | 44 (14.0%) | 29 (9.2%) | 13 (4.1%) | 26 (8.3%) |
| MBOs are suitable only for larger firms | 2 (0.6%) | 25 (8.0%) | 38 (12.2%) | 165 (53.1%) | 62 (19.9%) | 19 (6.1%) |
| MBIs rarely succeed because of the difficulties the new managerment team encounters with the existing employees | 12 (3.8%) | 53 (16.8%) | 85 (26.9%) | 89 (28.2%) | 26 (8.2%) | 51 (16.1%) |
| Only firms that are very profitable are suitable candidates for LBOs and LBIs | 51 (16.2%) | 99 (31.5%) | 31 (9.9%) | 89 (28.2%) | 22 (7.0%) | 22 (7.0%) |

**Table 7.6 continued**

| | Strongly agree | Agree | Indifferent | Disagree | Strongly disagree | No opinion |
|---|---|---|---|---|---|---|
| It is less dangerous for the firm to sell shares to another operating company than to implement an MBO | 29 (9.3%) | 87 (27.9%) | 57 (18.3%) | 86 (27.6%) | 21 (6.7%) | 32 (10.3%) |
| MBOs reinforce the motivation of the managers and strengthens the firm's performance | 84 (27.0%) | 159 (51.1%) | 31 (9.9%) | 8 (2.6%) | 10 (3.2%) | 19 (6.1%) |
| After an MBO the entrepreneur should stay totally away from the firm | 53 (16.8%) | 80 (25.4%) | 59 (18.7%) | 60 (19.0%) | 36 (11.4%) | 27 (8.6%) |
| An MBO or MBI values the company higher than a public stock offering | 3 (1.0%) | 40 (12.8%) | 71 (22.8%) | 100 (32.1%) | 26 (8.3%) | 72 (23.1%) |
| An MBO or MBI values the company higher than selling shares to another company | 6 (2.1%) | 36 (12.7%) | 77 (27.1%) | 91 (32.0%) | 18 (6.3%) | 56 (19.7%) |

**Table 7.7 Country-specific attitudes towards MBO/MBI as exit routes (mean percentage of respondents in each country agreeing or strongly agreeing with the statement)**

| | Belgium | France | Germany | Italy | Nether-lands | Scan-dinavia | Spain | United Kingdom |
|---|---|---|---|---|---|---|---|---|
| MBOs and MBIs are rarely successful | 4.2 | 42.7 | 12.1 | 4.0 | 0.0 | 16.3 | 50.0 | 1.7 |
| MBOs often result in the firm subsequently being sold to another company | 33.4 | 58.3 | 21.2 | 36.0 | 27.3 | 37.2 | 66.6 | 74.6 |
| It is difficult to find a group of managers inside the firm who are able and willing to buy the firm | 25.0 | 50.5 | 63.6 | 36.0 | 36.6 | 39.5 | 64.0 | 39.0 |
| MBOs are a good way to solve the succession problem | 66.7 | 72.6 | 78.8 | 60.0 | 63.6 | 44.2 | 64.0 | 59.3 |
| MBOs are suitable only for larger firms | 4.3 | 5.3 | 3.0 | 34.8 | 0.0 | 9.5 | 12.0 | 6.8 |
| MBIs rarely succeed because of the difficulties the new management team encounters with the existing employees | 16.7 | 22.9 | 9.1 | 24.0 | 9.1 | 39.6 | 20.0 | 11.8 |
| Only firms that are very profitable are suitable candidates for LBOs and LBIs | 45.8 | 71.9 | 36.4 | 64.0 | 9.1 | 44.2 | 41.6 | 20.7 |

**Table 7.7 continued**

| | Belgium | France | Germany | Italy | Netherlands | Scandinavia | Spain | United Kingdom |
|---|---|---|---|---|---|---|---|---|
| It is less dangerous for the firm to sell shares to another operating company than to implement an MBO | 41.6 | 55.3 | 18.7 | 45.8 | 18.2 | 37.2 | 36.0 | 16.9 |
| MBOs reinforce the motivation of the managers and strengthen the firm's performance | 90.9 | 75.8 | 75.8 | 60.9 | 72.7 | 81.4 | 60.0 | 91.5 |
| After an MBO the entrepreneur should stay totally away from the firm | 50.0 | 52.1 | 63.6 | 28.0 | 63.6 | 46.5 | 8.1 | 24.1 |
| An MBO or MBI values the company higher than a public stock offering | 0.0 | 7.3 | 18.2 | 23.8 | 18.2 | 16.3 | 32.0 | 13.6 |
| An MBO or MBI values the company higher than selling shares to another company | 0.0 | 8.3 | 26.7 | n.a. | 9.1 | 16.2 | 24.0 | 21.4 |

n.a. is not available due to limited sample size.

**Table 7.8 Attitudes of CEOs towards initial public offerings or equity shares as exit routes**

| | Strongly agree | Agree | Indifferent | Disagree | Strongly disagree | No opinion |
|---|---|---|---|---|---|---|
| Fees and commissions associated with stock-market flotations are too expensive | 39 (12.7%) | 142 (46.3%) | 39 (12.7%) | 34 (11.1%) | 4 (1.3%) | 49 (16.0%) |
| Managers of listed companies are forced to manage for short-term profits | 28 (9.2%) | 137 (44.8%) | 43 (14.1%) | 58 (19.0%) | 16 (5.2%) | 24 (7.8%) |
| Listed companies have to reveal too much information to the public | 16 (5.2%) | 104 (33.9%) | 75 (24.4%) | 79 (25.7%) | 14 (4.6%) | 19 (6.2%) |
| Chief executives of listed companies have to spend too much time dealing with the financial community | 21 (6.9%) | 118 (38.6%) | 71 (23.2%) | 62 (20.3%) | 10 (3.3%) | 24 (7.8%) |
| Listed companies are vulnerable to unfriendly takeovers | 19 (6.2%) | 137 (44.9%) | 64 (21.0%) | 45 (14.8%) | 12 (3.9%) | 28 (9.2%) |
| Shares of small companies that have gone public have performed poorly in the last few years | 41 (13.4%) | 105 (34.2%) | 57 (18.6%) | 46 (15.0%) | 2 (0.7%) | 56 (18.2%) |
| It is difficult to maintain investor interest in small companies after the initial listing on the stock market | 37 (12.0%) | 146 (47.4%) | 46 (14.9%) | 33 (10.7%) | 3 (1.0%) | 43 (14.0%) |

**Table 7.8** continued

| | Strongly agree | Agree | Indifferent | Disagree | Strongly disagree | No opinion |
|---|---|---|---|---|---|---|
| In general, investment banks neglect small company shares after the initial listing | 25 (8.3%) | 147 (48.7%) | 45 (14.9%) | 17 (5.6%) | 1 (0.3%) | 67 (22.2%) |
| In general, a stock-market flotation places the highest valuation on a company | 19 (6.2%) | 89 (29.0%) | 72 (23.5%) | 68 (22.1%) | 9 (2.9%) | 50 (16.3%) |
| A company gains considerable prestige by being listed on a public stock market | 40 (13.1%) | 164 (53.8%) | 53 (17.4%) | 21 (6.9%) | 2 (0.7%) | 25 (8.2%) |
| In general, a listed company can raise capital more easily than a non-listed company | 35 (11.5%) | 161 (53.0%) | 45 (14.8%) | 36 (11.8%) | 2 (0.7%) | 25 (8.2%) |
| A stock exchange flotation is the best way of enabling stockholders to realize the value of their investment | 29 (9.4%) | 115 (37.5%) | 70 (22.8%) | 59 (19.2%) | 5 (1.6%) | 29 (9.4%) |
| A listed company gets better terms from its lenders than a non-listed company | 16 (5.2%) | 113 (36.9%) | 77 (25.2%) | 48 (15.7%) | 4 (1.3%) | 48 (15.7%) |
| Getting listed in more than one country strengthens a company's competitive position | 27 (8.9%) | 111 (36.5%) | 75 (24.7%) | 31 (10.2%) | 2 (0.7%) | 58 (19.1%) |

Table 7.9 Country-specific attitudes towards initial public offerings of equity shares as exit routes (mean percentage of respondents in each country agreeing or strongly agreeing with the statement)

| | Belgium | France | Germany | Italy | Netherlands | Scandinavia | Spain | United Kingdom |
|---|---|---|---|---|---|---|---|---|
| Fees and commissions associated with stock-market flotations are too expensive | 47.8 | 49.5 | 50.0 | 77.3 | 72.7 | 48.8 | 40.0 | 48.8 |
| Managers of listed companies are forced to manage for short-term profits | 52.2 | 40.0 | 32.3 | 47.6 | 45.4 | 62.8 | 12.5 | 62.8 |
| Listed companies have to reveal too much information to the public | 78.3 | 40.0 | 46.7 | 54.5 | 81.8 | 44.2 | 32.0 | 44.2 |
| Chief executives of listed companies have to spend too much time dealing with the financial community | 60.9 | 63.8 | 36.7 | 28.6 | 63.6 | 41.9 | 12.0 | 41.9 |
| Listed companies are vulnerable to unfriendly takeovers | 43.5 | 61.7 | 62.1 | 27.3 | 63.6 | 67.2 | 32.0 | 67.2 |
| Share of small companies that have gone public have performed poorly in the last few years | 43.5 | 27.7 | 46.6 | 68.2 | 63.6 | 58.2 | 24.0 | 58.2 |
| It is difficult to maintain investor interest in small companies after the initial listing on the stock market | 60.9 | 59.6 | 61.3 | 41.2 | 90.9 | 60.5 | 20.0 | 60.5 |

**Table 7.9 continued**

| | Belgium | France | Germany | Italy | Nether-lands | Scan-dinavia | Spain | United Kingdom |
|---|---|---|---|---|---|---|---|---|
| In general, investment banks neglect small company shares after the initial listing | 50.0 | 62.8 | 43.4 | 38.9 | 72.7 | 51.2 | 52.0 | 51.2 |
| In general, a stock-market flotation places the highest valuation on a company | 39.1 | 39.4 | 20.0 | 59.1 | 18.2 | 37.2 | 76.0 | 37.2 |
| A company gains considerable prestige by being listed on a public stock market | 82.6 | 40.4 | 73.3 | 40.0 | 81.8 | 76.7 | 64.0 | 76.7 |
| In general, a listed company can raise capital more easily than a non-listed company | 47.8 | 54.3 | 75.9 | 40.0 | 63.6 | 60.5 | 76.0 | 60.5 |
| A stock exchange flotation is the best way of enabling stockholders to realize the value of their investment | 45.5 | 30.8 | 53.3 | 18.2 | 63.6 | 69.8 | 52.0 | 69.8 |
| A listed company gets better terms from its lenders than a non-listed company | 26.1 | 48.9 | 30.0 | 57.1 | 36.4 | 44.2 | 68.0 | 44.2 |
| Getting listed in more than one country strengthens a company's competitive position | 45.4 | 50.0 | 56.7 | 47.4 | 36.4 | 44.2 | 80.0 | 44.2 |

Spanish and Italian CEOs were much more likely to believe that a stock-market flotation placed the highest value on a company than were Dutch, German, British and French CEOs (Table 7.9). However, British, German, Swedish and Dutch CEOs were more likely to agree that a flotation was the best way of enabling stockholders to realize the value of their investment than were Italian and, to a lesser extent, French CEOs.

## DISCUSSION

The companies in our sample were on average growing robustly at a time when the European economies were sluggish. That's good news for the venture capitalists that backed them. The exception were the Italian firms, which were barely growing on average. As yet we have no convincing explanation for the slow growth of the Italian firms in our sample.

One of the overall findings of the survey was that there is not a single uniform view from Europe. While there may be a general tendency on many of the issues – and we have tried to present that – there is a great deal of variation in opinions concerning various aspects of IPOs, trade sales, and particularly, MBOs/MBIs. Statistical analysis reveals that with regard to many of the questions, there are significant differences in the pattern of responses country to country.

For instance, there are some very significant differences by country in the pattern of responses to the question of which sources of information and advice are most consulted (and how often). Similarly, there are significant differences in relative perceptions of various sources of long-term capital by country, Figure 7.3 illustrates the range of repsonses on the questions regarding the desirability of various sources of long-term capital. The implications of this are that while we can draw an overall sense of a European view from the survey, we still need to be mindful of the impact of the significant structural and behavioural differences within Europe.

For financing their companies, CEOs ranked retained earnings first, borrowing second, and selling equity third. Their preferences were rational from the perspectives of cost of capital and control of their companies (under asymmetric information, see Myers and Majluf, 1984); and – not incidentally – from the perspective of their personal wealth, as they had a significant part of their personal net worth tied to the success of their companies. Our CEOs were reluctant to involve family and friends in financing their companies.

Our CEOs viewed trade sales favourably, by and large. They thought trades sales were cheaper than IPOs, easier to execute and less costly in time.

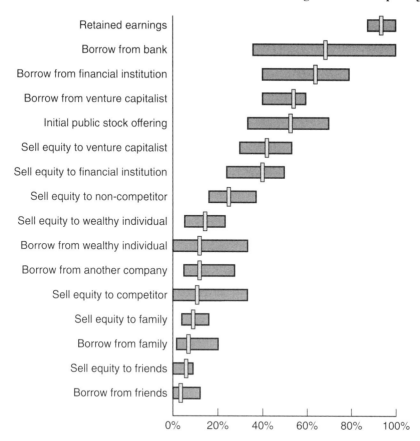

*Figure 7.3 Preferred sources of long-term capital (percentage responding 'like' or 'most like' and range of averages by country)*

Their attitudes towards trade sales in comparison with IPOs reflect the trends in Europe in recent years when trade sales have outnumbered IPOs; for instance, in 1991 trade sales accounted for 41 per cent of divestments by value, and stock flotations for only 10 per cent (EVCA, 1992).

In general, MBOs were thought to increase the motivation of the CEO and managers. That is in accord with agency theory (Fama and Jensen, 1983), which is one of the theoretical justifications for MBOs/MBIs (Jensen, 1991). But with respect to outcomes, the British CEOs were much more optimistic than the French. Almost 43 per cent of the French as against 2 per cent of the British believed that MBOs were rarely successful; 72 per cent of the French as against 21 per cent of the British thought that only very profitable firms were suitable targets for leveraged buy-outs; and only 32 per cent of the French as against 68 per cent of the British CEOs would consider an MBO for their firm. We know of no evidence that British MBOs/MBIs are more successful than French ones, so there is no glaringly obvious explanation of the British optimistic attitude. There are differences in the nature of MBOs/MBIs between the two nations. For instance, French MBO/MBI targets are substantially larger companies; a greater percentage of French MBOs/MBIs are family businesses (53 per cent in France and 32 per cent in the UK); a smaller percentage are domestic divestments by larger companies (24 per cent in France and 43 per cent in the UK) (Wright et al., 1992); and there are greater levels of protection of managers and employees in France (Franks and Mayer, 1990). Those may account for some of the differences in the perceptions of the French and British CEOs towards MBOs/MBIs. However, the British optimism may simply be due to the fact that the British CEOs are more familiar than the French with MBOs/MBIs. The differences in the perceptions of the French and the British CEOs correlate with the activity level of MBOs/MBIs in the two nations: from 1980 through 1991, there were 4176 MBOs/MBIs in the UK compared with 700 in France (a ratio of 6:1). By the beginning of the 1990s, that ratio had declined somewhat, but it is holding steady at around 4:1 (Wright et al., 1992).

Perhaps the most remarkable finding about the CEOs' attitudes towards IPOs was that they were still regarded positively in Europe despite unremitting bad news about secondary stock markets in the UK, France and The Netherlands. There were different perceptions among the nations and as might be expected, Dutch, British and French were not as upbeat as others. The Spanish CEOs were particularly sanguine.

Overall, 63 per cent of the CEOs of private companies said they would consider taking their company public on their national stock exchange. And what's more, they said that they would be more likely to take their companies public if a pan-European stock market existed (41 per cent agreed, 19 per cent disagreed).

## IMPLICATIONS

It is estimated that as many as 17 000 European companies received equity venture capital during the past decade (Batchelor, 1992). The majority of those investments have yet to be harvested, and the entrepreneurs and their venture capital backers will be looking to realize their investments. Of course, not all of them will be seeking a flotation, but flourishing stock markets will be essential for putting a price on these businesses. The secondary markets in Amsterdam, Brussels, London, Paris and other European financial centres have been struggling to maintain and even establish viable trading volumes. London scrapped its third market in 1990 and has announced its intention to close down its USM (Batchelor, 1992).

One of the important reasons for the decline of secondary markets is simply economics: the promoters, market-makers and stockbrokers cannot make an adequate profit on the low trading volumes. Hence they cannot afford to provide the level of support post-IPO that the CEOs expect (Onians, 1992).

Some CEOs might believe that they don't need a viable stock market because they believe they can realize their investments with a trade sale or an MBO/MBI. Leaving aside the fact that trade sales and MBOs/MBIs result in loss of control, they should ask themselves what determines the price of a trade sale or an MBO/MBI? It is usually the price-to-earnings ratio of comparable companies listed on public stock exchanges. Recent experience in the UK, where small-capitalization stocks have recently been out of favour, shows that price-to-earnings ratios realized on trade sales of smaller companies have been falling (Wright, et al., 1992). The sharp fall-off in the number of acquisitions in the UK has also probably depressed takeover prices.

British venture capital firms are alarmed by the proposed closure of the USM. A number of firms, including Causeway Capital, Grosvenor Ventures, Legal & General, Schroder Ventures and 3*i*, have joined together under the leadership of Ronald Cohen of Apax Partners to urge the London Stock Exchange to retain the USM if an alternative second market cannot be formed. According to Cohen the proposed closing of the USM will severely hamper the creation of business and jobs. He said, 'Unless a young company can have access to the public market at an earlier stage than is now possible there will be a brake put upon enterprises' (Batchelor, 1992).

While European stock markets for small-capitalization stocks are floundering in Europe, Nasdaq in the USA is thriving with the Nasdaq index hitting all-time highs. It lists 4000 stocks. It has on average 12 market-makers for each one of its stocks. And 98 per cent of its top 2200 companies are subject to regular analysts' reports (Wall, 1992). In the last couple of years it has set new records for initial public offerings. It appears that Nasdaq is trying to meet the concerns expressed by the CEOs in our survey. Small wonder that more and more European venture-capital-backed companies are having stock flotations on Nasdaq rather than on their national markets in Europe. Nasdaq now lists 181 European stocks. Nasdaq has tried to establish links with European exchanges but has been unsuccessful because it has not found a local partner who does not see it as a threat, according to its executive vice president, John Wall (1992).

Nasdaq has proven that a nationwide electronic stock market can be a huge success. It seems to us that the time has come to set up the European equivalent of Nasdaq. Our survey shows that CEOs of venture-capital-backed companies are interested in a pan-European stock market. The venture capital industry would welcome it. Perhaps it is now up to European policymakers in Brussels to take the initiative.

## APPENDIX TO CHAPTER 6

## QUESTIONNAIRE OF THE PAN-EUROPEAN SURVEY OF VENTURE-BACKED ENTREPRENEURS, 1992

### Q1
How regularly do you seek advice from each of the following sources about how to finance your company?

*(please circle one number in each row)*

| | | Weekly | Monthly | Quarterly | Yearly | Never |
|---|---|---|---|---|---|---|
| 1 | Your managers | 1 | 2 | 3 | 4 | 5 |
| 2 | Your accounting firm | 1 | 2 | 3 | 4 | 5 |
| 3 | Your board of directors | 1 | 2 | 3 | 4 | 5 |
| 4 | Your lawyer | 1 | 2 | 3 | 4 | 5 |
| 5 | Your investors | 1 | 2 | 3 | 4 | 5 |
| 6 | Your bankers (commercial & investment) | 1 | 2 | 3 | 4 | 5 |
| 7 | Consultants | 1 | 2 | 3 | 4 | 5 |
| 8 | Family | 1 | 2 | 3 | 4 | 5 |
| 9 | Fellow entrepreneurs | 1 | 2 | 3 | 4 | 5 |
| 10 | Friends | 1 | 2 | 3 | 4 | 5 |
| 11 | Academicians | 1 | 2 | 3 | 4 | 5 |
| 12 | Public agencies | 1 | 2 | 3 | 4 | 5 |
| 13 | Others (*please specify*) | | | | | |

### Q2
Suppose your firm could get long-term capital by any of the methods listed below. Please indicate how much your firm would like each method.

*(please circle one number in each row)*

| | | Most Dislike | Dislike | Indifferent | Like | Most Like | No Opinion |
|---|---|---|---|---|---|---|---|
| 1 | Borrow from a bank | 1 | 2 | 3 | 4 | 5 | 0 |
| 2 | Borrow from a financial institution | 1 | 2 | 3 | 4 | 5 | 0 |
| 3 | Borrow from family | 1 | 2 | 3 | 4 | 5 | 0 |
| 4 | Borrow from friends | 1 | 2 | 3 | 4 | 5 | 0 |
| 5 | Borrow from wealthy individuals | 1 | 2 | 3 | 4 | 5 | 0 |
| 6 | Borrow from another company | 1 | 2 | 3 | 4 | 5 | 0 |
| 7 | Retain earnings generated by your company | 1 | 2 | 3 | 4 | 5 | 0 |
| 8 | Sell equity to a financial institution | 1 | 2 | 3 | 4 | 5 | 0 |
| 9 | Sell equity to family | 1 | 2 | 3 | 4 | 5 | 0 |
| 10 | Sell equity to friends | 1 | 2 | 3 | 4 | 5 | 0 |
| 11 | Sell equity to wealthy individuals | 1 | 2 | 3 | 4 | 5 | 0 |
| 12 | Sell equity to another company | 1 | 2 | 3 | 4 | 5 | 0 |
| 13 | Make an initial public stock offering | 1 | 2 | 3 | 4 | 5 | 0 |
| 14 | Other (*please specify*) | | | | | | |

## Q3

In your own opinion, what is the right level of debt for your firm, expressed by the Debt to Equity ratio? (*please circle the most appropriate figure*)

0  0.1  0.2  0.3  0.4  0.5  0.75  1.0  1.5  2.0  2.5  3  4  5  6  7  8  9  10

## Q4

We would like to know your opinion on MBOs and MBIs.

A Management Buy Out, MBO, is when a company sells the majority of the ownership of the company to its existing managers. A Management Buy In, MBI, is when a company sells the majority of the ownership of the company to a group of new managers coming from outside the company.

To finance an MBO or an MBI, the buyers usually purchase the ownership of the company by borrowing money that is secured with the company's own assets. The interest on the debt is paid from the operating income of the company. This financing technique is referred to below as a Leveraged Management Buy Out (LMBO) or Leveraged Management Buy In (LMBI).

Please evaluate the following statements:

*(please circle one number in each row)*

| | Strongly disagree | Disagree | Indifferent | Agree | Strongly agree | No opinion |
|---|---|---|---|---|---|---|
| 1 MBOs and MBIs are rarely successful | 1 | 2 | 3 | 4 | 5 | 0 |
| 2 MBOs often result in the firm subsequently being sold to another company | 1 | 2 | 3 | 4 | 5 | 0 |
| 3 It is difficult to find a group of managers inside the firm who are able and willing to buy the firm. | 1 | 2 | 3 | 4 | 5 | 0 |
| 4 MBOs are a good way to solve the succession problem | 1 | 2 | 3 | 4 | 5 | 0 |
| 5 MBOs are suitable only for larger firms | 1 | 2 | 3 | 4 | 5 | 0 |
| 6 MBIs rarely succeed because of the difficulties the new management team encounters with the existing employees | 1 | 2 | 3 | 4 | 5 | 0 |
| 7 Only firms that are very profitable are suitable candidates for LMBOs and LMBIs | 1 | 2 | 3 | 4 | 5 | 0 |
| 8 It is less dangerous for the firm to sell equity to another operating company than to implement an MBO | 1 | 2 | 3 | 4 | 5 | 0 |
| 9 MBOs reinforce the motivation of the managers and strengthen the firm's performance | 1 | 2 | 3 | 4 | 5 | 0 |
| 10 After an MBO the entrepreneur should stay totally away from the firm | 1 | 2 | 3 | 4 | 5 | 0 |

11 Others (*Please specify*) _____

## Q5

Would you ever consider an MBO or an MBI for your company? (*please circle one*)

1 Yes (please answer the next question)
2 No  (please skip to Q7)

## Q6

Please list in order of decreasing importance the numbers of the items in Question 4 that caused you to answer "Yes" to Q5.

1st  Number___
2nd  Number___
3rd  Number___
4th  Other reasons (*Please specify*)
_____

## Q7

Please list in order of decreasing importance the numbers of the items in Question 4 that caused you to answer "No" to Q5.

1st  Number___
2nd  Number___
3rd  Number___
4th  Other reasons (*Please specify*)
_____

## Q8

Next, we would like to know what you consider to be the advantages and disadvantages of selling equity in your firm to another operating company (that is a non-financial company) instead of going public.  Please evaluate the following statements:

(*please circle one number in each row*)

| | Strongly disagree | Disagree | Indifferent | Agree | Strongly agree | No opinion |
|---|---|---|---|---|---|---|
| 1  It is easier to sell stock to another company than to go public | 1 | 2 | 3 | 4 | 5 | 0 |
| 2  The expenses associated with selling equity to another company are less than those of going public | 1 | 2 | 3 | 4 | 5 | 0 |
| 3  Another company would place a higher valuation on my firm than a public offering would | 1 | 2 | 3 | 4 | 5 | 0 |
| 4  I would not have to spend any time dealing with the financial community if I had a company rather than the public invested in my firm | 1 | 2 | 3 | 4 | 5 | 0 |
| 5  By selling stock to another company, my firm could get strategic assistance | 1 | 2 | 3 | 4 | 5 | 0 |
| 6  Even if I sold a minority share of my firm to another company, I would have less managerial control than if I took my firm public | 1 | 2 | 3 | 4 | 5 | 0 |

*(please circle one number in each row)*

| | Most Dislike | Dislike | Indifferent | Like | Most Like | No Opinion |
|---|---|---|---|---|---|---|
| 7  If I sold a majority interest in my firm to another company, I would be concerned that my managers and I might be replaced | I | 2 | 3 | 4 | 5 | 0 |

8  Other *(please specify)* _____

## Q9

Would you ever consider selling equity in your firm to another company?*(please circle one)*

1  Yes (please answer the next question)
2  No  (please skip to QI I)

## QI0

Please list in order of decreasing importance the numbers of the items in Question 8 that caused you to answer "Yes" to Q9.

1st   Number __
2nd  Number __
3rd  Number __
4th  Other reasons *(Please specify)* _____

## QII

Please list in order of decreasing importance the numbers of the items in Question 8 that caused you to answer "No" to Q9.

1st   Number __
2nd  Number __
3rd  Number __
4th  Other reasons *(Please specify)* _____

## QI2

Would you ever consider selling *all* of your firm to another company? *(please circle one)*

1  Yes
2  No

## QI3

We would like to know your opinions on raising money through a public stock offering.  Please evaluate the following statements:

*(please circle one number in each row)*

| | Strongly disagree | Disagree | Indifferent | Agree | Strongly agree | No opinion |
|---|---|---|---|---|---|---|
| 1  Fees and commissions associated with public stock offerings are too expensive | I | 2 | 3 | 4 | 5 | 6 |

*(please circle one number in each row)*

| | Strongly disagree | Disagree | Indifferent | Agree | Strongly agree | No opinion |
|---|---|---|---|---|---|---|
| 2 Managers of public companies are forced to manage for short-term profits | 1 | 2 | 3 | 4 | 5 | 6 |
| 3 Public companies have to reveal too much information to the public | 1 | 2 | 3 | 4 | 5 | 6 |
| 4 Chief executives of public companies have to spend too much time dealing with the financial community | 1 | 2 | 3 | 4 | 5 | 6 |
| 5 Public companies are vulnerable to unfriendly takeovers | 1 | 2 | 3 | 4 | 5 | 6 |
| 6 Stocks of small companies that have gone public in [name of country] have performed poorly in the last few years | 1 | 2 | 3 | 4 | 5 | 6 |
| 7 It is difficult to maintain investor interest in small companies after the initial public offering | 1 | 2 | 3 | 4 | 5 | 6 |
| 8 In general, investment banks neglect small company stocks after the initial public offering | 1 | 2 | 3 | 4 | 5 | 6 |
| 9 In general, a public stock offering places the highest valuation on a company | 1 | 2 | 3 | 4 | 5 | 6 |
| 10 A company gains considerable prestige by being listed on a public stock market | 1 | 2 | 3 | 4 | 5 | 6 |
| 11 In general, a public company can raise capital more easily than a private company | 1 | 2 | 3 | 4 | 5 | 6 |
| 12 A public stock offering is the best way of enabling stockholders to realize the value of their investment | 1 | 2 | 3 | 4 | 5 | 6 |
| 13 A public company gets better terms from its lenders than a private company | 1 | 2 | 3 | 4 | 5 | 6 |
| 14 Going public in more than one country strengthens a company's competitive position | 1 | 2 | 3 | 4 | 5 | 6 |

15 Other (*please specify*) _____

## Q14

Would you ever consider taking your company public on the [name of stock market(s) for a specific country]? (*please circle one*)

1 Yes (please answer the next question)
2 No  (please skip to Q16)

## Q15

Please list in order of decreasing importance the numbers of the items in Question 13 that caused you to answer "Yes" to Q14.

1st   Number ___
2nd  Number ___
3rd  Number ___
4th   Other reasons (*Please specify*) _____

## Q16

Please list in order of decreasing importance the numbers of the items in Question 13 that caused you to answer "No" to Q14.

1st   Number ___
2nd  Number ___
3rd  Number ___
4th   Other reasons (*Please specify*) _____

## Q17

If there were a *single* stock market on which small company stocks could be traded *throughout* Europe (referred to as the Pan-European stock market), would that influence your attitude toward taking your company public?

*(please circle one number in each row)*

| | Strongly disagree | Disagree | Indifferent | Agree | Strongly agree | No opinion |
|---|---|---|---|---|---|---|
| 1  My company would be more likely to go public if there were a Pan-European stock market | 1 | 2 | 3 | 4 | 5 | 6 |
| 2  Even if there were a Pan-European stock market, my company would still prefer to go public on the [name of specific national market] rather than a Pan-European stock market | 1 | 2 | 3 | 4 | 5 | 6 |

Finally, we would like to ask some questions about your industry, your company, and yourself. We want to assure you that your answers will be *strictly confidential* and that your *anonymity is guaranteed*.

## Q18

What is the age of your company?

____ years

## Q19

Is your business primarily a service or a manufacturing company? (*please circle one*)

1  Service
2  Manufacturing

**Q20**

What is the major industry sector that your company is in?

_____

**Q21**

Which of the following statements best describes the growth of your industry segment? (*Please circle one*)

1  slowly growing
2  rapidly growing
3  not growing
4  declining

**Q22**

Please indicate approximate figures for your firm in the following areas for the last year.  (Please use local currency where appropriate.)

| | |
|---|---|
| 1  Number of employees | _____ |
| 2  Total turnover | _____ |
| 3  Net income (bottom line) | _____ |
| 4  Turnover growth rate from 1991 to 1992 | _____ |
| 5  Percentage of turnover that was exported | _____ |
| 6  Amount of equity capital (paid-in capital plus retained earnings) | _____ |
| 7  Amount of financial debt (long-term and short-term) | _____ |
| 8  Average annual interest rate on your financial debt | _____ % |

**Q23**

What percent of your company's equity is owned by the following groups?

| | |
|---|---|
| 1  Owner-managers | ____ % |
| 2  Owner-managers' families | ____ % |
| 3  Your employees | ____ % |
| 4  Banks | ____ % |
| 5  Venture capitalists | ____ % |
| 6  Non-finance corporations | ____ % |
| 7  Individuals | ____ % |
| 8  Others (*please specify*) _____ | ____ % |
| Total | 100% |

**Q24**

What percentage of the equity effectively is controlled under written agreements by you and members of your family?

____ %

## Q25
If your firm is a family business, do your children or those of other family members work in the firm or plan to do so? (*please circle one*)

1 Yes
2 No

## Q26
How many members of your board of directors are insiders (that is yourself, other managers, and family members) and how many are outsiders?

1 Number of insiders                                    _____
2 Number of outsiders                                   _____
3 Number of others (*please specify*) _____    _____
4 Total number of directors                             _____

## Q27
What is your general level of education? (*please circle one*)

1 High school or lower (up to 12 years education)
2 University degree (13 to 16 years)
3 Post graduate degree (more than 16 years)

## Q28
What is your sex?

1 Male
2 Female

## Q29
How long have you been in charge of the firm?

___ years

## Q30
How did you get to be in charge of the firm? (*please circle one*)

1 Founded it
2 Bought it
3 Inherited it
4 Appointed manager

## Q31
If your company is a family business, which generation are you from? (*please circle one*)

1 First generation
2 Second generation
3 Third generation
4 Other (*please specify*) _____

**Q32**

What is the approximate percentage of your personal net worth that is tied up in the firm?

_____ %

If there is anything else you would like to tell us about the financing of your company, public stock markets, investors, lenders or any other issues related to our study, please use this space and if necessary the reverse side of this page.

Thank you very much for completing this survey. Your contribution to this effort is greatly appreciated. Please mail the completed survey in the envelope provided.

If you would like to receive a copy of the results of our study, please complete the postcard and mail it separately from the survey. We expect to have results of our survey by December 1992.

# References

Bannock, G. (1991).*Venture Capital and The Equity Gap*, London: Graham Bannock & Partners.

Batchelor, C. (1992). Enterprise looks for a way out, *Financial Times*, 22 Dec.

Brown, D. (1992). Venture capital returns. Presentation at the EVCA annual conference, Madrid, 4 June.

Bygrave, W. D. (1989). Venture capital investing: a resource exchange perspective. D.B.A. dissertation, Boston University.

Bygrave, W. D., and Timmons, J. A. (1992). *Venture Capital at the Crossroads*, Boston: Harvard Business School Press.

Bygrave, W. D., Muzyka, D., and Lelux, B. (1992). Pan-European study of harvesting attitudes. INSEAD working paper.

de Haan, M.(1993). Exiting in the US. Presentation at EVCA business seminar on Exiting in Europe, Venice, 11–12 Feb.

Elbertse, E. (1993). Developing exit mechanisms in your market. Presentation at EVCA business seminar on Exiting in Europe, Venice, 11-12 Feb.

EVCA (1991). *Venture Capital in Europe: 1991 EVCA Yearbook*, Zaventem EVCA.

EVCA (1992). *Venture Capital in Europe: 1992 EVCA Yearbook*, Zaventem EVCA.

Fama, E. F., and Jensen, M. C. (1983). The separation of ownership and control, *Journal of Law and Economics*, 26, 302–24.

Franks, J., and Mayer, C. (1990). Capital markets and corporate control: a study of France, Germany and the UK, *Economic Policy*, April.

Jensen, M. C. (1991). Foreword. In S. Green and D. F. Berry, *Cultural, Structural, and Strategic Change in Management Buyouts*, New York: St Martin's Press.

Myers, S. C., and Majluf, N. J. (1984). Corporate financing and investment decisions when firms have information that investors do not have, *Journal of Financial Economics*, 13, 187–221.

Onians, R. (1992). A pan-European stock market. Presentation at the EFER 92 Forum, London Business School, 12–14 Dec.

Onians, R. (1993). A European secondary market. Presentation at EVCA business seminar on Exiting in Europe, Venice, 11–12 Feb.

Wall, J. (1992). Nasdaq. Presentation the EFER 92 Forum, London Business School, 12–14 Dec.

Wood, B. (1993). Exiting in the US. Presentation at EVCA business seminar on Exiting in Europe, Venice, 11–12 Feb.

Wright, M., Robbie, K., Romanet, Y., Thompson, S., Joachimsson, R., Bruining, J. and Herst, A. (1992). Realizations, longevity and the life-cycle of management buy-outs and buy-ins: a four country study. Presented at the EFER 92 Forum, London Business School, 12–14 Dec (See also Chapter 4 above).

# 8

---

# A EUROPEAN MARKET FOR ENTREPRENEURIAL COMPANIES

*Jos. B. Peeters*

## INTRODUCTION

In June 1993 *The Economist* pointed out in 'European stock markets: too many trading places' that the 12 member countries of the European Community boast 32 stock exchanges and 23 futures and options exchanges. Of these, the markets in London, Frankfurt, Paris, Amsterdam, Milan and Madrid – at least – aspire to significant roles on the European and world stages. And the number of exchanges is growing. Recent arrivals include futures exchanges in Italy and Spain (*The Economist*, 19 June 1993) In contrast the USA has eight stock exchanges and seven futures and options exchanges. Of these only the New York Stock Exchange, the American Stock Exchange, Nasdaq and the two Chicago future exchanges have substantial turnover and nationwide pretensions.

Even though the European Community is not yet as integrated as the United States, it is clear that the local loyalties that sustain so many European exchanges look increasingly out-of-date. A single European market for financial services is on its way, and the competitive forces which this will release will inevitably lead to a rationalization of the European stock markets and to painful closures, mergers and takeovers.

But even with so many trading places around, there appears to be no stock market which satisfies the needs of the European venture capitalists. As pointed out in the introduction to this book, illiquidity has become a major concern to the European venture industry as opportunities for successful exits of venture capital investments have become less abundant in Europe. Nowhere is that more apparent than for flotations, with the number of initial public offerings by medium-size and small companies becoming relatively infrequent. As a result European venture capitalists are more agreed than ever before on the urgency of creating new exit mechanisms. The glaring lack of liquidity which distinguishes those holding venture capital assets in Europe from their counterparts in the USA has become a problem of such magnitude that it is not only top priority for EVCA but is also now perceived by the European Commission as needing urgent attention.

Despair at the failure of Europe's IPO markets to offer a consistent exit route for private equity investments has become so widespread that venture capitalists have been forced to take matters into their own hands (Anslow, 1993, p. 14). In an unusual move, members at the annual meeting of EVCA in June 1993 voted to make a mid-year modification to the annual budget to allocate funds for an emergency action programme to support the development or creation of European capital markets for smaller companies.

The idea that venture capitalists can create, run and regulate their own stock exchanges to trade blocks of shares in private companies would have seemed almost ludicrous a few years ago. But the degree of frustration that has built up over the existing stock markets has reached a point where serious organizations are prepared to put their credibility on the line to try any innovation that might resolve the current deadlock.

Is there an apparent contradiction between the oversupply of stock markets and the frustration of European venture capitalists about their lack of exit possibilities, or is this frustration a symptom of the European disease of a proliferation of disappointingly performing markets? This chapter will analyse some of the key issues which European entrepreneurs and their equity providers are facing in a situation where the options for realizing their investments in a successful way are limited.

The contrast between the situation of the European secondary markets and the success of Nasdaq, the US over-the-counter market, has been well documented in Chapter 2 by Yves Fassin and Churchill Lewis. Understanding the key factors which contribute to the success of this American market can help to identify the reasons why the trading volume of all European secondary markets combined is a tiny fraction of that of Nasdaq, which is rapidly approaching its first $1000 billion year.

Not surprisingly a range of organizations, including the London Stock Exchange, the Dutch Venture Capital Association and the European Venture Capital Association all have their home made cures for the illness. But the schemes which have been proposed don't measure up to the real opportunity which lies ahead. This opportunity can best be summarized as a green-field start-up of an electronically based pan-European trading system for stocks in high-growth entrepreneurial companies. The case for such a pan-European market will be made and an outline proposal for such a market will be presented as a conclusion to this chapter.

# THE EUROPEAN LIQUIDITY HEADACHE

## European venture capital – entry without exit?

By the end of 1992 European venture capitalists had raised a cumulative ECU 38.5 billion since the start of organized private equity investing in Europe. Of this amount ECU 20.4 billion or 53 per cent was locked up in some 10 000 small and medium-sized businesses across Europe. Total divestments at cost in 1992 totalled a mere ECU 2.3 billion, whereas ECU 4.7 billion of new venture capital investments were made. These numbers clearly show that the European venture capital business is building an ever larger portfolio of largely illiquid holdings.

This point has been further highlighted in the introduction and Chapter 4 of this book in relation to the study by the Centre for Management Buy-out Research. By the end of June 1992, only 27 per cent of the 1981–2 generation of small MBOs/MBI had been exited by an IPO, trade sale or secondary MBO/MBI. The perceived wisdom in venture capital is that MBO/MBI investments are made in companies which are in a more mature phase of their business development and hence that they are much easier to exit than, for example, early stage businesses. However, the figures from Mike Wright and his colleagues seem to indicate that there is no investment area in venture capital which provides easy exits.

In the past the need for disposals may have been more limited in Europe as private equity and venture capital managers were building their first portfolios. But this is changing rapidly. European managers have to demonstrate their ability to divest and to distribute cash in adequate amounts to their investors. Demonstrating returns which satisfy the expectations created during the raising of funds is not just a matter of proving the viability of one's own business but the viability of the whole venture capital industry.

Mergers and acquisitions and initial public offerings are the two main routes to liquidity for a venture capitalist. The only viable alternative is a sale to the management of the company, but this rarely results in returns for the investors significantly above average bond rates. Mergers and acquisitions or corporate takeovers require a specific strategy and careful planning, but can provide highly successful exits, as was discussed by Kaj-Erik Relander, Antti-Pekka Sryjänen and Asko Miettinen in Chapter 6. In general, trade sales cater for the bulk of venture capital exits. For example, in the United States, with the exception of 1983 and then of 1991 and 1992, trade sales were the primary exit vehicle (Vachon, 1993). In the years between there were about two or three trade sales for every IPO.

At the present time, exit possibilities in Europe are largely confined to trade sales and management buy-backs, while public markets have failed to provide a significant contribution. Of the divestments made by European venture capitalists in 1992 fewer than 5 per cent by number were public offerings whereas 30 per cent were trade sales (EVCA, 1993); by amounts invested the figures were respectively 17 per cent and 41 per cent. The shortfall of IPOs in Europe adds to the liquidity problem, but it cannot in itself explain the full extent of this problem.

## The missing cream

Public offerings are considered only for the most successful ventures. But though they might be limited in number, as William Bygrave pointed out in Chapter 1 they are incredibly important for the overall performance of a venture capital portfolio. It is the few spectacular successes that generate the above-average returns for a venture capital fund. The US experience shows that there is a one-to-one correlation between the Nasdaq index and the returns of venture capital funds (see Figure 1.4 and Bygrave and Timmons, 1992, pp. 277–82). In the long term an overall shortfall in performance would undermine the ability of fund managers to raise new funds and would jeopardize the whole European venture capital business. But in the absence of functioning public markets for high-growth stocks, the prospects for interesting returns for the European venture capital industry look bleak.

The current IPO problem seems to have taken the venture capital industry by surprise and one wonders why nobody anticipated this problem earlier in the game and why no action was taken sooner. It is clear that the importance of secondary markets for the development of venture capital was recognized from the beginning. For example, Harry Fitzgibbons pointed out at a venture capital conference in 1985 that venture capitalists could not afford to ignore the health and welfare of the equity marketplace, which was so integral to their ambition for liquidity (Fitzgibbons, 1985). In addition he urged the governmental agencies, which had started to spend a lot of time and money promoting venture capital as the antidote to the economic decline of the early 1980s, not to view their national secondary markets as an afterthought, merely hoping that they would spring automatically from the brow of Zeus as venture portfolios matured.

The creation of national secondary markets was a key factor in the development of venture capital businesses in the various European countries. Belgium saw the creation of four venture capital funds within a year once there was an announcement that a secondary market was to be created. The United Kingdom, The Netherlands and France, which were the first to introduce secondary markets, have also enjoyed the most active development of their venture capital industry.

It is clear that the issue of exits, and particularly exits through IPOs, was not a belated afterthought but was very much on the agenda at the time of the creation of the European venture capital industry. The launch of the Unlisted Securities Market in London, the Second Marché in Lyon, the Marché Hors-Côté in Paris, the Parallel Markt in Amsterdam, the Mercato Restritto in Milan and the Secondary Market in Brussels were significant contributors and enabling factors for the introduction of venture capital in these European countries.

The problem with the IPO exits started with the general stock market crash of October 1987. Unlike the primary markets and unlike the secondary market in the United States, the secondary markets in Europe didn't recover. On the contrary, the tornado which caused havoc in the world stock markets seems to have unrooted the emerging European secondary markets and they continued to wither and die after the storm calmed down, rather than to bounce back and put out new shoots. Later in this chapter we will analyse in detail why these European growths were so sensitive and didn't recover from the first storm that tested the strength of their roots.

## The yardstick

As noted before, with the exception of a few years with white-hot IPO markets, even in the United States venture capitalists see two to three times more exits by way of a trade sale than by a public offering. IPOs will always be limited to the highest performing companies of a portfolio, and other transactions in shares will dominate exit discussions. But all these other transactions, whether transfers between family owners of a business, between private investors and entrepreneurs or between institutional investors and corporations, will always involve a valuation of the company and an agreement on a price. Many valuation techniques are in use, from net asset value calculations, via compounded earnings considerations, to multiples of current or future cash flows and earnings. But at the end of the day the real value of the *Sunflowers* of Van Gogh or the real value of 7.5 per cent of the shares of Antwerp Bionic Systems n.v., a small medical device company in Antwerp, is what somebody is prepared to pay for such an asset. A market which sees regular transactions in a given asset becomes a reliable indicator and reference point for the value of that asset and for the value of any related or similar assets.

When a group of venture capital investors led by Alta Berkeley & Associates and Development Capital Corporation sold their holdings in Noctech Ltd, a small, privately held Irish biotech company, to the US-based, publicly quoted Cambridge Biotech Corporation, it was the valuation of the latter which served as a guideline in the price discussion, and, not surprisingly, the Noctech investors were paid in Cambridge Biotech shares. This type of scenario has been the exit route for many small, technology-based companies. However, this type of transaction is only possible if at least one of the parties to the deal is publicly quoted and if the pricing used by the public markets can be used as a yardstick for the unquoted entity.

## Financial backbone

People in the venture capital industry such as Bert Twaalfhoven, Chairman of Indivers and shareholder in Gildenventures, a Dutch venture capital fund, regard it as a tragedy that a good company in a strong position, with good prospects, is not as well appreciated by financial markets in Europe as it would be in the US. The danger is that in the European situation, where trade sales predominate, there is a tendency to exit relatively early to a competitor or a large acquirer, whereas in the US, if the prospects are there, it is possible for a firm to undergo many more financing rounds, particularly in the case of highly specialized, growth companies (Twaalfhoven, 1993).

The story of Cambridge Biotech Corporation, and similar companies, illustrates how access to public markets allows companies to find the risk capital to finance their growth faster and how it provides them with a competitive advantage which can put them in the driving seat when it comes to discussions about possible mergers and acquisitions. In a recent Commentary in the *European Venture Capital Journal* I pointed out that the lack of a European equivalent of Nasdaq had a dominant impact on the failure of European venture capital to spawn major global businesses out of technology-based start-ups. The fact that risk-bearing, high-growth companies in the US can call on the public at large for their financing provides them with the financial muscle to attract top-class people, to foster their ongoing research and development and to establish appropriate marketing channels (Peeters, 1993, p. 28).

## Real money please

Moments of truth come for venture capitalists when they show their cash returns to their investors. For entrepreneurs and their staff there are similar moments. It is often a problem for them to retain the confidence of their families in the enterprise they are building. Exciting technical breakthroughs, achievements of strategic sales, influence on the direction of the company, stock options and paper equity holdings seem a feeble compensation in the eyes of a family deprived of the attention and presence of a parent or living with the uncertainties of a young business in return for no more than an average salary. When Alan Sugar first introduced Amstrad on the London Stock Exchange in April 1980 he personally raised £2 million by parting with a quarter of his company. Showing his father, a semi-skilled worker in the garment trade in London's East End, evidence of the fruits of the flotation was a significant rite of passage, as Sugar explains: 'It wasn't until I physically put a cheque for two million pounds under his nose that he realized it was OK for him to stop worrying, because I actually could make a living without working for somebody' (Thomas, 1990, p. 15).

Realizing parts of their holdings allows entrepreneurs to convert the theoretical value they have built into cash. This provides them with a real return on their investment in creativity, time and commitment. It allows them to honour the loyalty and support of their families and of those who have been part of the building process. It enables entrepreneurs to spread their risks and to reduce dependence on the company alone for future wealth.

Selling shares on the stock market is the only way of realizing enterprise value without losing control of the enterprise and without depleting the financial resources of the company. Many disputes in family-held companies are related to the perceived discrepancies between the shareholders who play an active role in the company and receive a remuneration for their work and the passive shareholders who only see a dividend, if any. Since Europe is facing the succession problems of tens of thousands of family-owned businesses, a suitable public market for the stocks in these companies could be the magic solution which provides liquidity on demand for the non-active shareholders and which makes the company attractive for external professional managers.

The liquidity issue may be the most pertinent for the key entrepreneurs, with significant stockholdings, and for the return-oriented venture capitalist, but it extends well beyond that. High-growth companies are in need of fast-moving, result-oriented employees and of experienced, well-connected non-executive board members and advisers. Both categories are in high demand and are expensive to attract and difficult to retain if a company can only provide current income through salaries or fees. Stock options are crucial for binding these important allies to a business. An interest in the future of a business tomorrow buys commitment to solving the problems of today. But such commitments can only been obtained if there is a real prospect for liquidity in these shares or options on shares. Non-liquid stock option plans are a nightmare and can turn quickly into major disincentives.

## Divide and rule

Entrepreneurs are motivated by independence. If trade sales are the only option open to them, they will not be attracted to the venture in the first place (Cohen, 1993). Compared with a trade sale or a corporate buy, the market gives the entrepreneurs continued management freedom, even if it may be slightly less freedom than they were used to as a private enterprise (Onians, 1992). The expanded shareholder array provides entrepreneurs with more options for raising finance in the future and with personal liquidity, and at the same time it leaves them largely in control of their enterprise. This is the dream of all entrepreneurs: to be in control of resources which vastly exceed their own means, in order to be able to capitalize on the opportunities they perceive around each turn of the road. This point is illustrated by the findings of the pan-European survey (see Figure 7.1). In choosing their finance, the entrepreneurs in the survey not only preferred the route that appeared to be the cheapest, but also the routes that implied the least influence on their business. For long-term capital their first choice was retained earnings, followed by borrowing money and, next, initial public stock offerings. Only as a last resort would they sell equity to parties who could exercise some degree of control. Within each category they preferred the source which had the least impact on their independence.

It is important to understand that in the absence of functioning stock markets for high-growth companies, private equity investors, who have a limited time horizon of, say, five to 10 years and whose only exit is to sell their holdings at some point in time to a corporation, will no longer be welcomed by the independently minded entrepreneurs. The stock markets are crucial to venture capitalists to keep their investors happy, but they are equally important to maintain the interest of opportunity-driven entrepreneurs, and to continue to be the preferential equity partners for them.

The issues faced by European venture capitalists and high-growth entrepreneurs can be summarized as follows:

- the venture capital industry has built a huge portfolio, but is short of spectacular realizations;
- failing a public stock market, there is no reference point for the valuation of shares in other transactions;
- high-growth companies are deprived of the required equity to grow really big and become major companies;
- entrepreneurs and their staff can only enjoy the fruits of their work by depleting the cash flow of their company;
- entrepreneurs cannot provide an exit for their venture capital investors without losing control over their business.

# THE NASDAQ FORTUNES

The glaring success of Nasdaq was well described by Yves Fassin and Churchill Lewis above. Created in 1971, Nasdaq saw nearly 50 billion shares of high-growth and small-capitalization companies change hands in 1992. A mere $890.8 billion was involved in these transactions. This amount is higher than the annual transaction volume on any primary stock exchange anywhere in the world, with the exception of the New York Stock Exchange, and is about 70 per cent of the total transactions on all European primary stock markets combined. But, as William Bygrave points out in Chapter 1, the market for small-capitalized stocks has been going through 'ecstasy–agony' cycles. After the collapse of the hot market of 1983, small-capitalized stocks went through eight lean years; only in the last years has Nasdaq been reviving. An increase from 134 initial public offerings in 1990 to 432 new issues in 1992 and 56.8 per cent and 16.5 per cent rises in the composite index in 1991 and 1992 respectively prove the current health of this market and its resilience with respect to cycles. We will try to analyse below the main factors that have contributed to the remarkable overall success of Nasdaq.

## Transparency

The most important point about going public is that the entrepreneur develops a publicly held attitude. For John Wall, Executive Vice President of Nasdaq, that is crucial to any successful IPO or public company subscribing or selling shares to other investors, because without that publicly held attitude, information is not going to be provided to the new partners. If you do not provide information to them, you are not going to have a happy or long relationship with those partners (Wall, 1992). What starts with a red herring, the preliminary prospectus, the key selling document in the run-up to a public listing, ends with quarterly 10 Q statements and regular and extensive disclosures of holdings and potentials for conflict of interest. These reporting obligations are onerous for the companies and their management, but, together with the imposed holding periods of several months to years for significant investors, they have contributed significantly to the above-board image of this market. Major scandals involving fraudulent representations or insider dealings have been avoided, which has given individuals as well as institutional investors confidence in this market.

## Money makes the market go round

Market-makers are the key to why markets work. The support market-makers bring to companies is that they are indeed trading and they bring a commitment that they are willing to continue to make a market in those securities. They are willing to stand there and get hit for 1000 shares at a clip at the prices they are showing on the screens. And this happens automatically; they cannot move out of the way, even if they wanted to. The only way they can take evasive action is to change the price and that can only be done for the next order, not for the one just executed.

The market-makers are providing the capital necessary to make Nasdaq work. John Wall points out that without the capital all you have is a purely mechanical system, a black box. You take all the sell orders and all the buy orders, put them together, and when the prices match they will go off. Everybody can do that – all you need is a computer program (Wall, 1992). Nasdaq is successful because it offers much more than a black box service; the positions taken by the market-makers provide an intrinsic liquidity to this market and that is very different from a passive matching system.

The simple secret of why market-makers are prepared to take an exposure and commit themselves to buy and sell shares is that the system allows them to make money. To make money there must be a difference between the ask and the bid prices. This spread is part of what makes the market work. The spread is the profit to the market-maker on one side and possibly the loss on the other side. Only markets that provide a spread can attract capital and provide liquidity.

## Global presence, local action

Another key to the success of Nasdaq is that the market is taken to where the investment capital is. Local brokers anywhere in the world can access the computerized trading system and complete a transaction while being still on the telephone with their client. If a client wants to buy shares in Apple Computer, the broker will instruct the computer, 'Buy 1000 shares of Apple,' and hit the button. The computer is linked to the Nasdaq computers. Nasdaq guarantees the broker that that customer will receive the best price at that time for the Apple stock or for whatever other security might be wanted. The Nasdaq computers will find the best price and ship the order automatically through the screen back to the broker's terminal. So the broker immediately knows the deal is executed and at what price. That transaction has involved comparisons between market-makers who could be in St Louis, New York or London; but wherever they are they will find the transaction on the screen. The broker, still on the telephone with the customer, can say, 'You have just bought x number of Apple shares at y dollars per share.' That transaction is then registered in the Nasdaq computers and sent to the clearing corporation. The point is that the market-maker knows that it is a completed trade, no risk, all done through the system, and the institutional or individual investor can move on to other investments.

The transaction has been handled fully electronically, with buyer and seller at different ends of the world and with full knowledge of what is on offer anywhere on that market. Today about 60 per cent of all transactions on Nasdaq are effected in this fully automatic way, the balance being handled by telephone. Nasdaq has 425 firms that are active market-makers. On average a listed company has about 12 market-makers that compete by price in the system, and those prices are obviously firm and can be hit automatically by computer. As in most situations, 80 per cent of the business is done by 20 per cent of those market-makers. But the 80 per cent of the market-makers doing only 20 per cent of the business are very valuable because those market-makers are making markets in the smaller local issuers: issuers that their investors are in, issuers that their customers are investors in, issuers that are located in their local community and issuers that would not be public and could not reach the capital market if it were not for those smaller broker dealers who are willing to put their capital behind them.

## Success breeds success

Nasdaq is operating in a competitive environment with the New York Stock Exchange and the American stock exchange as main contenders. Companies seeking a listing have basically a choice as to where they can list. Nasdaq has created an identity as the distinct market for 'small-capitalization' and 'high-growth' investing. Customer satisfaction on this type of market can only be maintained if it shows superior performance compared to other markets over a long period of time. The 191 per cent increase in the Nasdaq composite index over the past 10 years is an indication of this overall performance.

Nasdaq has grown because the companies listed on Nasdaq have grown. Nasdaq adapted to permit a market where large companies also want to participate. It is not a second-choice market, but considers and projects itself as a primary market with its own identity. It seems that companies such as Apple, Intel, Microsoft and many similarly admired companies continue to believe in Nasdaq and stick to their listing on this market. These megastars in entrepreneurial performance provide a significant part of the Nasdaq business: in 1992 over 500 million Intel shares and over 400 million Novell shares changed hands on Nasdaq. These stocks clearly retain investors' interest in the market and set a role model for hundreds of other high-growth enterprises whose main ambition is to obtain a listing on Nasdaq and be part of this select club of companies that have made it.

Not only has Nasdaq enjoyed and managed to keep major successful companies, at the other end of the spectrum it has seen relatively few failures. According to Ellen Hipschman, Director of International Services at Nasdaq, only 8 per cent of the companies overall don't succeed (Hipschman, 1993). A relatively low failure rate, a convincing performance and a number of brilliant stars have build Nasdaq's reputation and have kept both its client companies and its client investors, institutional and private, happy and loyal to this market.

## Customers first

In a competitive environment you have to be aware of who your customers are and how you can keep them happy. John Wall puts it in the following way: 'When you look at our corporate structure, go through our strategies and look at the vision of the market, you see that our mission is to exist in order to facilitate the capital-raising function of companies. That is our purpose, that is why we do exist. If we cannot do that cheaper, better and quicker than anybody else then we should not exist. Quite frankly that is what we have tried to build Nasdaq on' (Wall, 1992).

In summary, we believe that the key ingredients which have made Nasdaq into the success it is today are:

- a steady and high-quality flow of information from the companies to the investors;
- a system of market-makers who always take one side of a deal;
- a fully automated electronic system providing overall market information and local presence;
- a better than average performance and highly successful role models;
- a professional, customer-oriented organization.

## BLINDFOLDED AND IN THE DARK

The creation of national secondary stock markets in Europe in the first half of the 1980s was more a matter of showing the appropriate intentions than of a rational analysis and a commitment to an agreed strategy. National governments and stock-market authorities were obliged to create public markets for small companies as part of their efforts to stimulate entrepreneurship. Most of the resulting secondary markets had no sense of direction and not surprisingly they got nowhere. As if blindfolded, they struggled and stumbled in the dark and finally fell flat on their face, feeling hurt and aggrieved and disappointed by the lack of success, not realizing that they were so handicapped at the start that they never had a chance of finishing anyway.

In this section we will identity some of the blind spots of the European secondary markets and discuss how they contributed to the current situation.

## Force-fed industry

Dick Onians, Managing Partner at Baring Venture Partners, traces one of the major problems of the European venture capital industry back to the way this industry was created, in contrast to the origin of venture capital in the United States. Back in the 1960s and 1970s many US investment bankers started to deal in stocks of small companies that needed a market. It should not be overlooked that Nasdaq was created by an association of security dealers who perceived an opportunity in the combination of the demand for capital by high-growth, small and medium-sized businesses and the public interest in owning stock in rapidly growing companies.

Then, in the late 1970s, having discovered that there was a business based on dealing in this small-capitalization, high-growth stock, the individual partners of investment banks suddenly cottoned on to the idea that if they personally could get into these stocks five years before they were brought to them for initial public offering, they themselves could get significantly richer. They started to raise venture capital funds, because having identified an opportunity like that it followed that they should not only put their own money into it but also recommend it to their friends. That is how many of the professional venture capital companies in the USA began. They got into business with investment bankers who wanted to share in the process earlier for the purpose of taking the first big gain.

In Europe the venture capital managers went about things the other way around. Starting in the late 1970s and early 1980s, they force-fed their industry as managers of capital, giving rise to the problem they have today. They created the industry without having a shred of evidence as to whether they could be liquid at a later date. The Americans started with the liquidity mechanism and backed into professional venture capital management techniques afterwards. This is the distinction between Europe and America and explains to some extent why the European venture capital industry is where it is today (Onians, 1992). This top-down start-up deprived the European venture capital industry of the essential network of specialized investment bankers and analysts who are the vital link between emerging growth companies in need of equity and the public at large who are interested in more exciting investment opportunities than government bonds or blue chips.

## For Your Ears Only

Europeans are paranoid about disclosing information. Historically they might have good reasons for taking this attitude. Only in the last 20 years has this continent been building some degree of multilateral cooperation and unification in a peaceful way. In earlier times it was the scene of violent wars, and different nationalities were always trying to be superior to their neighbours. Furthermore, anti-entrepreneurial and anti-free market attitudes of powerful trade unions and the political parties allied to them have not created an environment where companies and entrepreneurs alike have felt secure to disclose critical information. Punitive taxation in many European countries of company profits, capital gains and accumulated assets certainly did not help to solve this problem. The result is that companies and individuals are not forthcoming with information, and as a consequence there is a fair amount of unscrupulous activity going on in Europe. This is particularly true in the area of privileged information and its use.

As the regulations with respect to the disclosure of information vary widely from country to country, and as the enforcement of these regulations sees even wider discrepancies, investment bankers are using the grass-roots approach to manage their portfolios. Françoise Vappereau, Vice President of Banque Lombard-Odier and Manager of the SMIC fund, a fund specialized in investing in stocks listed on the French second market, is very clear about the information issue. In order to invest in secondary markets you have to adopt a bottom-up approach, which means that you have to establish direct contact with the companies that you manage in your portfolio. You have to visit them yourself, see the offices, meet with employees and management, in particular the financial management, and also be able to contact them on the phone several times a year when necessary. The key is to hear the news first, and obviously this will help you to decide when to invest and when to divest (Vappereau, 1993).

On order-driven markets the brokers rely on the commission income from transactions. Given that companies on second and third markets are smaller, enjoy less liquidity and suffer from smaller transactions, very few brokers will find it economically justifiable to produce research on these companies. Hence it falls to the company itself to arrange for credible and useful information on its activities to be circulated. If it wants an active and reliable market in its shares, there is an incentive to produce more attractive information (Wallinger, 1992).

It should be no surprise that when the task of providing information is left to the discretion of companies, there is going to be a bias towards the good news, and there are also liable to be elements of overselling and insider dealing. Companies guilty of these practices have not only ruined their own reputations, but they have at the same time destroyed the reputation of the markets where they were trading. Some bad occurrences shortly after introductions on public markets have caused significant losses for investors, and this has created mistrust and given some markets a bad reputation.

On the other hand, many entrepreneurs have been disappointed in the stock market. After the euphoria of the initial public offering and an initial upsurge in price, they have seen only a deterioration of this price and a gradual drying up of the market in their shares. The reason is simple: after the roadshows leading to the IPO, these companies have just not bothered to keep their investors informed and hence have forfeited all their interest.

## A second-class citizen

The secondary markets in Europe were in general organized by the same organizations that run the primary stock markets. The Second Marché in Brussels was organized by the Brussels stock exchange, the Parallel Market in Amsterdam by the Amsterdam Stock Exchange, etc. Hence, the secondary markets were never meant to compete with the primary markets or to have their own identity. These markets were mainly set up as a stepping stone to the main markets. The idea was to accept public trading in the stocks of smaller companies on a separate market so that these companies could better prepare themselves for an entry on the first market. One of the reasons for the underperformance of the French Second Marché is that the second market itself acted as a springboard for the smaller companies to be listed on the main market. In the early 1990s, 24 companies which were listed on the Second Marché moved to the main market, and almost all of them were stars of the second market. Among them was Canal Plus, which came to be included in the CAC 40 index of the 40 largest stocks on the Paris Stock Exchange (Vappereau, 1992).

Thus the secondary stock markets in Europe never had a competitive advantage or a positive identity or market image of their own. The primary markets which had organized them competed with them for the better deals and lured the companies that made the grade away from the secondary markets. A complaint often heard is that the conditions and cost of entry on the secondary market are not different enough from those for the primary market. With the higher prestige offered by the primary markets, companies are likely to prefer to wait longer and seek a listing on that market straight away.

In many respects the secondary markets have been treated like stepchildren by the main exchanges. The name itself, 'secondary' in contrast to 'primary', tells more than anything else how these markets have been perceived by their parents and by the financial community of stockbrokers, investment bankers, fund managers and authorities. This situation is unlikely to change in the near future. In a personal comment, Baron Boudewijn van Ittersum, Chairman of the Amsterdam Stock Exchange and President of the Federation of Stock Exchanges of the EC, admits that the issue of a market for small company stocks is not a first priority for the European stock exchanges. They are already quite busy enough organizing the professional trading in the bigger stocks in Europe and promoting cross-border trading between their markets (van Ittersum, 1992). A single European market for financial services will further increase the competition between national stock markets in Europe. Their current preoccupations relate to the introduction of computerized trading systems, lobbying their governments on stamp duties, adapting the new regulations and seeking to find alliances in the battle for market share. European high-growth entrepreneurs and their venture capital investors would be naive to expect a solution to their liquidity and performance problems to come from their national stock exchanges.

## A white elephant?

Was the creation 10 years ago of secondary stock markets in Europe a solution looking for a problem? In other words, were there willing buyers and sellers of shares in small-capital, high-growth companies? The point made by Dick Onians that the European venture industry was force-fed clearly indicates that the secondary markets didn't come into existence in a response to pressure from buyers and sellers. They were largely the result of governmental plans to revitalize the ailing European economies at the beginning of the 1980s.

In a speech in 1988 delivered at the annual symposium of the European Venture Capital Association, John Cope MP, Minister of State for Employment in the UK, stated: 'Since 1979 this Government has recognized that the creation of wealth, which in turn leads to the creation of jobs, comes from a thriving economy built upon a successful and profitable business sector. The Government recognized that it had to provide a framework of financial stability and that it had to remove impediments to enterprise and individual initiative.' He went on to stress the importance of spreading individual share ownership and involvement and described the development of the Unlisted Securities Market and the Third Market as another vital element in the growth in equity finance (Cope, 1988).

When the secondary markets in Europe were created it was very unclear that there would be enough companies to seek a listing on those markets and that there would be sufficient public and institutional interest in buying the types of stocks on offer. Hence our poor blindfolded stepchild had a real uphill battle.

Today the situation appears to be very different. On the offer side there are at least 10 000 companies currently in venture capital portfolios eagerly looking for exit possibilities. From the pan-European survey we learn that, overall, 63 per cent of the CEOs interviewed said they would consider taking their company public on their national stock exchange, and 41 per cent claimed that they would be more likely to take their companies public if a pan-European stock market existed. Only 19 per cent believed that the existence of such a market would have no influence on their intentions of going public.

Early in 1993 Ronald Cohen from Apax Partners took five of his colleagues to the London Stock Exchange authorities to discuss the decision to close the USM. Between the six of them they had 96 companies in their portfolios with market capitalizations of less than £20 million, and these could have gone to Nasdaq. Their approach at least resulted in temporarily preventing the closing of the USM and in the establishment of a working party (Cohen, 1993). At the end of 1992, over 150 European companies were trading on Nasdaq; in principle they are all potential candidates for a second listing on a properly functioning European market.

If the sellers are there, will there be any buyers? The conventional wisdom is that Europeans are risk shy and hence are less interested in buying stocks in small-capital, high-growth companies. There is definitely less of a tradition in buying stocks in Europe than there is in the United States or Japan. But Europeans are no fools and they buy when they can make money. When in the mid-1980s France introduced the Monory law and Belgium the Cooreman–De Clercq law, making investments in stocks fiscally attractive, millions of new stockholders emerged overnight. The privatization programmes in the United Kingdom, which worked with very attractive pricing, equally created millions of first-time stock owners. A lot of these newcomers to the European stock markets have made money; equally quite a number of them learned the hard way about the cycles of the market and lost money in the downturn. The hope is that they will realize that there is an expectation of better times after a decline and they will come back to the market.

A major competitor for the stock markets are of course the bond markets and, in particular, the government bonds. Given their preferential fiscal treatments compared to equity holdings and high interest rates, it should not be a surprise that Europeans prefer safe bonds over risky stocks. However, interest rates are coming down, making bonds less attractive. Furthermore, European governments are desperately looking for initiatives to stimulate their economies; soon they will rediscover the recipe book of the early 1980s and turn back to stimulating entrepreneurship and equity holdings. An additional aspect is that under the Maastricht treaty the European governments have committed themselves to drastic reductions of their budget deficits and their public debt as a percentage of GNP. Any reduction in these deficits is going to free up vast amounts of capital, which can be reinvested in productive companies.

At the 1993 EVCA symposium, Bill Fields, Chairman of Prudential Equity Investors, Inc., predicted that US institutional investors would go global with their investments in small-cap stocks (Fields, 1993). Such a development could indeed bring major liquidity and expertise to European markets for small-cap stocks.

There are many more reasons now for optimism about the potential and need for European markets for small-capitalization, high-growth companies than there were 10 years ago.

In this section we have not highlighted the fact that the national secondary stock markets in Europe were too small to be viable and never reached a critical mass, neither in terms of companies listed, nor in terms of institutional buyers and investors. This was definitely the case for the secondary markets in the smaller countries such as Belgium, The Netherlands and Italy. But the Unlisted Securities Market in London or the Second Marché in Lyon could have become specialized European markets for small-capitalization, high-growth stocks if they had followed different and more ambitious strategies.

The key problems which the national secondary markets in Europe have been facing can be summarized as follows :

- a top-down approach when markets were created which was not a response to an emerging need of individual and institutional investors and which failed to create the indispensable network of advisers and analysts;
- a lack of openness and rigour in the supply of information which has led to mistrust and abuse;
- a lack of competitiveness and identity which resulted from the relationship with the parent prime markets.

A number of elements indicate that at present the conditions for a successful development of a pan-European stock market for small-capital, high-growth companies are more favourable than ever before.

# A CHOICE OF SOLUTIONS

The work of the European Foundation for Entrepreneurship Research and the European Venture Capital Association and the general reaction of dismay at the announcement of the closure of the USM in London have resulted in a major debate on the question of specific stock markets for small-capitalization, high-growth companies in Europe. The discussions have already produced a number of proposals and some concrete actions. We will briefly review the key aspects of the main proposals.

## The European Private Equity Exchange

In 1992 Baring Venture Partners, a leading European venture capitalist, launched a study on the exiting of venture capital to find out why certain things were not happening in Europe and how better things might be made to happen. The results and recommendations of this study were presented at the EVCA business seminar in Venice (Onians, 1993).

The Barings proposal is to set up a European Private Equity Exchange (EPEE) which would be owned by full members of EVCA; it would be operated with limited liability and run, essentially, as a 'club' with no external regulations. The basic idea is that what Europe needs most to increase the transactions in shares of emerging growth companies is good-quality information, produced and presented on a consistent basis and resulting in a sustainable valuation. EPEE is designed to do exactly that.

The exchange would employ a full-time staff which would be a mixture of market/technology analysts, lawyers, financial analysts and accountants. This team would form a self-contained unit disposing of the most advanced data-processing and communication equipment. The group would operate from one central location and undertake assignments on a pan-European basis. This resource would be in a position to produce due diligence and come up with an evaluation for each company wishing to submit itself to the process. EPEE as a professional organization could guarantee absolute confidentiality and be totally neutral in publishing its comprehensive information memoranda on its client companies.

Under the scheme, members of the club, which could include selected investment banks in addition to the venture capitalist owners of EPEE, could propose companies from their portfolios for evaluation by EPEE. The company would pay a fee to EPEE to go through this process, and the company would of course become the owner of the resulting information memorandum. This memorandum can then be circulated by the company to the members of the club to see if there are any potential buyers among them. Alternatively, the company might use it as a basis for discussions with investors who are not necessarily members of the club, or use it for internal discussions requiring a valuation of the company, such as stock option plans, for example.

EPEE would also have the skills and resources to complete transactions if its client companies wished it to do so. In such cases EPEE would take a commission on the transaction. Once a sufficient flow of transactions was established, EPEE could provide a quotation service and start to publish information on the completed transactions.

EPEE would not be subject to the brokerage or stock exchange laws of any country. It would be totally self-regulating and have a supervisory board imposing strict supervision of standards and dealings.

An interesting aspect of EPEE is that the valuation methodology used could include strategic as well as financial arguments. The published memoranda might evaluate, for example, the economies of scale in marketing, distribution and maintenance through a large corporation in combination with the innovative skills and the flexibility of a small entrepreneurial company. As a result, the memorandum might be used equally well in negotiations with corporate buyers.

Because financial markets undervalue the strategic aspect of small companies, there is a strong argument to be made, according to Richard Onians, for focusing on the corporate market and not even bothering with any financial markets at all (Onians, 1993). This point is illustrated by one venture capitalist involved in the sale of Origin Medsystems to Eli Lilly & Co in 1992. The IPO market looked at Origin Medsystems as a stand-alone company worth X amount, whereas Lilly looked at it and, because they really wanted to get into that market, regarded the company as worth 1.3X (Vachon, 1993).

The key point about the proposal of Baring Venture Partners is the creation of a respected valuation mechanism which investors of all types learn to trust. EPEE would be very much about confidence building and be designed to have an effect over the long term rather than to provide a short term 'fix' for the problems of illiquidity (Anslow, 1993).

The Baring proposal has been discussed at the level of the board of EVCA, but has failed so far to find their members committed enough to it to finance the launch of EPEE.

## The Dutch Participation Exchange

Faced with the problems typical of a national secondary market, which are already well documented and with the imminent closing of the Parallel

Market in Amsterdam, the Dutch Participation Exchange (Parex) was created in December 1992. The initiative was taken jointly by the Dutch Venture Capital Association (NVP) and the Dutch Stock Exchange and received support from the Dutch Ministry of Economic Affairs. Parex is owned by a foundation and is run by a board comprising officials from the NVP and the Dutch Stock Exchange and an independent chairman. Membership of Parex is restricted to members of the NVP. It will be based in Amsterdam.

Basically Parex is an auction which is held twice a year, in May and November. Two months prior to trading day, investors wishing to sell blocks of shares have to register these shares with Parex. Blocks of shares offered for sale have to represent a minimum holding of 5 per cent of the stock of the company and have to have a minimum value of Dfl.1 million. Only shares in profitable companies are accepted and only NVP members can register shares. Issues of new shares are not allowed.

The board of Parex evaluates the applications and checks the accuracy of the offering memoranda. One month before trading day the information on the registered and accepted shares is circulated to interested buyers. These include the members of the NVP and institutional investors. Steady ownership has to be assured so that there is no risk of a takeover for the company.

On trading day potential buyers place sealed bids for the shares they wish to acquire. A vendor can create a floor price below which there is no sale by also putting in a sealed bid. After potential buyers have handed in their bids, sellers are allowed to reposition their floor prices. The highest bidder wins the bid; if the bid is undecided because more than one party offers the same price then a second round of bidding is organized.

The organizational costs and overheads of Parex will be paid for by applying a surcharge – on a sliding scale of 3.5 to 1 per cent, depending on size – on the transaction. Compared to EPEE there is no need for exhaustive due diligence and valuation. All that is needed is a relatively simple information memorandum.

In its well-established tradition of being action oriented, the Dutch Venture Capital Association has created in Parex an instrument which might well serve a very useful role, particularly in the Dutch environment, and its development will be followed with great attention by other European countries. Although Parex cannot be considered a fully fledged replacement for the Parallel Market, it is providing a new exit route for the Dutch venture capital industry. If it is successful, it could become a major instrument for institutional investors who want to invest in small-capitalization companies and want to build a non-quoted portfolio alongside their quoted holdings.

The lower cost and limited publication requirements of Parex are attractive to venture capitalists wishing to dispose of an investment. The potential broadening of a shareholder base without the risk of a straight takeover are appealing features for the entrepreneurs. To them Parex would become even more interesting if they could sell new issues of shares on Parex and raise new money for their company. Dr Evert Elbertse, Secretary General of the NVP, acknowledges these points, but emphasizes that the current restrictions on Parex have been designed to create confidence in the market from an early stage. Once successful trading has been established, restrictions will be lifted and the scope of the market extended, greatly increasing its potential for liquidity. 'After all,' he concludes, 'it would be unwise to try to run before we can walk' (Elbertse, 1993, p. 13).

Not everybody is equally optimistic about the future of Parex. Bert Twaalfhoven, from his venture capital experience, believes that there is a danger that venture investors will look at their portfolios to assess what they want to get rid of, which could result in Parex becoming a market for 'lemons' (Twaalfhoven, 1993).

The launch of Parex planned for May 1993 had to be postponed for administrative reasons, and the first auction is scheduled for November 1993.

## The Enterprise Market

After closing the Third Market in 1990, the London Stock Exchange announced at the end of 1992 that it would close the Unlisted Securities Market. This decision was based on a fall in demand both from small companies wishing to list and from investors wishing to buy. On 7 December, 1992 a diversified lobby group of London-based intermediaries, investors and venture capitalists launched CISCO, the City Group for Smaller Companies. The objective of Cisco is to defend the cause of smaller companies threatened by the increasing unwillingness of big securities firms to trade in their stocks. Cisco's concern at the lack of adequate dealing facilities for less liquid securities has convinced the London Stock Exchange to suspend its decision to close the USM until a valuable replacement is available. A working party to assess the need for and the potential characteristics of a new market was set up.

In the meantime Cisco formulated a proposal to restructure the UK equity markets and to create a three-tier market (Cisco, 1993). A first segment would include the top 350 securities of the London Stock Exchange and would be called the International Equity Market. This segment would also include other leading European shares traded on SEAQ International. The second segment would be a National Market oriented at well-developed companies listed in the UK with a capitalization of less than £50 million. The third segment, the Enterprise Market, would be a market focused on high-growth, entrepreneurial-type companies. This market would attempt to establish itself in the UK as the market of choice for exciting new companies, as Nasdaq has done in the United States.

The plan for the Enterprise Market envisages that listing requirements will aim to be as low as national and EC legislation allows, both to keep the cost of listing low, and to open access to as wide a range of potential entrants as possible. Companies will not be barred from this market and from access to capital on the grounds that they represent a significant business risk; this will be left to investors to assess. Nor will companies be barred on the grounds that there is unlikely to be a significant turnover of the shares in the aftermarket. Low liquidity is considered by Cisco a feature of small companies; the lack of liquidity in itself does not deter investors from investing in small companies.

According to the proposal, companies seeking a listing on the Enterprise Market will not be required to have a trading history. Hence the market will be open to new start-ups seeking seed capital, so long as a recognized sponsor supports the application. Companies must be prepared to issue at least £500 000 of shares at the time of listing, but no minimum or maximum market capitalization is imposed; the market must be distinguished by kind and not by size (Cohen, 1993). Companies meeting the listing requirements will not be granted access automatically. As with Nasdaq, the quality both of reputable sponsors and of companies wishing to list will be vetted. Initially this market will be seeking to list high-tech, entrepreneurial companies in order to establish its brand image. The plan is to run the Enterprise Market as a private venture and not as a public service.

The admission requirements to this market will be based on the legal minimum requirements; this will include the production of a prospectus. Once listed, companies will be expected to provide quarterly reports on performance, including an updated profits estimate, in addition to interims and audited financial statements. All price-sensitive information must be released through the market news service. This information will include the sale or purchase of significant assets, significant orders won or lost and results data.

The exact *modus operandi* of this market is still under discussion, but it is possible that the existing trading facilities of the London Stock Exchange could be used, or alternatively a collaboration with Nasdaq on the use of its computer facilities might be envisaged. The trading is likely to become a combination of market-makers making firm quotations and an order-driven, matched-bargain service. The Enterprise Market will be available to institutional investors and to private investors through qualified agents. This new market ideally should have independent governance and financial management. Whether or not the Enterprise Market should be organized by the stock market authorities or independently from them is still very much a matter of debate. Ronald Cohen from Apax Partners believes that the development of this market cannot be left to the Stock Exchange. He points out that it is needed now, not after years of discussion about whether or not it is necessary or possible. In his view the industry has to develop a credible alternative of its own and then ask the Stock Exchange whether they will run it or whether the industry should do it (Cohen, 1993).

With its proposals for the Enterprise Market, Cisco is providing a clear and potentially interesting alternative for the USM in London. For the moment this proposal appears to be addressing only the UK problem. There is a need and an opportunity to extend this type of initiative to the rest of Europe. However, if the Enterprise Market itself is harbouring the ambition to become the European equivalent of Nasdaq, then companies based in other European countries must be brought in now rather than later. Like-minded intermediaries, investors and venture capitalists from the continent should be invited to the drawing board to design a more ambitious vehicle that would serve the needs of entrepreneurial businesses across Europe.

## The Nasdaq International Board

With 4400 entrepreneurial growth companies listed on a buoyant market on one side of the Atlantic and fading market activity on the other side, it should be no surprise that European venture capitalists and entrepreneurs have been looking eagerly at what's going on on the American side of the pond. Nasdaq is the perfect role model for what they need. The question is how to get access to it.

Why has Nasdaq not established a truly European operation, knowing that there are a large number of companies out here desperately seeking a listing and that there is only very fragmented local competition? As John Wall, Executive Vice President of Nasdaq, has explained more than once: 'We have tried to establish links with European exchanges; but we have not found a local partner who did not see us as a threat' (Batchelor, 1992). It is understandable that an American organization would seek local support and partners in establishing such a complex and politically sensitive operation as a pan-European stock market for high-growth companies. The other aspect, of course, is that Nasdaq has been created by the Association of American Equity Dealers. As their business is in making transactions in the quoted stocks themselves, they can expect little benefit from a European Nasdaq operation.

What is more interesting to these dealers is that European companies come and list on the American exchange. As a result the strategy of Nasdaq has been to welcome foreign companies and to encourage them to seek a listing on Nasdaq. At the end of 1992 this policy had brought 181 foreign stocks to the two main Nasdaq markets. To support its European marketing effort, Nasdaq has opened an office in London with a brief to create more visibility and to attract customers to its American market. To make life still easier for European companies and investors, Nasdaq created Nasdaq International in January 1992, as a market dedicated to the European time zone.

At the EVCA business seminar in Venice on the topic of Exiting in Europe, Michiel de Haan of Atlas Venture Holding b.v. and Brian Wood of Alta Berkeley Associates were unanimous about the role which Nasdaq can play for European companies (de Haan, 1993; Wood, 1993). Both have taken several of their European companies public on Nasdaq and their comments were based on first-hand experience. While there are pitfalls with a transatlantic IPO, a Nasdaq listing currently produces the best valuations and the best exit prices. In the absence of any European equivalent, the recommendation is to use Nasdaq. It is a first-rate mechanism and European venture capitalists should not be chauvinistic; their duty to their investors goes beyond worrying about that (Onians, 1992).

The main disadvantages for European companies listed on Nasdaq are that they have to comply with SEC rules and they must produce their accounts in the US format and in US dollars. To keep the interest of American institutional investors alive, it is absolutely essential to establish and maintain communication lines. These obligations can be expensive and onerous on the company and its management. Susi Belli, an executive from the Luxottica Group, which is one of the largest manufacturers of spectacle frames in the world, explains that being listed on the New York Stock Exchange as an Italian company involved a trip to New York every single quarter. Each trip meant meetings and letters to 300 to 400 investors telling them the story from the beginning to the end, without forgetting a single detail. Being a company which consolidates its figures in Italian lire and converts the consolidated numbers into US dollars, the company saw its net earnings decline in dollar terms when the dollar was gaining strength. Although Luxottica was enjoying a 24 per cent compound growth rate in income, its share price was going down (Belli, 1992).

Listing of the better European companies on foreign stock markets such as Nasdaq is a pragmatic temporary solution. With the valuations that can be obtained there, it is an option which has to be considered, failing an equivalent European alternative. But the real answer to the European liquidity headache is for the Europeans to grasp the nettle and create a proper pan-European stock market for entrepreneurial, high-growth companies.

In the light of the previous analysis, it should be clear that the needs for equity and liquidity of entrepreneurial, high-growth companies in Europe are not going to be solved by the existing stock markets. These have their own problems to deal with and are fundamentally not interested in these higher risk stocks. Nasdaq is only interested in Europe to attract European companies to its American markets. Both the EPEE and the Parex proposals bring original solutions to some aspects of the problem, but neither of the two provides a full solution. The concept of the UK Enterprise Market comes closest to what is needed, but falls short in the absence of a European dimension and approach – unless it adopts some of the ideas expressed by Ronald Cohen during the annual symposium of the European Venture Capital Association (Cohen, 1993).

Ronald Cohen suggests calling the new market he proposes EASDAQ, the European Association of Securities Dealers Automated Quotations, to benefit from Nasdaq's entrepreneurial identity. His proposal is a variation of the Cisco proposal. For him the Enterprise Market should operate independently from the London Stock Exchange and adopt a European scope. In his view national markets should be responsible for organizing themselves but use broadly harmonized membership and selection criteria. Together they could lead a concerted effort to create a proper European public market for emerging growth companies.

However, this approach might lead to slightly different rules applying in different countries, creating uncertainty and complexity for investors. One of the keys to the success of Nasdaq is the quality and consistency of the information supplied. Furthermore, to become a successful private venture, a Europe-wide market has to be in charge of its own destiny and take its pan-European marketing and organization into its own hands, rather than leave this to fragmented national markets.

## THE CASE FOR A PAN-EUROPEAN MARKET

Our proposal for a more far-reaching European market is deeply rooted in the ideas for the Enterprise Market in London and in Ronald Cohen's suggestions for EASDAQ. Our proposal is to create EEMEC, the European Electronic Market for Entrepreneurial Companies. It would have the following characteristics :

1 EEMEC must build a clear identity as the European market for entrepreneurial, growth companies. It should profile itself as the European equivalent of Nasdaq.

2 EEMEC should operate as a private venture and be self-regulatory. This means no public service obligations and a freedom to be selective in accepting companies presenting themselves for a listing; meeting the set criteria gives no automatic access.

3 This market should develop into a high risk/high reward market. Rigorous disclosure requirements will protect against fraud, but it will be left to the investors to judge the business risks.

4 Companies seeking a listing will be required to have at least two independent market-makers who will provide firm bid and ask prices. The system of market-makers provides liquidity to the market, and the spreads, the differences between bid and ask prices, can attract intermediaries and provide the incentive for researching the listed companies.

5 EEMEC will be a fully electronic market, with screen services similar to those on Nasdaq. This provides full transparency and all buyers always get the best available price at the time of buying. An electronic market can be everywhere the customers are.

6 The market will be for institutional and private investors, both operating through registered brokers.

7 EEMEC will have its legal base in a European country whose legal requirements allow it maximum flexibility in its operation and whose regulations come closest to the minimum criteria for equity dealing as imposed by the European directive.

8 EEMEC will have its own independent governance body, which will ensure the good standing and integrity of the organization.

9 Companies seeking a listing will not be required to have a trading record, there will not be a minimum or a maximum in terms of capitalization. There will be a criterion for the minimum amount of equity raised or sold.

10 The admission requirements will be based on the legal minimum requirements; this will include the production of a prospectus.

11 Listed companies will be required to provide quarterly reports on performance, including interim financial statements and profit forecasts. All price-sensitive information, such as purchase or sale of significant assets and major orders won or lost, must be released through the EEMEC news service.

12  All prices will be denominated in ECU and all transactions will be executed in ECUs. This is the most practical way of dealing with the various European currencies and might help in promoting the use of the ECU.

13  The market will have its own news service. All information will be produced in English. Consideration should be given to the use of pan-European satellite television as a way of communication to the investors.

The main objection against EEMEC is likely to be that its pan-European dimension is too ambitious and cannot be implemented in a realistic time-frame. There are bound to be some legislative and regulatory problems. But the European Commission has been an attentive observer in the debate and will almost certainly encourage and support the creation of a truly pan-European solution. Even today the Commission is supporting changes to its directives to allow blue chip stocks to trade more easily on the various European stock markets. Europe is more unified now than it was 10 years ago and every day more directives eliminating practical and legal obstacles for a truly pan-European operation come into force.

We are convinced that the pan-European dimension for EEMEC is essential to give it a fair chance of success. The European economy cannot afford to repeat its previous experience with fragmented national markets for entrepreneurial companies, in which the markets failed to meet the challenges of identity, competitive advantage and critical mass.

Furthermore, the advent of cheap and reliable electronic networks has already changed the face of national stock markets. Future success will be based on service and costs, and less and less on tradition. What, after all, is an exchange? It is no more than a system to bring together as many buyers and sellers as possible, preferably under an agreed set of rules (*The Economist*, 19 June 1993).

Nasdaq has proved that a nationwide electronic stock market can be a huge success. An equivalent of the Nasdaq market, using its key operating principles, but adapted to the European situation, as in our EEMEC proposal, could present a major step forward in releasing the logjam the European venture capital industry is facing. This market could become the harvesting place for the prime crop of venture capital portfolios and hence provide a significant boost to the rates of return for venture capital in Europe. This is vital for the long-term health of this industry.

But perhaps most importantly, a stock market such as EEMEC would give the entrepreneurial, growth companies of Europe access to the equity financing they badly need to compete in world markets. The pan-European research shows that our European entrepreneurs are in support of such a pan-European stock market and can see its benefits to their businesses (Chapter 7).

It is now, at a time when the European economies are at the bottom of a cycle, that action should be taken to create this badly needed instrument for our entrepreneurial companies; they must be enabled to attract the necessary capital to ride the next wave. It is really up to the European venture capitalists, the investment bankers and stockbrokers who are amenable to the EEMEC proposal to get together and create this new venture.

# References

Anslow, M. (1993). Two ideas for a private equity exchange, *European Venture Capital Journal*, Feb.–Mar.

Batchelor, C. (1992), Enterprise looks for a way out, *Financial Times*, 22 Dec., p. 7.

Belli, S. (1992). Presentation at the EFER 92 Forum, London, Dec.

Bygrave, W. D., and Timmons, J. A. (1992). *Venture Capital at the Crossroads*. Boston: Harvard Business School Press.

Cisco, (1993). A blueprint for the smaller companies' market. Paper.

Cohen, R. (1993). Presentation at EVCA symposium on Ten Years of Venture Capital, Brussels, June.

Cope, J. (1988). Presentation at EVCA symposium on The Internationalization of Venture Capital, London, May.

de Haan, M. (1993). Presentation at EVCA business seminar on Exiting in Europe, Venice, Feb.

Elbertse, E. (1993). Plans for the Parex unveiled, *Initiative Europe Monitor*, Mar.–Apr.

EVCA (1993). *Venture Capital in Europe; 1993 EVCA Yearbook*, Zaventem: EVCA.

Fields, W. (1993). Presentation at EVCA symposium on Ten Years of Venture Capital, Brussels, June.

Fitzgibbons, H. E. (1985). Secondary markets in Europe. Presentation at the conference on Venture Capital, Geneva, Nov.

Hipschman, H. (1993). Presentation at EVCA symposium on Ten Years of Venture Capital, Brussels, June.

Onians, R. (1992). Presentation at the EFER 92 Forum, London, Dec.

Onians, R. (1993). Presentation at EVCA business seminar on Exiting in Europe, Venice, Feb.

Peeters, J.B. (1993). High tech at the crossroads, *European Venture Capital Journal*, Feb.–Mar.

Thomas, D. (1990). *Alan Sugar – The Amstrad Story*, London: Pan.

Twaalfhoven, B. (1993). Viewpoint, *Initiative Europe Monitor*, Mar.–Apr.

Vachon, M. (1993). An uptick in M&A exit activity, *Venture Capital Journal*, Feb.

van Ittersum, B. (1992). Presentation at the EFER 92 Forum, London, Dec.

Vappereau, F. (1992). Presentation at the EFER 92 Forum, London, Dec.

Wall, J. (1992). Presentation at the EFER 92 Forum, London, Dec.

Wallinger, J. (1992). Presentation at the EFER 92 Forum, London, Dec.

Wood, B. (1993). Presentation at EVCA business seminar on Exiting in Europe, Venice, Feb.

# INDEX